Walking to America

How "American Indians" Discovered America, then Settled It.

Mark Thompson

Copyright Page

Mark Thompson

7821 US-23 North

Rogers City, MI 49779

(989) 351-9787 or

Calcitetwo@yahoo.com

About The Author

A high school dropout, Mark Thompson is a decorated veteran of the Vietnam War, a former member of the Michigan House of Representatives, and he holds degrees from Lake Superior State University and Michigan State University. Mark's varied career has included working as a reporter, college professor, maritime academy administrator, merchant mariner, and executive director and curator of an award-winning historical museum. He and his wife Linda live along the shores of Lake Huron in Rogers City, Michigan.

INDEX

Dedications

For Eve, the African child who became the mother of us all. And for my incredible grandchildren, Jack Alspach, Madison Alspach, and Maximus Thompson, in the hope that they will always cherish honesty, treat others with kindness, give aid and comfort to those who are in need, and "do their best" Remember, despite the many differences that exist between individuals, cultures, and races, we are all born with the hearts of human beings.

PREFACE

Seven years ago, I was working on a local history book that included an introductory section on Native Americans in Northern Michigan. While doing research, I soon found that there were significant differences in the accounts of relations between Indians and Whites, depending on their sources. In trying to gain an accurate understanding, I read more and more books and articles related to that topic. I gradually began to get a sense for just how complex the relations between the Indians and the Whites were, involving as they did every aspect of life for each of the two groups—groups that had little in common other than belonging to the species homo sapiens and wanting to live in the Americas.

Relations between the Indians and Whites were also significantly affected by the U.S. government and several government agencies, including the Bureau of Indian Affairs and the U.S. Army. There were even times when White-Indian relations were affected by the actions of foreign governments, including those of France, Britain, Spain, Mexico, Holland, Russia and even the Confederate States of America, all of which claimed portions of North America at one time.

If those factors didn't complicate things enough, most of the hundreds of Native American tribes spread across the continent spoke different languages, had different values, different lifestyles, different religious practices, lived in different geographic regions with different flora and fauna, and had different experiences with government agencies, White settlers, and their Indian neighbors. Whites weren't all that homogeneous either, representing a wide variety of interests and ideals that impacted how they viewed Indians in general or the specific tribe, or tribes, that they interacted with.

In his Rites of Conquest, Charles Cleland, Professor Emeritus of Anthropology at Michigan State University, also pointed out that, "like all historical accounts, the history of Indian groups is the product of the historian who selects and interprets the facts to conform to some preconceived theory or perspective. Too often,

Indian history or the role of Indians in American history has been written to either glorify or to vilify Indian participants rather than to gain a perspective on their special place in historical events."
[Charles E. Cleland, Rites of Conquest: The History and Culture of Michigan's Native Americans (Ann Arbor: The University of Michigan Press, 1992), p. viii]

That claim instantly brings to mind all the "Cowboy and Indian" movies that used to be shown Friday evenings at the Rogers City Theater in my hometown. No matter how desperate the cowboys' situations might have been mid-movie, you knew they would be victorious by the time the big purple curtain came down. The cowboys always won.

By the time Charles Cleland wrote his Rites of Conquest in 1992, attitudes about Native Americans and assessments of historical events involving Indians and Whites had shifted considerably. Cleland tried to be very honest with his readers: "I intend this book to present the facts of history objectively, it must be admitted that it does so with a perspective sympathetic to the trials of the Great Lakes Indians in the three hundred years of contact with Europeans and Americans. I will confess to both empathy for their suffering and admiration for their long and decidedly uphill struggle to maintain their cultures, dignity, and pride."

So, after an extensive career with much of his time devoted to objectively studying Native American cultures and their interactions with each other and with White cultures, Professor Cleland has concluded that the Indians got a raw deal. I have reached the same conclusion. In fact, I'm pretty sure that many of the authors who have written about Indians share that overarching opinion. I think a person would have to be very cold-hearted to make an in-depth study of the topic and reach any other conclusion.

That does not, however, totally exonerate or hold blameless many Native Americans, both individuals and tribes, who lived here during the period from the late fifteenth century through the nineteenth century—from the time Columbus arrived in the hemisphere until December 30, 1890, when Sioux warriors ambushed the 7th U.S. Cavalry at Drexel Mission on the Pine Ridge, South

Dakota, reservation, "exacting a slight measure of revenge" for the massacre that had taken place at Wounded Knee the previous day...and substantially ending the Indian Wars."
[Robert M. Utley and Wilcomb E. Washburn, Indian Wars (Boston: Mariner Books, 2002), p. 300.]

Needless, to say, it also doesn't exonerate generations of Whites, most of them immigrants from Europe or the children, grandchildren, or great-grandchildren of immigrants, most of whom came here to escape the horrors of ongoing wars in Europe, religious intolerance, assaults on minorities, or who were attracted by the almost unbelievable promise of land ownership…land that had at one time belonged to American Indians.

I am the descendant of a number of those immigrants. Great-grandfather Joseph Nedeau arrived in Canada in the 1640s and settled at what became Mount Royal, better known today as Montreal. Great-grandfather Francois de Youville arrived in the company of Robert de LaSalle between 1669 and 1678. One of LaSalle's most trusted aides, he would serve at Fort Michilimackinac and accompany LaSalle on his first voyage of exploration down the Mississippi River. He eventually left LaSalle's service, having been awarded the honorary title of "the explorer," and established a highly lucrative fur business at Montreal, until his early death. I am also proud that two of my Great-grandmothers were Filles du Royal, or "Daughters of the King," whose resettlements in New France were sponsored by the French King. Today they are regarded as among the "Founding Mothers" of Canada.

Another notable Great-grandfather was Robert Navarre, a young French Royal, who arrived at Fort Detroit in an Indian canoe in 1721 to serve as the French Sub-Intendent and Royal Notary. Navarre was to fill the administrative vacancy created by the death of the famous Henri de Tonti and establish the first civil government at the small community on the western margin of New France. Navarre developed an excellent reputation with the numerous local Indian tribes and the local chief of the Potawatomi eventually awarded him a portion of his tribe's lands south of Detroit. That may have taken place in 1763 when the Britain and their allies defeated French forces in what we know as the French and Indian Wars, taking control of Fort Detroit and other forts in the region of the Great Lakes, and potentially resulting in Navarre's expulsion from the fort.

Carl and Amalie Tosch, my maternal ancestors, arrived here from Germany in 1870 and homesteaded land in a small German settlement that had just been planted about five miles west of the lumbering village of Rogers City, Michigan. While they were relative newcomers compared to my French ancestors, they founded a branch of our family that now includes several hundred people who still live in the area, or who still refer to it as "home."

Members of our family have lived in the Great Lakes region ever since Nedeau, Youville, and Navarre arrived from France in those early years. In the intervening years, we have been government officials under French, British, and U.S. governments, and we have toiled as farmers, timbermen, miners, railroad men, autoworkers, educators, reporters, business owners, a doctor, and several Great Lakes' sailors. Most of the men in the family have also served in U.S. armed forces during times of war.

With ancestors who were here for 100, 200, 300, and almost 400 years, we are still "newcomers" when compared to our American Indian friends whose families could easily have roots back thousands of years. The homelands around the Great Lakes that our family members cherish so passionately, were once their lands—Indian lands.

The historical record tells us that the Indians came up losers in a struggle where the cards were stacked against them by disparities in critical elements of culture, technology, and population. They fought many valiant battles and were victorious in a surprising number of them, but when the last blood had been spilled the Indians had been defeated, and with that they essentially lost dominion over most of the lands they had occupied for untold generations. In some important ways, however, the Indians never totally capitulated, and many native cultures, or remnants of native cultures, exist yet today. Now, more than a century after the Indian Wars ended, we find that the struggle continues for many of those Indians who are trying to hang on to some aspects of their traditional cultures, and their traditional homelands, that are fundamental to their being…or just trying to survive in the White Man's world.

One phenomenon that quickly became obvious to me as I began researching the history of Indian and White relations is that more and more Indians are being portrayed as the innocent, the aggrieved, the just, the victims. To an extent, that's accurate; to an extent, it's not. At the same time, today the United States is all too often painted as the neighborhood thug, violator of sacred lands, tormenter of the innocent Indigents, destroyer of Native cultures, perpetrator of genocide. Sadly, to an extent, that too, is accurate; to an extent, it's not. If you study the histories of Indian and White relations and come to different conclusions, you're probably wrong. You've missed something! Maybe your personal biases have overshadowed your honesty? Maybe the sources of your information have been biased, or simply inaccurate? Maybe your sources are just telling you what they know you want to hear?

I believe there is a growing gulf between Indians and Whites in North America, due in part to the inaccuracy of the information bases being used by the respective parties and the lack of this country's commitment to improving the statuses of American Indians. In particular, data on the living conditions of many Indigenous peoples in North America, data on their health and health care, data on their educational opportunities and achievements, and data on their employment opportunities are, for many tribes, unacceptable. They are frequently so bad that I want to cry for the poor souls trapped by their heritages.

Those problems are not likely to get the needed attention until both Indians and Whites are operating on facts. Progress will be driven by facts, not fantasy or fiction that is presented as fact. Progress today is often being hindered when too much attention is focused on events that occurred a hundred years ago, or more, especially when the accounts of those events are seldom completely accurate.

—Mark Thompson

Rogers City, Michigan

CHAPTER 1

HOME ON THE ICE BRIDGE

> Beliefs about Indian origins that are drawn from myths and legends that have been passed down by word of mouth from generation-to-generation contrast sharply with the story that emerges through the examination of artifacts unearthed by archaeologists or documents carefully studied by learned ethnohistorians. One is left to wonder, which version of history is correct.
>
> —**Charles E. Cleland**
> Rites of Conquest

We homo sapiens— and all of us humans are homo sapiens regardless of the color of our skins, our eyes, or our hair–took long and circuitous routes to get to our present homes scattered throughout the terrestrial areas of planet Earth. Few routes, if any, were longer or more circuitous than those of the Americans for whom the Western Hemisphere is now home.

Our most distant ancestors originated in Africa about 300,000 years ago and are believed to have begun their migration out of Africa about 60,000 years ago. Based on sophisticated DNA analysis on both living subjects and ancient skeletons, researchers have concluded that, "Modern humans left Africa about 60,000 years ago and swiftly expanded across six continents."
[Greshko, Michael, "Ancient DNA reveals complex migrations of the first Americans."]

The oldest homo sapiens fossils outside of Africa have been found in Israel and Greece, dated to 177,000 to 210,000 years ago. By 50,000 years ago, our ancestors had spread along the south coast of Asia and southeast to the continent of Australia and the more than ten thousand islands in the South Pacific region, including those of New Zealand, Melanesia, and Micronesia. The thousand widely scattered islands comprising Polynesia appear to not have been settled until 1500 BC to 1200 AD.

By 40,000 years ago, our ancestors had spread out across what is now Europe. There, they came in contact with other early human species, including Neanderthals and Denisovans. Our ancestors are known to have interbred with the early humans they encountered throughout the region and, as a result, many of us carry small amounts of DNA the ancient ones unknowingly contributed to our biological makeup that survives all these many years later.

By 40,000 years ago, most of our ancestors were ensconced in Africa, Asia, Europe, or the Middle East, but their migrations had not ended. Humans have always been highly mobile creatures, probably a result of the combination of our large brains and our ability to walk upright, combined with our long history of wandering around looking for something better. Their wanderings were motivated by a variety of reasons: following the animals they relied upon for food, moving into an area with better sources of food, escaping their enemies, or looking for areas with better weather conditions, just to name a few. In many cases, migrations were probably the result of a combination of factors. Many scientists believe there is evidence that once the early humans decided to move out of Africa, they "moved fast and frequently." [Ewen Callaway, "Ancient genomics is recasting the story of the Americas' first residents," Nature, November 9, 2018.]

We may never know exactly why the ancestors of America's Indigenous peoples left their historical homelands in Asia, but the weather was probably a factor. From about 115,000 years ago until 11,700 years ago, planet Earth was in a period of extended bad weather in the northern latitudes…the Last Glacial Period, commonly referred to as the Ice Age. Much of the planet north of the 45th parallel of longitude was buried under unimaginable glaciers that were as much as a mile or two thick. Weather conditions along the southern edge of the glaciers would have been bitterly cold with brutal winds, worse than just about anything found on Earth today north of Antarctica. If that wasn't enough of an incentive for humans to migrate in search of warmer climes, food sources in the area were also undoubtedly limited, especially sources of protein—mainly meat.

Some Aboriginal Siberians migrated to the east into an area between northeastern Siberia and the western region of present-day Alaska that came to be identified as Beringia. There, they found their way blocked by glaciers for as much as 15,000 years.

Because of the tremendous amount of water eventually locked up in the planet's massive ice cap, water levels in the oceans gradually dropped to as much as 200 to 390 feet below present sea levels. As the sea level declined, what had been a narrow strait on the Bering Sea between the two continents became a "broad plain, perhaps 600 miles wide" between Siberia and what is now Alaska. (It was actually closer to 900 miles wide from north to south.)

The term "Land Bridge" is somewhat of a misnomer. It was not a "bridge" in the sense that we commonly use the word today to denote a raised, usually steel or wood structure, carrying a road, path, railroad, or canal across a river, valley, or other obstacle. It was, however, a "bridge" in that it spanned—or bridged—the gap between Siberia in the west and Canada and Alaska in the east. As the northern waters were converted to ice and became part of the massive glaciers, what had been the bottom of the sea was exposed, making it possible to travel across the region on dry land. The term "Land Bridge" appears to have been first used by Swedish botanist Eric Hultén in his doctoral dissertation in 1937. While studying plant life in the region he discovered that "there had probably been a land area capable of sustaining flora in the area" between eastern Siberia and what is now western Alaska. He named his find after Vitus Bering, the Scandinavian explorer who first sailed through the strait that separated Asia and what is now America.

In his brilliant Atlas of a Lost World, author and researcher Craig Childs described it as "a flat subcontinent fully exposed when sea levels were at their glacial low, its center five hundred miles from the nearest coast." It was the exposed bottom of the Bering Sea and Bering Strait, which Childs describes as "a steppe grassland," with "with the occasional birch and black spruce grove, summers free of snow, ground grazed and turn to grass by large herbivores, loess blown in from the edges of distant ice caps, allowing the soil to hold and retain organic matter. This would have been a habitable landscape."

In his research, Eric Hultén documented that "the land bridge supported a great variety of plant and animal life, including wooly mammoths, grounds sloths and could weigh up to six thousand pounds, fierce saber-toothed cats, bison, muskoxen, horses, saiga antelope, and giant moose, among others." The intertidal zone was also "rich in algae, seaweed, kelp, mussels, clams and a variety of fish." [en.wikipedia.org/wiki/Settlement of the Americas; Alan M. Milner, "Ice Age Migrations Populated America and Siberia From Beringian Refugees," www.guardian.com/2014/03/12; Childs, Chris, "Atlas of a Lost World: Travels in Ice Age America, (New York, Random House, 2018), pp. 4-5; O'Neill, Dan, The Last Giant of Beringia: The Mystery of the Bering Land Bridge, (Boulder, CO: Westview Press, 2004), pp. 59-65.]

When the ice started to recede at the end of the Last Glacial Maximum, about 20,000 years ago, some of the Siberian natives returned westward toward their former homes while others headed east, supposedly entering what is now Alaska, their gateway to the previously unknown continent of North America and the Western Hemisphere, which they didn't know existed. Remaining in Beringia was not an option because the rising levels of the oceans would soon submerge their land bridge refuge, forcing them to move to land that would not be submerged as the glaciers continued to melt. We don't know how many chose to return to the west, to Siberia. Three groups of the Siberian-Beringians who had been trapped in Beringia are believed to have left the land bridge and headed east and south into what was then the great unknown…into what became the Americas, or what Craig Child's called, "Earth's last major vacant landmass to be populated by homo sapiens." The refugees from Beringia would eventually travel south into the Americas in three waves of migration over a considerable period of time. They knew nothing of the lands that lay before them. It was a great unknown.

[Tom D. Dillehay, "Probing deeper into first American studies," Proceedings of the National Academy of Sciences. January 27, 2009.]

We can only guess why they chose to head in a generally southerly direction. Historically, they had come from the west, from Siberia. That was many years in the past, but by going west and southwest they would have been returning to lands their ancestors had known. Maybe that's exactly why they chose a different route. After all, their ancient ancestors had chosen to abandon their homelands in Siberia, probably in search of new lands that were more hospitable. I use the word "hospitable" in a very general sense. In this application it suggests that the ancient Siberians were looking for lands with a warmer climate, or a better supply of foodstuffs, to escape unfriendly neighbors, or maybe all of those things—more hospitable lands.

Maybe they had some knowledge that the climate was more amenable in lands to the south. Maybe someone had gone on ahead and eventually returned to describe the lands south of the glaciers. Maybe a returnee had made a map of a route south. Maybe it was just that they saw birds migrating toward the south when temperatures began to plummet in the fall of the year. Maybe they were simply following the movements of the animals that were the number one source of their protein, especially the megafauna? We don't know, and we will probably never know. It is one of many great mysteries surrounding the movements of the people who seem to have become the First Americans. "They probably didn't have any idea of the scale of emptiness that lay ahead," observed Craig Childs in a classic understatement. It is safe to assume that they didn't.

I have spent an inordinate and frustrating amount of time pouring over maps of Beringia, Alaska, North America, and South America, trying to make an educated guess at what route each of the groups of migrants might have followed. I look at a detailed map of Alaska and it's like a puzzle with half the pieces missing. I think it was Craig Childs who was writing about the route that might have been followed and his wisdom was, "follow the rivers." Friends, find a map of Alaska and take a close look: Alaska is coast to coast rivers! The areas that aren't rivers are mountains! And remember, those first travelers had no maps, so there is no way they could have comprehended and anticipated the complex river systems that spread across the face of Alaska, the hundreds of rivers they were probably going to have to be crossed to get anywhere, and the mountains and mountain ranges that would undoubtedly block their routes south.

"Follow the rivers," just isn't an easy solution, but the predominance of rivers isn't the only problem. At the time of the first migrations into the Americas, none of the virgin forests had been lumbered. Thick woods of ancient pines and leggy hardwoods ran right up to the banks of most rivers, as they do yet today. That makes for hard walking. In fact, I concluded that the easiest travel using the river systems would probably have been in the winter when the rivers were frozen and a traveler could have walked along an ice sidewalk. Seriously. Walking along the banks of most rivers would have been like fighting your way through a jungle.

In addition to the overwhelming proliferation of rivers throughout Alaska, the other predominant geographic feature shown on today's colored maps are the mountain chains that line the north and south of the state. Mountains! The Aleutian Range, Alaska Range, Brooks Range, Adam Mountain, Kenai Mountains, Denali, Capitan Mountain, Cascade Range, Mount Capps, Mount Hunter, Chugach Mountains, Mount Crosson, Wrangell Mountains, Jade Mountains, and Mount Foraker. If I missed any, I apologize. Anyway, there's a pretty good chance that without a map you are going to stagger out of the almost endless forest one day and find yourself starring at a mountain. Sorry. It's likely to slow you down a little.

While you are studying your map of Alaska, you will notice that Alaska and Russia almost touch at the Bering Strait off the western end of Alaska's Seward Peninsula. The narrow strait is just over 62 miles wide. In fact, the two-island group in the middle of the strait is split by the International Border and Big Diomede Island is located in Russian territory, while nearby Little Diomede Island is U.S. property. As one would expect, the waters of the strait are relatively shallow, only about 164 feet deep. In fact, during the Last Glacial Period (LGP), from about 27,000 years ago until 11,000 years ago, when seawaters rose again as the glaciers melted, the bottom of Bering Strait became dry land—what we now refer to as the Bering Land Bridge. The "bridge," as it was, became the home for refugees from Northeast Asia who would eventually become the "First Americans." Conditions on the land bridge were apparently, and understandably, more habitable than conditions on the Russian peninsula they were occupying during the LGP. David Meltzer described the land bridge as:

A flat, ice-free, almost featureless highway trafficked by plants, animals and people for Millenia. That the same mammals inhabited Siberia and Alaska testifies to the ease of travel back and forth: only Siberia's woolly rhinoceros and a few Alaskan species (including the giant short-faced bear), failed to make the cross-Beringia commute…From the absence of evidence for trees or lakes, and the presence of extensive sand dunes, loess, tracts of permafrost, and ice-wedge casts, it appears that the LGM climate was significantly drier and colder than at present…it was a tundra unlike that in the Arctic today. Its productivity was much higher, and it included plenty of grasses for grazers. Humans on this landscape may not have found many plants to eat, but there would have been animals to hunt as they made their way across from Siberia."
[Meltzer, David J., First Peoples in a New World: Colonizing Ice Age America, (Berkeley, CA: University of California Press, 2009), pp. 34-35.]

CHAPTER 2

CLOVIS, MORE THAN JUST A TOWN IN NEW MEXICO

We can never know with certainty that we have found the earliest remains in North America because there may always be something that we have not found.

—**Robert L. Kelly**
Quaternary International

While figuring out when and by what route, or routes, the first Indians came to the Americas has proven exceedingly difficult and continues to be the subject of ongoing research and debate, finding evidence of human occupation as early as 15,000 or 16,000 years ago, or more, makes finding a needle in a haystack look like a "slam dunk." While hundreds, or potentially thousands, of migrants from Beringia undoubtedly made the long trek south to escape the white world of the seemingly endless Ice Age, it wasn't until November of 1932 that the first evidence of them was discovered. Even then, it was a fluke that they were found and a fluke that anyone thought enough of the find to contact archaeologists, and a fluke that an archaeologist from Pennsylvania would actually hop on a train and travel to south-central New Mexico to take a look at a large cache of big animal bones that came to be known as "Clovis First."

Clovis, Clovis, Clovis! "Clovis" isn't some magical archaeological term, it's actually the name of a town in New Mexico that was attached to a unique type of stone or bone "points," mainly arrowheads, spear points, blades, scrapers, or knives that were found at several locations in the area in the 1920s and 1930s. The points were dramatic improvements over all previous points, to the extent that they have been referred to as "killing machines." About four inches long and one to two inches wide, Clovis points are bifacial—

sharpened on both sides—with a slightly concave base. It is also common for the points to have flutes, or grooves, beginning at the base and continuing midway up the point on both sides.

The distinctive and totally unique points that were labelled as "Clovis" were first found in 1932 in a mass of large old bones that had been accidentally uncovered by a road crew looking for a source of gravel. Archaeologist Edgar B. Howard of the University of Pennsylvania Museum heard about the discovery at what came to be known as the Blackwater Draw site, and he led archaeological activities at the location over the next four years.

The "Clovis points," as they came to be known, were found amongst the bones of extinct Pleistocene mammals, including horses, camels, bison, and mammoths that lived during the last Ice Age that extended from 2,580,000 to 11,700 years ago. Blackwater Draw became "the first site to demonstrate that Paleo-Indians—the earliest Native Americans—lived alongside Ice Age mammals." The ancient people who knapped the points were also judged to have been "the first [human] inhabitants of the Americas," and descendants of the people with roots in Siberia and Beringia who made their ways south into the Americas near the end of the Ice Age. [Edgar B. Howard, "Evidence of Early Man in North America,"
[The Museum Journal, University of Pennsylvania, Vol. 24, 1935; Charles C. Mann, "The Clovis Point and the Discovery of America's FirstCulture," www.achaeologysouthwest.org/2021/02/08; and wikipedia.org/wiki/Clovis_culture]

"Howard and others looked for Clovis points in collections from Siberia, the origin of the first Americans. None have ever been found. Clovis points, it seems, were an invention by those first occupants—perhaps the first American invention. Since then, more than 10,000 Clovis points have been discovered, scattered in 1,500 locations throughout North America…They seem to have materialized suddenly, by archaeological standards, and spread fast. The oldest securely dated points, discovered in Texas, trace back 13,500 years. Over a few centuries, they showed up everywhere from Florida to Montana, from Pennsylvania to Washington State."

[Charles C. Mann, "The Clovis Point and the Discovery of America's First Culture," www.archaeologysouthwest.org/2021/02/08.]

For about four decades, adherents of what came to be known as the "Clovis First" explanation of the settling of the Americas held sway over the archaeological community. "Clovis First" soon came to represent the majority opinion of archaeologists and others studying the settlement of the Americas. The first Americans, it declared, were the Indigenous peoples who had developed and used Clovis points. Clovis, Clovis, Clovis!

Clovis was more than just a small town in New Mexico, or a unique style of point, however. Craig Childs said, "Clovis was a way of working stone in an almost identical fashion from coast to coast…a single cultural complex across the Americas with a stupendous killing force."
[Childs, Craig, Atlas of a Lost World: Travels in Ice Age America, (New York: Vintage Books, 2019), pp. 169-170.]

In an insightful analysis, and without really taking sides in what is an ongoing dispute, respected archaeologist David Meltzer of Southern Methodist University, acknowledges that the dozens of proponents of sites they felt were pre-Clovis were quite literally toyed with by their colleagues. Even the legendary Louis Leakey's claim that the Calico site in California was several hundred thousand years old—certainly pre-Clovis—was rejected. Professor Meltzer noted that, "Other pre-Clovis claims were made by lesser mortals, but in all cases the result was the same: a purportedly ancient site burst on the scene with great promise, only to quickly tumble down what I came to call the pre-Clovis credibility decay curve…Dozens, even scores of sites failed to withstand critical scrutiny."
[Meltzer, David J., First Peoples in a New World: Colonizing Ice Age America, (Berkeley: University of California Press, 2009), pp. 10-12.]

Needless to say, the advocates for those supposedly pre-Clovis sites were unhappy. Some of the rejections of proposed pre-Clovis sites were clearly justified by problems with the supposed evidence they contained. In other cases, however, it appeared that leaders of the archaeological community were simply looking for every possible excuse to deny that sites were pre-Clovis. In case after case, sites that were tentatively identified as "possibly pre-Clovis," were dismissed by the "Clovis Firsters," the "Clovis gatekeepers," as being unreliable or somehow not meeting the profession's standards for proof of antiquity. As a result, Clovis First remained supreme and was seldom seriously challenged for close to seven decades.

The actions of the "Clovis gatekeepers" reminded me of something that Arthur C. Clarke, the noted science author, is quoted as having said: "When a distinguished scientist states that something is possible, he is almost certainly right. When he states that something is impossible, he is very probably wrong." My experience suggests Clarke's observation is almost certainly accurate more times than it is not. Claiming that something is impossible is a tacit acknowledgement that current knowledge is probably accurate, or at least that it is likely to be more acceptable than the change that has been suggested. In the minds of scientists and academics, "Change" is basically a four-letter word, a vulgarity. Status quo is safer; change is full of risks.
[Clarke, Arthur C., Visions of Future Past, (London: Biddle and Sons, Ltd., 1977, quoted in Joseph, Frank, Advanced Civilizations of Prehistoric America, Rochester, Vermont: Bear & Company, 2010, p. 8.]

It wasn't until 1997, after twenty years of work at the Monte Verde sites in Chile, that Thomas Dillehay found a way to convince some of the staid and traditional archaeology community that the Clovis people were not the first to move into the Americas. He and his colleagues arranged for a group of highly respected archaeologists to visit the University of Kentucky and inspect the wide range of materials they had removed from Monte Verde. Following that, they actually traveled to Chile to physically observe the site and evaluate the geological layers in which the various remnants of early human activities were found. The archaeologists attending were polled at the conclusion of their visit and overwhelmingly agreed that the Monte Verde sight was legitimate and predated Clovis. To a degree, it opened the door to those who were uncomfortable with, not just Clovis and the issue of when humans began to occupy the Americas, but where those people came from and how they might have travelled.

[Raff, Jennifer, Origin: A Genetic History of the Americas, (New York: Twelve, 2022), pp. 77-78.]

CHAPTER 3

LEAVING BERINGIA

When rising waters at the end of the Last Glacial Period forced residents of the Bering Land Bridge to evacuate, some moved back to the west, into Siberia, while others moved into the Seward Peninsula region of Alaska, east of the land bridge. How far to the east they might have moved, is a mystery. There are indications that some of the migrants could have traveled east as far as the Alaska-Yukon border where there are interesting archeological sites at Old Crow and Bluefish Caves, both of which may be pre-Clovis sites that are among the oldest every found in the region. What is missing is any clue about how, or why, the Beringians ended up in the Americas. Without a map, you could wander around in Alaska for a very long time without arriving at what became the northern entrance to the Ice-Free Corridor or the southeast shore of Alaska, along the Pacific Coast. Those two routes being those most widely accepted as having been used by the First Americans to enter what became North America. It could simply have been good luck. It could have partially resulted from a decision by the travelers to move south in an effort to find a superior habitat. Maybe "scouts" were sent out find the best routes to the south. The travelers could have spent hundreds of years in roaming around in Alaska before they made the decisive move to the south. It is also possible that they encountered indigenous people who could point them in the right direction. We just don't know, and we probably never will.

I spent many largely unproductive hours trying to determine what routes Indians might have taken. Of course, I was using a map. They had no idea what lay ahead of them. They didn't even know what they were going to find at the end of their travels. Fortunately for us, we have pretty good ideas where they ended up and general ideas of where they started from. That information allows us to "reverse engineer" the routes they took...potentially with some modest degree of accuracy.

If we look carefully at where the different groups ended up, it is quite obvious that their routes diverged considerably. (That's what happens when you don't have a roadmap or Google Maps.) Other researchers have also offered the opinion that the groups of Beringians traveled at different times, without necessarily specifying how much time might have separated the travels of the three groups. Some researchers suggest that the first group entered what became the Americas about 13,000 years ago, the second group 10,000 years ago, and the last group 4,000 years ago. Altogether, it appears to have taken about 13,000 years for the three groups to make their ways into the Americas, or more than 500 generations. It must be an incredible story. [Nichols, Johanna, "Linguistic Diversity and the First Settlement of the New World," Language, 66(3):475-521; Dan O'Neill, Last Giant of Beringia: The Mystery of the Bering Land Bridge, (Boulder, CO: Westview Press, 2004), pp. 169-175, p. 171-176.]

Once the First Americans crossed into what is now the United States, their travels were still far from being over. They would eventually spread over virtually all of the Americas. Todd Surovell, an archaeologist at the University of Wyoming, developed a model to estimate the possible speed at which the travelers could move south through the Americas. His model covered the route from the southern limits of the Cordilleran Ice Sheet near Seattle, Washington, to Monte Verde on the coast of Chilean Patagonia, about 10,000 miles south of the land bridge. He estimated that once a group of travelers would reach an optimum population density of 175 people within a 1,000-kilometer strip of coastline, the next group would leapfrog about 200 kilometers to the south, largely in search of new sources of food. Under Surovell's conditions, the trip from Seattle to the prehistoric settlement at Monte Verde would have taken an estimated 2,267 years! Craig Childs, a very experienced hiker, canoeist, and kayaker, felt that he could cover the same distance in only about two years. The answer to how long it might have taken the migrants from Beringia is undoubtedly somewhere in between—between two years and 2,267 years! What's your estimate?
[Childs, Chris, "Atlas of a Lost World: Travels in Ice Age America, (New York, Random House, 2018), p. 6, 94-95.]

Another one of the mysteries of the peopling of the Americas is whether some of the early arrivals came from someplace other than Beringia. Candidate locations could include Japan, the islands of the Pacific, Africa, Europe, and possibly even Beringia or Alaska. (Excuse me if I have overlooked any potential candidates.) I sort of poo pooed the possibility until I tried to find some feasible explanation for the growing number of pre-Clovis sites being found in South America. We would clearly assume that the first migrants into the hemisphere would have settled in North America. That makes sense, doesn't it? If you were arriving from a lifetime in Beringia, there are many, many, locations in North America that would have been extremely attractive sites for your new home, so why would you go farther south? If that statement is reasonable, and I feel that it is, why then are most of the pre-Clovis sites found in South America?

One explanation would be that the first group of pre-Clovis settlers followed the Pacific Coast south from Beringia, Alaska, and British Columbia—then found themselves trapped on the west side of the Rocky Mountains, forcing them to continue along the west side of the Pacific Coast all the way to South America. Remember, they undoubtedly wouldn't have known what was east of the mountain chain. In fact, it is unlikely that they knew there was anything east of the mountains. Over time, the group dispersed throughout South America. If you don't find that answer satisfactory, I don't either. I just can't imagine walking from Beringia, getting to southern California, or Mexico, or Columbia, and continuing to head south! Amazingly, some went all the way to the tip of South America at Tierra del Fuego. (I always thought the name probably meant "The End of the World," or something of that nature, but it translates from the Spanish as "Land of Fire." The name originated when a Spanish ship passed the tip of the peninsula at night and the sailors could see the campfires of the Natives dotting the countryside.) I still think "The End of the World," would be more accurate.

Another feasible explanation for why we find the first settlers in the hemisphere in South America is that they didn't come from Beringia at all, but by water from other locations. The most likely point of origin would probably have been somewhere in the South Pacific islands, although they could originally have come from literally anywhere in Southeast Asia…or from Japan or Korea in the Northern Pacific.

There is actually also no real reason that migrants could not have come from Africa or Europe. That, too, is feasible. All they would have needed would have been a boat of some sort. Unfortunately, our knowledge of the earliest marine vessels is very sparce, and since they were built of wood, reeds, and other natural products that deteriorate over time, few examples have survived. It is questionable, however, whether a vessel crossing the Atlantic at that time could have carried enough migrants to produce and populate the South American pre-Clovis sites that have already been identified.

The route the travelers chose would have had significant consequences for both how they traveled and where they went. There are two basic models that are widely discussed and deserve a closer look: the Ice-Free Corridor or the Coastal Migration Route, sometimes referred to as the Kelp Highway.

Perhaps appropriately, the "genesis" of the Ice-Free Corridor model dates to Jose de Acosta, a sixteenth-century Jesuit priest who theorized that those who migrated into the Americas "must have walked across dry land from Asia." At that time, there probably wasn't any realistic alternative explanation: "How did the First Americans get to the New World?" "They walked!" It seemed logical, except that it would have been necessary for the ancient travelers to find some way to cross the Bering Sea that lies between Asia and what we now know as the Western Hemisphere. If that wasn't enough of an obstacle, the region between Asia and the Western Hemisphere had been covered by massive glaciers during the last Ice Age, which occurred from 115,000 to 11,700 years ago.

A little light was cast on a portion of the puzzle in the mid-1800s by Jules Marcou, a French geologist who spent much of his career working in the United States. Marcou hypothesized that so much of the planet's water was consumed by the glaciers during the Ice Age that water levels throughout the world dropped, often by hundreds of feet. Researchers exploring Marcou's construct eventually determined that a number of "land bridges" had existed at various times in history related to periods of glaciation. Included was the Isthmus of Panama that was created and connected what is now North America to South America, the Sinai Peninsula that connected Africa with Eurasia, "Doggerland" that connected Great Britain to Continental Europe…and the 620-mile-wide Bering Land Bridge that connected Asia to what is now North America.

The Bering Land Bridge, up to 600-900 miles wide and constituting a land area totaling about 160,000 square miles, formed and disappeared a number of times as glacial lobes extended and retreated as the result of minor fluctuations in temperatures. As temperatures went up, the glaciers melted and retreated, forming the land bridges; and when temperatures dropped again, the glaciers extended, and the land bridges disappeared. Researchers tell us that the Bering Land Bridge would probably have existed intermittently from 60,000 to 30,000 years ago; and again from 30,000 to 11,000 years ago, the period when the people who would become the "First Americans" are believed to have found their way to the Western Hemisphere, "the New World."

The Bering Land Bridge got the Asians from Siberia onto the Western Hemisphere and what we know today as Alaska. They were still living in a cold and icy world, however, their way east or south blocked by glaciers. The Cordilleran Glacier extended from what is now the State of Washington north along the Pacific Coast to what is today the Alaskan Range and inland—west—until it met the Laurentide Glacier at the Rocky Mountains. The Laurentide Ice Sheet covered most of the balance of what is now North America, extending north from about the 45th parallel to the Canadian Ice Cap. From its contact with the Laurentide ice sheet along the Pacific Coast, it quite literally covered the rest of the United States and Canada that lie north of about the 45th parallel, although there were times when it extended south to the State of Missouri and the Ohio River Valley.

For thousands of years, the two glaciers blocked entry into what is now the northwestern sections of the United States and Canada. About 13,000 years ago, however, during a warm period that resulted

in the recession of the glacial sheets, the retraction of the east edge of the Cordilleran Glacier and retraction of the west edge of the Laurentide Glacier created what is known today as the "Ice-Free Corridor." The corridor "would have stretched 2,500 kilometers from the limits of glaciation along the Arctic coast in northern Yukon to northern Montana." Other research suggested that "the actual opening of a corridor to the south could not have occurred until about 13,000 YBP and extensive glacial lakes occupied much of the area until around 12,000 YBP."
[Lionel E. Jackson, Jr., and Michael C. Wilson, "The Ice-Free Corridor Revisited," from geotimes.org/febo4/feature, February 2004]

More recent research, however, has shown that, "The passable opening was likely only partially ice-free, so it is sometimes called the 'Western interior corridor' or 'deglaciation corridor' in the scientific literature." The limitations on when the Ice-Free Corridor could have accommodated the movement of the Siberian-Beringian-Alaskan migrants into the Western Hemisphere conflict with the accepted dating of archaeological sites throughout both North and South America.
[K. Kreis Hirst, "Is the Ice-Free Corridor an Early Pathway into Americas?" ThoughtCo, July 3, 2019, at www.thoughtco.com/ice-free-corridor-clovis-pathway.]

Researchers argued that "Even though the corridor may have opened up 13,000 years ago, there wasn't much vegetation until 12,600 years ago, when grasses and grazing animals such as bison and woolly mammoths started to appear, along with smaller animals like jackrabbits and voles. About a thousand years later, it was colonized by trees, moose, elk and bald eagles. That's when humans could finally move in," one researcher suggested. "Having a tree suddenly changed the game, because now we have fuel, we have shelter, we have a raw material that could be used for making tools."
["Popular theory on how humans populated North America can't be right, study shows," www.cbs.ca/news, August 11, 2016, and Mikkel W. Pederson, Anthony Ruter, Charles Schweger, et. al., "Postglacial Viability and Colonization in North America's Ice-Free Corridor,"

Nature, 537, no. 7618 (2016), pp. 45-49, referenced in Jennifer Raff, "Origin: A Genetic History of the Americas, (New York: Twelve, 2022, pp. 81-87.]

Under the best of circumstances, traveling the route should never be considered to have been a walk in the park. The opening between the two gigantic ice sheets is estimated to have been about twenty-five kilometers wide…and about 1,243 miles long. It would have been littered with all sorts of debris that would have been gathered up and deposited there by the glaciers. The route would have been strewn with rocks of all sizes, from cobblestones to massive boulders larger than Volkswagens, rivers formed by runoff from the glaciers would probably have frequently blocked the route, as would numerous glacial lakes of varying sizes and depths. A variety of soils would have been encountered along the route, ranging from some akin to beach sand and others that would have been heavy, water saturated clay that would have taxed the travelers.

The most recent scientific assessments, certainly still subject to scrutiny and challenge, suggest that "the pre-Clovis migrations occurred by at least [about] 15.5 to 16.0 [thousand years ago], or earlier than most recent assessments of the age of the Ice-Free Corridor opening at [about] 14.0 to 15.0 [thousand years ago], lending support to the use of a Pacific Coast migration route instead." The researchers acknowledge, however, that there is still some "uncertainties in ages from the Ice-Free Corridor" that could affect whether the corridor would have been available for use by the migrants.
[Clark, Jorie, Anders E. Carlson, Alberto V. Reyes, et. al., "The age of the opening of the Ice-Free Corridor, implications for the people of the Americas," March 21, 2022, www.researchgate.net.]

Chapter 4

Becoming "Americans"

> What is certain is that the initial colonization of the New World was the last great continent-wide expansions of Homo sapiens. Indeed, it may well be the last great large-scale peopling episode of our kind, unless we ultimately choose or are forced to leave our planet to colonize other worlds and even stranger lands.
>
> **—J. M. Adovasio, and David Pedler**
>
> Strangers in a New Land

It is probably important to note that no archaeological evidence has ever been found of any humans moving from Beringia south through the corridor toward the Americas. No human burials, no bones of animals killed by humans, no remains of fire pits, no footprints. Nothing. Not a sign of any sort. Interestingly, some evidence has been found that some people eventually moved northward toward Alaska and the Yukon several millennia after Clovis, perhaps attempting to return to their hereditary homelands. [Heather L. Smith and Ted Goebel, "Origins and Spread of Fluted-Point Technology in the Canadian Ice-Free Corridor and Eastern Beringia," Proceedings of the National Academy of Science, USA, 115 (2018): 4116-4121.]

Anthropologist and Geneticist Jennifer Raff has concluded that "due to glacial conditions, people moving through the area of the Ice-Free Corridor could only have migrated before 26,000 years ago or after 19,000 years ago," unless there was a yet undiscovered path through the walls of ice. Raff's assessment is that most researchers tend to favor the "after 19,000" scenario, delaying entries into the hemisphere from Beringia by about 6,000 to 9,000 years. Raff, however, is quick to point out that there are numerous archaeological sites in South America that date to 30,000 years ago, or more, well beyond the Clovis time period.

"It may be that people were in the Americas by 25,000 years ago," states Professor Raff. "Figuring out how that finding fits with genetic evidence is a new puzzle to solve. But I think that while we exercise a healthy skepticism, we must learn our lessons from the erroneous Clovis First paradigm and not simply dismiss evidence because it doesn't fit with a model we happen to favor."
[Raff, Jennifer, Origin: A Genetic History of the Americas, (New York: Twelve, 2022), pp. 93-98; Christina Larson, "Evidence points to footprints being the oldest sign of humans in America," The Alpena News, October 6, 2023, p. 3B; Strickland, Ashley, CNN Science – Wonder Theory at cnn.com.]

In The Indigenous Paleolithic of the Western Hemisphere, published in 2021, Professor Paulette F.C. Steeves of Canada's Algoma University, identified a total of 111 sites in North America that appear to be between 11,200 and at least 22,000 years old. Another 58 sites of similar age are identified in South America.
[Steeves, Paulette F. C., The Indigenous Paleolithic of the Western Hemisphere, (Lincoln: University of Nebraska Press, 2022), pp.104-150.]

One of the sites described by Professor Steeves was the Cerutti Mastadon site near San Diego, California, that was first discovered in 1992. It yielded fractured Mastodon bones that appear to have been worked by humans. Testing showed them to be at least 130,700 years old. When the mammoth bones underwent testing, they generated dates of at least 130,000 years old. When news about the sight was published in Nature magazine in 2017, it generated "an immediate firestorm of criticism from American archaeologists.

An archaeological site that generated more attention than the Cerutti mastodons were the sixty-one human footprints discovered along the edge of an ancient lakebed in what is now the White Sands National Park in New Mexico. First made public in 2021, dating the fossil footprints required the complex analysis of a variety of seeds found at the same level as the footprints. Results of those analyses have convinced a growing number of researchers that the tracks made in the mud thousands of years ago could really be evidence that there were humans in the Americas 23,000 to 21,000 years ago, either during the last Ice Age, or, even more startling, before the Ice Age.

Professor Thomas D. Dillehay's Monte Verde site in Chili contains a variety of evidence that dates at 15,500-18,500 years old. Dillehay of the University of Kentucky has been the principal investigator at the Monte Verde site that contained a unique and diverse collection of animal bones, some with what appeared to be cut marks on them. Resting with the bones were rope, what was left of meals, even mammoth remains that still included soft tissue. Like White Sands, Monte Verde also contained human footprints, but made by a young child, left in what had been a layer of mud and clay. Discovered in 1977 and radiocarbon dated at 14,600 years before the present, many archaeologists refused to accept the Monte Verde results, due mainly to their conflict with the dates of Clovis sites. Widespread acceptance of the "Clovis First" explanation for when the Americas were peopled seems to have blinded members of the archaeology community to other possible hypotheses.
[Wernecke, D.C. and M.B. Collins, (2016). Institute for Archaeological Studies: "Pre-Clovis in the Americas Conference" Smithsonian Institution Washington, D.C. Retrieved from http://prehistoricterritory.org/pre-clovis-in-the-americas-conference-smithsonian-institution-washington-d-c/; Steeves, Paulette F. C., The Indigenous Paleolithic of the Western Hemisphere, (Lincoln: University of Nebraska Press, 2022), pp.104-150.]

In addition to the Cerutti Mastodon, White Sands, and Monte Verde sites, Steeves includes information on sites from Oregon to Tennessee, Pennsylvania to the Yukon, and Florida to Wisconsin, all claiming to be older than Clovis sites, but not necessarily widely accepted by the archaeology community at this time.

Some of the issues that were raised with respect to the widely accepted Ice-Free Corridor explanation focused attention on the Coastal Migration Route, or the Kelp Highway. A Coastal Migration explanation had been suggested by archaeologist Knut Fladmark of

Simon Fraser University in 1979. His advocacy of a coastal route for entrance into the Americas was based largely on the need to find an explanation for the astonishingly rapid movement of the migrants from Beringia to both North and South America. Theoretically, the route down the Pacific Coast has a number of advantages over the inland route that was based on there being a traversable gap developing between the Laurentide and Cordilleran ice sheets. First of all, the western perimeter of the Cordilleran ice sheet is at the western-most extreme of the glaciation of North America. That would undoubtedly have provided surface area for melting that would have been well in excess of that that could have occurred with an ice sheet that abutted another ice sheet, as the east side of the Cordilleran does. It abuts the massive Laurentide glacier, and it is the melting of the seam between those two ice sheets that created the Ice-Free Corridor. However, a glacial perimeter abutting an ocean would undoubtedly be expected to melt at a significantly faster rate than one that leaned against another glacier. Fladmark felt that there would potentially be major difficulties in using a corridor between the ice sheets as a means of access to the Americas and that boat travel would be a much simpler way to get to the unglaciated shores of Oregon and California.
[Adovasio, J.M., and David Pedler, Strangers in a New Land: What Archaeology Reveals About the First Americans, (Buffalo, NY: Firefly Books, 2016), pp. 19-21.]

While there were various iterations of the Coastal Migration model proposed, they all basically involved a route along the Pacific Coast of Canada and the U.S., usually by boat. That could get the migrants to the unglaciated shorelines of British Columbia and Washington. Others felt the migrants could have followed the Pacific Coast all the way to Tierra del Fuego, and that could have accounted for the rapidity with which the migrants reached South America.

"The coastal migration hypothesis was bolstered by findings such as a report that the sediments in the Port Eliza caves on Vancouver Island indicated the possibility of a survivable climate as far back as 16,000 years ago in the area, while the continental ice sheets were then just approaching their maximum extent." In 2017, a

Canadian archeological team excavated a hearth on Triquet Island, northwest of Vancouver, British Columbia, that was radiocarbon dated to be between 13,613 and 14,086 years old, making it one of the oldest settlements in North America. The finding seems to have confirmed the First Nation oral history that said Triquet Island was inhabited during the Ice Age, and it definitely added substance to the Port Eliza findings.
[Surovell, Todd A., "Simulating Coastal Migration in New World Colonization," Current Anthropology, Wenner-Gren Foundation for Anthropological Research," (2003), 44 (4): 580-591; Wikipedia: Coastal Migration Route; Majid Al-Suwaidi (2006), "A Multi-disciplinary Study of Port Eliza Cave Sediments and Their Implications for Human Coastal Migration," Library and Archives Canada, archived from the original on 2020-02-29; Thomas D. Dillehay, The Settlement of the Americas: A New Prehistory, (New York: Basic Books, 2000), p. 246; Wikipedia: Coastal Migration (Americas).]

A related, but somewhat different model, explained in a Discover Magazine article by Roy W. Lowe of the U.S. Fish & Wildlife Service, hypothesized that the First Americans may have followed a "Kelp Highway" of marine resources via a coastal route from Siberia to the New World. Nutrient-rich kelp beds, such as those that proliferate near Crook Point on the Oregon coast, attract salmon and other sea life that would have sustained the early explorers. In fact, "different types of seaweed—or kelp—were once a staple food for Europeans for thousands of years..." Referred to as a, "21st Century tweak of a Coastal Migration Theory," the Kelp Highway model postulates that, "16,000 years ago, someone traveling along the northern Pacific Ocean coastline eastward from Siberia would have encountered an essentially unobstructed route at sea level, with plenty of fish, shellfish, kelp, seabirds, and other resources — and no dangerous open ocean."
[Hunt, Katie, "Wonder Theory," Weekly Spaceand, Science, Digest; Gemma Tarlach, discovermagazine.com/planet-earth/did-the-first Americans arrive via- kelp-highway? November 2, 2017.]

Researchers in colleges and universities and on the staffs of museums around the world immediately began searching for evidence that would support the Coastal theory…or, perhaps more commonly, send it to the midden of failed archaeological theories. Researchers on the mainland east of Wrangell Island in southeast Alaska even found the remains of a dog that were radiocarbon dated as 10,150 years old. Genetic studies showed that the dog's lineage split from Siberian Zhokhov Island dogs 16,700 years earlier, a time that coincided with the likely opening of the coastal route into North America.
[Wikipedia: Coastal Migration (Americas)]

Linguist Johanna Nichols of the University of California, Berkeley, was among the first to offer support for the Coastal Migration Route, based on her finding that "the centers of greatest language diversity are located along the Pacific Coast of North America and the northwest corner of South America." Given presumed rates of linguistic change and the diversity of languages, Nichols had reached the conclusion that either there had been a single entry of the original settlers 50,000 years ago, or there had been multiple entries beginning at least 30,000 years ago. She made no apologies for the fact that archaeologists had failed to find sites that old. "As a linguist, that's not my problem," she explained.

Stanford University linguist Joseph Greenberg reached a conclusion very similar to that of Nichols, based on the supposition that each of the first three groups to enter the Americas spoke a core language. Greenberg's research suggested that the hundreds of Native American languages spoken during the historic period could be grouped into three families: Eskimo-Aleut, Na-Dene, and Amerind, each spoken by various indigenous populations. Greenberg had concluded that the differences between the three groups were so pronounced that their use "must have dated back to Old World populations, and that each of these must have crossed the land bridge at different times."

He determined that the first migration would have been by members of the Amerind linguistic group, the largest of the three, and whose language is least similar to those of the Old World. "Next to arrive," according to Greenberg, "must have been the Na-Dine family" that occupies a more southerly location than the Eskimo-Aleut and whose languages are least similar to those of the Old World. They also retained some connection with Asian languages but had undergone more internal language differentiation than the Eskimo-Aleut group. The Eskimos Aleuts occupied lands closest to the land bridge, they were the last to cross into the New World, and their speech "shows close affinities with Siberian and Old-World languages."

Not to be outdone by the linguists, Christy G. Turner, an American anthropologist known for his research in dental anthropology, noted that teeth are often excellent indicators of a population's history or their relatedness. In such cases, the best clues to relatedness are genetic traits that depend on many genes and do not change rapidly in response to use, diet, health, or other factors, according to Turner. "Teeth," he states, "meets these requirements." Turner said they also have an advantage of being dated and generally preserve extraordinarily well, outlasting bones.
[O'Neill, Dan, The Last Giant of Beringia: The Mystery of the Bering Land Bridge, (Boulder, CO: Westview Press, 2004), pp. 171-176); Meltzer, David J., First Peoples in a New World: Colonizing Ice Age America, (Berkeley: University of California Press, 2009), p. 192.; Nichols, Johanna, "Linguistic Diversity and the First Settlement of the New World," Language, 66(3):475-521; Dan O'Neill, Last Giant of Beringia: The Mystery of the Bering Land Bridge, (Boulder, CO: Westview Press, 2004), pp. 169-175, p. 171-176; Adovasio, J.M. and Jake Page, The First Americans: In Pursuit of Archaeology's Greatest Mystery, (New York: Random House, 2003), pp. 275-276.]

Most of those who studied the Coastal or Kelp theories agreed that either route would have provided the sustenance needed by the travelers, especially until they reached the ice-free regions of North America…or South America. In fact, according to J. M. Adovasio and Jake Page, "it turns out that the Cordilleran glacier was never in total command of the coast. There were what scientists call 'refugia' along the way, ice-free spots that sailors would think of as safe harbors where they could gather themselves, kill a few seals or whatever, and then be on their way. Most, including Knut Fladmark, also linked the Coastal route with the likelihood that the travelers would have used boats of some sort to travel along the Pacific Coast. In fact, many people specifically mentioned "rafts" or "boats" as if it was a foredrawn conclusion that since the migrants were expected to travel along the shore of the Pacific Coast, they would inevitably use some kind of marine vessel. It must have slipped their minds, however, that the peoples who had been residents of Beringia for many centuries were not part of maritime cultures. As far as anyone knows, they didn't have boats of any sort, nor did most have any place where they could have used boats. Even the Aleuts or Eskimos had not yet developed their kayaks and unimaks and they did their hunting for seals on the ice. So, it appears that it is unlikely that the migrants could have come up with boats of some type and "sails made from skin or woven plants" that would have allowed them to be "whisked down the coast in fairly short order."

David J. Meltzer of Southern Methodist University puts the issues in a proper context. "Opinion is divided over whether in-migrating groups coming down the coast would have traveled on foot or by boat. Since we've not found any late Pleistocene watercraft, much of this debate rests on speculation and circumstantial evidence—both for and against the possibility."

J. M. Adovasio and David Pedler said, "For some incomprehensible reason, many New World archaeologists have maintained longstanding biases against the potential role of watercraft in the initial dispersal of the First Americas..." They go on to note that, "Current data suggest that Homo erectus was utilizing boats to populate islands off southeastern reaches of Asia's continental shelf by 880,000-780,000 yrs. BP, and there is gathering evidence that some Mediterranean islands such as Cyprus and Crete that were colonized via boats much earlier than previously believed." They conclude that, "If watercraft were indeed operational in the open waters of Southeast Asia by at least 40,000 yrs. BP, it is virtually certain that ancient coastal populations further to the north also had access to boats.

[Adovasio, J. M., and David Pedler, Strangers in a New Land: What Archaeology Reveals About the First Americans, (Buffalo, NY: Firefly Books, 2016), pp. 29-30.

That, of course, isn't evidence, it's speculation. It's the old "If A, then B" model: If they had watercraft in Southeast Asia, they should have had watercraft along the Pacific Coast. That's definitely arguable.

University of New Mexico anthropologist E. James Dixon makes a similarly unsupportable claim in his Bones, Boats & Bison. He starts by stating, "The initial colonization of the Americas used watercraft and occurred about 13,500 B.P. and possibly earlier." That hypothesis is then "supported by" nine other statements, one of which relates to watercraft: "Evidence from other regions of the world demonstrates that humans had watercraft and the ability to navigate near-shore ocean waters prior to 14,000 B.P., and possibly more than 40,000 B.P."

Obviously, in his desire to make it possible for the First Americans to have paddled down the Pacific Coast, Dixon also subscribes to the "If A, then B" model. I totally agree with his statements but can find no evidence that the Beringians or the First Americans had gained any marine experience during the 15,000 years, or so, that they had been trapped in Beringia by the Ice Age. Could they have built some sort of boat? I think that might have been possible and will discuss that later. But I have been unable to find any evidence that the Beringians, Yup'ik, Eskimos, or Aleuts had any sort of boats during the Beringians' move into the Americas. If they did, they apparently didn't take them along on their trip south.

The kayak and umiak and their various derivations were boats developed by Indigenous Peoples in the far north—Yup'ik, Inuit, and Aleut—but it is nigh impossible to find any mention of them as boat builders or sea-mammal hunters before 4,000 years ago. The earliest written records would have been those prepared by Russian explorers beginning in about 1759. A kayak was also beached along the shore of Scotland in the late seventeenth century. It is not in the collection of the museum in Aberdeen, Scotland. "The kayak seems to prove that Eskimos, probably from Greenland, were able to paddle their light skin boats across the North Atlantic, and that they are to be identified with the 'Finn-men' of Scottish legend."

In her article "Small Boats upon the North Atlantic," that appeared in the 1971 collection Man Across the Sea: Problems of Pre-Columbian Contact, Professor Alice B. Kehoe of Marquette University in Milwaukee, said that records documented hundreds of small boats that had been used to cross the Atlantic Ocean. Her list included, "at least two rafts, two dugout canoes, two dories propelled only by oars, several dories fitted with sails, conventional sailboats as small as five feet eleven inches in length, and unconventional boats including kayaks, folding boats, an inflatable life raft, and an amphibian jeep."

It is not a question of whether small boats, like those that might have been used by the Indigenous Peoples who subsequently founded and populated the Americas, were capable of reaching the Americas from Beringia. That feat could definitely have been performed. There is, however, no evidence of any kind that indicates that it actually happened, that boats played a role in the initial peopling of the Americas. The first "boat people" who reached the Americas via the oceans were the Norse, or Vikings, who visited the northern Atlantic Coast around the year 1000. They even maintained a small settlement at L'Anse aux Meadows in northern Newfoundland for several years before abandoning the site, possibly in reaction to ongoing conflicts with the local Indigenous Peoples.

[Dixon, James E., Bones, Boats & Bison: Archaeology and the First Colonization of Western North America, (Albuquerque: The University of New Mexico Press, 1999), pp. 254-255; Laughlin, William S., Aleuts: Survivors of the Bering Land Bridge, (New York: Holt, Rinehart and Winston, 1980), pp. 35-41, 128-131; Wikipedia: Kayak; Kehoe, Alice B., "Small Boats Upon the North Atlantic," in Riley, Carroll L., J. Charles Kelley, Campbell W. Pennington, and Robert L. Hands, eds., Man Across the Sea: Problems of Pre-Columbian Contact, (Austin, TX: University of Texas Press, 1971), pp. 275-292, and 276f, quoted from I. Whitaker, "The Scottish Kayaks and the Finn-men, Antiquity, 28:110.]

Clovis ruled for decades. The creators of the Clovis points were widely recognized within the archaeological community as being the first Indians to settle in the New World. Any sites that were represented as possibly being pre-Clovis were almost summarily rejected. Thomas Dillehay who spent two decades trying to get the

Monte Verde in Chile accepted as being older than the Clovis sites summarized the problems he experienced with many of his archaeological colleagues: These critics have a long history of rejecting any site that counters the Clovis-first model. In their haste to defend the Clovis model, they fantasize floods and other natural events to explain the association of the different cultural traits often found at non-Clovis sites, or, worse, they invent mistakes in the analysis of these sites to give cause for dismissing them. What all this boils down to is the politics of science and the replacement of one paradigm by another.
[Thomas D. Dillehay, The Settlement of the Americas: A New Prehistory, (New York: Basic Books, 2000), pp. xvi-xviii.]

Challenges to "Clovis First" really began to mount in the 1980s, eliciting a comment from anthropological geneticist Jennifer Raff of the University of Kansas, that "the field is bonkers right now. I think there's a new important paper coming out every three or four months."
[McSporran, Joanne, "The Knotty Question of When Humans Made the Americas Home," The Anthropology Newspaper, September 4, 2019, at www.sapiens.org.]

In addition to Professor Dillehay's well-known Monte Verde site, some of the sites in the Americas offering interesting alternatives to "Clovis First" include:

—Coprolites (desiccated human feces, sometimes referred to as fossilized human feces), found in Paisley Five Mile Point Caves in south-central Oregon, were dated to 14,500 years ago. One of the eight caves found at the site may contain "DNA evidence of the oldest definitively dated human presence in North America." The site has been investigated by anthropologists since 1938, but the antiquity of the caves were disregarded because they conflicted with the

predominant "Clovis First" model accepted by most researchers. They were wrong.
[Adovasio, J. M., and David Pedler, Strangers in a New Land: What Archaeology Reveals About the First Americans, (Ontario, Canada: Firefly Books, 2016), pp.236-245.]

—Discovered by the landowner in 1955, the Meadowcroft Rockshelter site in southwestern Pennsylvania would have been south of the area of glaciation during the last Ice Age. Radiocarbon dating of the site indicated occupancy beginning 16,000 years ago and possibly as early as 19,000 years ago, a full 2,000 years before Clovis sites. The site has been made very accessible for tourists and other visitors. [Adovasio, J. M., and David Pedler, Strangers in a New Land: What Archaeology Reveals About the First Americans, (Ontario, Canada: Firefly Books, 2016), pp. 200-215.]

—More than 200 stone artifacts were recovered from the Cooper's Ferry site in Idaho and subsequently dated at 16,000 years old. Some points were similar to points found in Japan, which could provide some support for a Pacific Coastal route for the immigrants peopling the west coast of the Americas.
[ww.sci-news.com/archaeology/coopers-ferry-tools-07546.html]

The Buttermilk Creek Complex in Texas, with two sites totaling just over 42 acres, has produced more than fifty well-formed artifacts in a layer of clay soil below typical Clovis material. Historically a very resource rich site, its principal investigator has referred to it as "a special place" and claims it has been special for "a very long time." In fact, it appears that the sites have been in use for over 13,000 years. The larger of the two sites has yielded more than 15,000 artifacts from its pre-Clovis strata.
[ancientexplorermagazine.wordpress.com/2016/10/20/pre-clovis-presence-in-the-americas; Adovasio, J. M., and David Pedler, Strangers in a New Land: What Archaeology Reveals About the First Americans, (Ontario, Canada: Firefly Books, 2016), various pages.]

Not all the sites that have been presented as being "Pre-Clovis" have been accepted, or "generally accepted" by the archaeological community. Two "possible Pre-Clovis sites" that are still controversial are the Bluefish Caves in the Yukon and the Topper site in South Carolina.

—The Bluefish Caves are located along the Bluefish River in the Canadian Yukon, just less than 30 miles north of the Arctic Circle and a little east of the U.S. and Canadian border, an area spared from the glaciation of the Pleistocene. The caves, located on a ridge about a distance of two-and-a-half football fields above the river, provide a panoramic view of the terrain along the river that would have been visited by many species of wildlife that would have been included in the diets of humans. Discovered in 1975, bone tools from the three caves have produced radiocarbon dates in the range of 14,000 years before the present to 28,560 years before the present. The date of 14,000 years before the present is considered to be well-documented, while the older dates are "problematic."
[Adovasio, J. M., and David Pedler, Strangers in a New Land: What Archaeology Reveals About the First Americans, (Ontario, Canada: Firefly Books, 2016), pp. 306-313.]

—Another site that has been proposed as a Pre-Clovis site, but has not been widely accepted by members of the archaeological community is the Topper site on the Savannah River in southern South Carolina, about seventy miles north of Savannah. It has produced findings, that if validated, could indicate a pre-Clovis presence of over 50,000 years ago. Radiocarbon tests of carbonized plant remains recovered from the site by University of South Carolina archaeologist Dr. Albert Goodyear indicate that the sediments containing these artifacts are at least 50,000 years old. Acceptance of that age would mean that humans inhabited North American long before the last ice age." The age of the site is still being debated, however. Many archaeologists who have examined the findings believe that the pre-Clovis materials actually migrated downward from the site's large Clovis stratum. A reexamination of the findings in 2015 claimed that the supposed Pre-Clovis materials had been found in situ in a Pre-Clovis layer and did not migrate from a higher level. Stay tuned! [en.wikipedia.org/wiki/TopperSite;sciencedaily.com/releases/2004/11/041118104010.htm; Adovasio, J. M., and David Pedler, Strangers in a New Land: What Archaeology Reveals About the First Americans, (Ontario, Canada: Firefly Books, 2016), pp. 272-285.]

If validated, these seven archaeological sites, as well as the other 162 possible pre-Clovis sites on Professor Steeves' list would challenge the widely accepted "Cloris First" story of the settling of the Americas. One, the Cooper's Ferry site in Idaho, would also present the possibility of Japanese involvement in the settling of America, including adding some possible evidence supporting a Pacific Coastal route of migration, as opposed to the "Bering Land Bridge to the Ice-Free Corridor" route. It's probably safe to say that researchers around the world are studying these ten sites in an effort to make some sense of the multitude of varying findings. I think we are getting closer to the day that they can make definitive decisions, due in large part to the growing "toolbox" that researchers have available to them for establishing ages.

In their magnificent Strangers in a New Land, J. M Adovasio and David Pedler conclude that Clovis First has collapsed "on both chronological and behavioral grounds." The chant, "the King is dead, the King is dead," has probably rattled the test tubes and coffee mugs in many research facilities throughout the world. At the same time, the mantra, "Clovis First, Clovis First," is undoubtedly still heard in many sites, possibly being intoned more quietly than before. Adovasio and Pedler feel that today, "Clovis represents the cusp or threshold of archaeological visibility in North America—the establishment of a resident population in some portions of the hemisphere." The unique Clovis point, "is not the lithic banner of a rapidly moving group of migrants, but rather a stone icon passed quickly for still unknown reasons between and among some pre-existing populations. As there are no real functional advantages to fluting, either for hafting or killing, we presume its dispersal is somehow socio-ideological in origin."

On the somewhat related question of "who were the first humans," Adovasio and Pedler, have concluded, "we will probably never know for certain." They added, "What is certain is that the initial colonization of the New World was the last great continent-wide expansions of Homo sapiens sapiens. Indeed, it may well be the last great large-scale peopling episode of our kind, unless we ultimately choose or are forced to leave our planet to colonize other worlds and even stranger lands." [Adovasio, J. M. and David Pedler, Strangers in a New Land: What Archaeology Reveals About the First Americans, (Buffalo, NY: Firefly Books, 2016), pp. 314-315.]

CHAPTER 5

EARLIER ARRIVALS?

> People were likely present in the Americas long before their traces appear on our archaeological radar screen.
>
> **—David J. Meltzer**
>
> First Peoples in a New World

Could people from Africa, Europe, Asia, or the Pacific Islands have visited the Americas in the distant past? Absolutely. Could they have visited the Americas before the arrival of the Beringian migrants? That's entirely possible. While we don't have evidence of boats anywhere in the Americas that could have been used by the First Americans to travel from Beringia into North America or South America, boats with those capabilities did exist elsewhere. Voyages to the Americas from the other continents could even have been accidental—ships blown off course in storms, ships without means of propulsion carried to our shores by the currents in the Atlantic and Pacific. They could even have predated the arrivals of the American Indians—arriving on our shores without means to return to their homes, perhaps they tragically died here; or they eventually blended with the American Indians when they arrived, and no record of them having been here has ever been found. That is made understandably feasible because the shorelines of the Americas that existed in the Pleistocene are now several hundred feet underwater due to the increases in water levels that resulted from the melting of the glaciers.

In Atlas of a Lost World, Craig Childs discusses the Fukushima Earthquake and its effect on the West Coast of America:

The Fukushima Earthquake hit the coast of Japan on April 22, 2011. The following tsunami washed nearly five million tons of debris, including boats, cars, parts of houses and factories, and some of the twenty thousand dead, into the Pacific. Debris entered the gyratory Kuroshio Current and was swept toward North America, where objects began to arrive a month later. The first landing was April 28, when a cargo box from Yamamoto in Miyagi prefecture, the hardest hit from the quake, washed onto a heavily forested island of Haida Gwaii on the west coast of British Columbia. The box opened as it hit the beach and a Harley-Davidson motorcycle rolled onto the sand. This was the first offering from Japan.

It had taken the Harley-Davidson and the tons of other tsunami debris a month to reach our Pacific Coast "under no power but wind and sea to make the four-thousand-mile trip from Japan to the edge of North America."

Stories about boats and ships that intentionally or unintentionally landed on the shores of the Americas are not difficult to find. In addition to those cited by Craig Childs, Gavin Menzies, a former Royal Navy officer, and author Ian Hudson, make the case for Asian migrations, including by the Chinese, Japanese, and Koreans. Professor Ivan Van Sertima of Rutgers, a noted linguist and anthropologist, makes strong arguments for the presence of Africans in ancient America. Medieval records in Europe include reports that St. Brendan, an Irish monk, sailed to the Atlantic Coast of America…and back to Ireland…in a wood-framed sailboat sheathed in skins in the sixth century. There are many other similar accounts. [Childs, Craig, Atlas of a Lost World: Travels in Ice Age America, (New York: Vintage Books, 2019); Menzies, Gavin, and Ian Hudson, Who Discovered America? The Untold History of the Peopling of the Americas, (New York: HarperCollins, 2013); Van Sertima, Ivan, They Came Before Columbus: The African Presence in Ancient America, (New York: Random House, 2003); Craig Childs, Atlas of a Lost World, (New York: Vintage Books, 2019), pp. 62-66.]

Based on my own experience as a hiker and boater, I immediately saw what seemed to have been a weakness of the Ice-Free Corridor hypothesis, as expounded by Pederson, et. al., and the potential advantages of the Coastal Migration Route with its comparatively generous availability of food along the entire route. While I don't have any experience along the Pacific Coast of the Americas, I have walked hundreds of miles on beaches in Florida and along the shores of Lake Michigan and Lake Huron. Walking along a beach, particularly above the high-water mark, is generally easier than walking through an area of young vegetation, debris ice, and frequent lakes and ponds, like the situation that would probably have been found along the Ice-Free Corridor.

The ease of walking the Coastal Migration Route is a critical factor to me, because I seriously doubt that the migrating bands would have traveled by boat. Since they apparently did not have seafaring backgrounds, I question the travelers' ability to even construct a functional boat. It is even questionable whether the Indigenous people traveling south had any experience in the construction or use of boats, which would have been totally useless in the ice-covered country they had lived in for Millennia. We have to remember that for thousands of years they and their ancestors had existed in the frozen north of the hemisphere, an environment totally unsuited to the use of boats most of the time. Even if they managed to build something like a dugout canoe, raft, or skin-covered vessel of some sort, paddling a crude vessel of that nature down the Pacific Coast would have been a dicey feat and one known historically to frequently lead to disaster.

The boat we think of most often in use by the Inuit, Yupik, Aleuts and other residents of the far north is the kayak, or one of its various iterations. However, the first kayaks are believed to have first been built only 4,000 years ago, long after the "First Americans" would have traveled down the Pacific Coast.

Advocates of the Coastal Migration Route will also often mention the "coracle" as being a type of vessel that might easily have been built by the First Americans. Coracle-type vessels are small, round or oval, wood-framed or bone-framed, skin-covered boats that can be found in use in many areas of the world. They are said to have been in use in the United Kingdom, particularly in Wales, Ireland, and Scotland, for at least 2,000 years and may actually date to prehistoric times. Lacking a keel to make them more directional, they are often referred to as a "roundabout boat," because when paddled they are just as likely to go in circles as in a straight line.
[See Kayak, Umiak, and Coracle in Google.]

Lacking a maritime tradition or experience in boatbuilding, it is questionable whether the First Americans could have produced a functional vessel with the few stone-age tools they had and a critical lack of knowledge. If they did, the raft or boat would undoubtedly not have been very maneuverable and paddling the crude vessel down the shore of the Pacific Ocean would undoubtedly have been a challenging feat. From my experience on the Great Lakes, I can attest that even a canoe or dugout would have been very difficult to keep off the beach with an onshore wind or even small waves, and both of those conditions would have been almost continuous along the Pacific shore. The wind or waves would tend to constantly be pushing your crude little boat onto the beach, forcing you to paddle out into deeper...and more dangerous...waters, a time-consuming and energy draining activity.

The easiest "vessel" to build is probably a raft made from logs that have been tied together to fashion a platform of sorts, the top of which is commonly just above the top of the water. While they are simple "vessels," it is difficult to build one that is sturdy and most have a tendency to come apart in any sort of seaway. Unless you have some strong paddlers, rafts are also extremely difficult to navigate; without a keel and usually absent any sort of rudder, they want to go wherever the wind and current want to send them. (An excellent treatise on the hazards of raft travel can be found in the story of Spanish conquistador Cabeza de Vaca and his party who were lost along the Gulf Coast of Florida in 1527. Only four from his party of four hundred men survived the march through what is now Florida and a treacherous raft passage along the coast of what is now Louisiana, a journey that took ten years.) [Andrés Rseséndez, A Land So Strange: The Epic Journey of Cabeza de Vaca, (New York: Basic Books, 2007.]

Professor David Meltzer acknowledges that the first people to settle what is now Australia arrived there by boat more than 40,000 years ago. To do that, they didn't just paddle down a friendly shore, they had to cross open water. The amount of open water and the nature that water and weather would have been far different for the

Beringians, however, and could easily have resulted in the trip ending in a maritime disaster.

Meltzer also points out "The first evidence watercraft were used in the North Pacific—the occupation of islands off the Pacific Northwest coast and the hunting of marine mammals—mostly postdate 10,000 years before the present, too late for initial colonizers skirting south around the ice sheets."

My reservations about the ability of our traveler friends to construct a suitable boat in which to parallel the Pacific Coast, are tempered only by my confidence in the creativity of human beings. As a child of 8 or 10, living along the Lake Huron shore, my friends and I frequently built small rafts in the summertime. They embodied every negative attribute a "vessel" could have, but they floated. Given time and a few resources—mainly just wood and rope—I am confident that by the time we were 12 or 14 we could have had a raft or boat that would have been the envy of our friends. Given the amount of time it would have taken to make a trip from Beringia to British Columbia…or anywhere on the coast north of Tierra del Fuego, I think our Pleistocene pals could have fashioned some sort of vessel that would have made their travels easier and maybe even faster. Professor Meltzer isn't far off when he concluded that "For the moment, Occam's Razor points to the groups walking down the coast—if they came via that, route." (Occam's Razor, attributed to 14th century friar William of Ockham, posits that scientists should accept the simplest possible explanation for the existing situation being considered. In other words, "pick the simplest explanation." That, of course, has been proven to be the wrong answer many times over the years. It may be wise advice in this case…or not.)
[Meltzer, David J., First Peoples in a New World: Colonizing Ice Age America, (Berkeley: University of California Press, 2009), pp. 129-130.]

CHAPTER 6

THE WORLD OF OTHER POSSIBILITIES

We're not sure where everyone came from—maybe everywhere.

—Craig Childs
Atlas of a Lost World

The preceding seven potential pre-Clovis cases are not, however, the only contenders in the archaeological puzzle competition. There are all sorts of archaeologists and wannabe-archaeologists out in the field right now, hoping to find something old or something new—something like a new Clovis site or, better yet, a pre-Clovis site, or a site that contains something we haven't seen before in the way of tools, weapons, clothing, bones, or bodies.

In addition, there are already many competing explanations for who the First Americans were. Author and researcher Robert D. Morritt, a protagonist of alternative explanations for who first settled the Americas, or who visited here before the groups from Siberia-Beringia-Alaska, or who might have visited here and interacted with the First Americans to the extent that they influenced them in some identifiable way. His website presents at least twenty-three explanations for who settled the Americas that are at odds with the Bering Land Bridge, Ice-Free Corridor, Coastal Migration Route, Kelp Highway, and even the Clovis First positions. Articles on the site would add Early Europeans, Solutreans, Semites, Sumerians, Egyptians, Phoenicians, Hebrews, Minoans, Israelites, and Irish to our list of possible First Americans…among others.

The articles provide a lot of "facts," not all of which are actually factual, so read them with some skepticism and be cautious about subscribing to any of them without doing some research of your own. My take is: if they had any likelihood of being true, they would be on lists like the one above that challenges Clovis First.

They do make interesting and sometimes thought-provoking reading, however, especially if you're on a long flight, or you have insomnia, or you are forced into watching a Detroit Lions football game. [Morritt's information can be found at www.faculty.ucr.edu/~legneref/bronze/archaic.htm.]

One possible group that is not included in Morritt's list is mentioned in Buddy Levy's excellent book River of Darkness, about the first known voyage by Europeans down the Amazon River in 1541-42:

One day a delegation of Indians arrived who, more than any before them, captivated and engaged (Francisco) Orellana and his men. They came to see the Captain and his men, four Indians who approached us, and they were each of such a stature that each one was taller by a span than the tallest Christian, and they were quite white and had very fine hair which reached down to their waists, and they came all decked out in gold and splendid attire; and they brought much food; and they approached with such humbleness that we were all amazed at their manners and good breeding; they took out a great quantity of food and placed it before the Captain and told him how they were vassals of a very great overlord, and that it was by his command that they came to see who we were and what we wanted or where we were going.

The tall White visitors soon departed to report back to their great overlord and "the Spaniards were never to learn where the distinctive natives were from." Some thought they were pituitary giants or possibly "from one of the farther-reaching tribes, such as one of the various Arawak groups. These groups were very sophisticated, which would explain the regal bearing, humility, and fine manners of the [tall, White Natives], as well as their formal regalia."
[Buddy Levy, River of Darkness: Francisco Orellana and the Deadly First Voyage Through the Amazon, (New York: Division Books, 2022), pp. 87-88.]

There have also been developments regarding exactly who the Siberians were who immigrated and eventually became "American Indians." The ability of scientists to explore that important issue has been dramatically enhanced in recent years by the development and continuing growth of DNA analysis. (Note that the Siberians who came here from Beringia didn't actually become "Indians" until after Columbus got lost and stumbled into the West Indies in 1492. In fact, some of those we lump together as Siberians may have been living east of the Bering Sea land bridge for thousands of years, certainly long enough that they probably deserve to be referred to today as "Alaskans," or at least "proto-Alaskans.")

It is only several years ago that researchers could make the claim that Indigenous Americans, who include Alaska Natives, Canadian First Nations, and Native Americans, descended from humans who crossed the ancient land bridge connecting Siberia to Alaska tens of thousands of years ago. But scientists are still unclear about the routes these people, who were to become the first Americans, used to reach what are now the Americas. Two relatively new studies shed light on this mystery and actually identify the most closely related Native American ancestors outside North America.

In a 2019 study, researchers led by Eske Willerslev, a geneticist at the University of Copenhagen, sequenced the whole genomes of 34 individuals who lived in Siberia, the land bridge Beringia, and Alaska from 600 to nearly 32,000 years ago…Using DNA analysis, "researchers did find a group that eventually moved into Siberia, splintered, and crossed Beringia into North America." A woman known as Kilyma1, who lived in northeastern Siberia about 10,000 years ago, was found to share about two-thirds of her genome with living Native Americans. "It's the closest we have ever gotten to a Native American ancestor outside the Americas," Willerslev says. "Still, notes Ben Potter, an archaeologist at the University of Alaska in Fairbanks who was not involved with the study, "the relation is nevertheless distant."
[Price, Michael, "Closest-known ancestor of today's Native Americans found in Siberia," www.sciencemag.org, June 5, 2019.]

"Based on the genetic data, the researchers determined that humans populated Siberia in at least three major migratory waves. The now-extinct Ancient North Siberians arrived first, from the west; they were followed by two migratory waves from eastern Asia. The third of those waves was a group known as Neo-Siberians, to which many contemporary Siberians can trace their ancestry."

Around 18,000 to 20,000 years ago, a descendant of the Ancient North Siberians intermingled with people from the two eastern Asian groups. A partial skull found at a site near Siberia's Kolyma River dates to about 10,000 years ago and shows genetic similarity to Ancient North Siberians and to the eastern Asian group that became ancestors to Native Americans, according to the study."

"This indicates that the previously unknown Siberian group participated in the interbreeding that eventually resulted in humans who migrated to North America...This individual is the missing link of Native American ancestry."

"According to the authors, while the Ancient North Siberians were not the direct ancestors of Native Americans or contemporary Siberians, "traces of their genetic legacy can be observed in ancient and modern genomes across America and northern Eurasia," revealing that the human history of populating ancient Siberia—and the New World—is a far more complex tale than the present genetic record would suggest," the researchers concluded.

"Analysis of the collection of genomes suggests the population that became the ancestors of native North Americans was the result of liaisons about 20,000 years ago between East Asians, who travelled north, and a group distantly related to the Ancient Northern Siberians. The East Asians also mixed with other descendants of Ancient Northern Siberians to give rise to another group, who the team dub the Ancient Paleo Siberians who went on to supplant the existing group.

Ancestors of Native Americans were not the first people in northeastern Siberia as most people, if not everybody, thought, said Willerslev, adding that DNA recovered in northeastern Siberia from what is believed to be an Ancient Paleo-Siberian was crucial to the work. "This is the first evidence we have, real evidence, of something very close genetically to Native Americans," said Willerslev, director of the Lundbeck Foundation Centre for Geogenetics at the University of Copenhagen.

The Ancient Paleo-Siberians seem to have been supplanted by another band of East Asians heading north about 10,000 years ago that gave rise to a group dubbed the "Neo-Siberians." The vast majority of the genetic makeup of present-day Siberians comes from this last push, "said Willerslev, "This is also the reason you don't have any very close connection between contemporary Siberians and Native Americans." [Nicola David, "Ancient Siberia was home to previously unknown humans, say scientists," The Guardian, June 5, 2019; www.sciencenews.org>article>dna-reveals-ancient-siberians-set-stage-first-americans.]

CHAPTER 7

ICE-FREE OR COASTAL MIGRATION?

> I used the words First Americans, Ernestine Hayes, a Tlingit and Alaskan State Writer Laureate,said the people entering from Beringia were not becoming American, but becoming Tlingit, becoming Navajo, becoming Lakota.
>
> **—Craig Childs**
> Atlas of a Lost World

Most researchers used to believe that it was most likely that the former Beringians made their way south through the ice-free corridor that developed between the Cordilleran and Laurentide glaciers. While this has been the most widely supported explanation for how the Americas were populated, it is not unanimously accepted. There are those who question the existence of a "land bridge" link between Siberia and the Western Hemisphere, or the willingness of humans or animals to leave their normal territories to track across such a route. It has also been postulated that hopping continents via the land bridge would have required travelers to negotiate two formidable mountain ranges bordering the Bering Strait.
[George Gaylord Simpson, "Mammals and Land Bridges," mentioned by Vine Deloria, Jr., Red Earth, White Lies, p. 106-107]

The functional viability of the Ice-Free Corridor" route connecting Beringia with areas that are now British Columbia, Alberta, Idaho, and Montana has also been challenged. In the summer of 2016, the journal Nature carried an article by noted evolutionary geneticist Eske Willerslev and his international team of researchers

who studied the area of the Ice-Free Corridor to determine whether it could actually have been the route humans used to enter the Americas near the end of the last ice age. Their results determined that there was a "choke point" near the southernmost end of the 1,000-mile-long corridor between the Laurentide and Cordilleran ice sheets that "lacked the basic necessities for survival, such as wood for fuel and tools and game animals to be killed for sustenance…The bottom line is that even though the physical corridor was open by 13,000 years ago, it was several hundred years before it was possible to use it. That means that the first people entering what is now the U.S., Central, and South America must have taken a different route." David Meltzer, co-author of the report with Willerslev, summed up the findings: "The first people to reach the Americas in Ice-Age times would have found the corridor itself impassable."
[Klein, Christopher, "New Study Refutes Theory of How Humans Populated North America," August 29, 2018, at www.history.com/news/new-study-refutes-theory-of-how-humans-populated-north-america.]

While some researchers still cling to the Ice-Free Corridor route, a growing number favor a "Coastal Migration Theory," "Marine Migration Hypothesis," or "Kelp Highway Hypothesis," each of which has Beringians travelling along the deglaciated Pacific coast on foot or through the use of vessels of some sort. Some proponents of the coastal movement argue that was the only route that contained sufficient sources of food to support the extended migration. [Fladmark, Knute R., "Routes: alternate migration corridors for early man in North America," American Antiquity, 44 (1), January 1979; Erlandson, John M. and Braje, Todd J., "From Asia to the Americas by Boat?," Quaternary International, 239 (1-2): 28-37 (20ll); Erlandson Jon M. and Michael H. Graham, and Bruce J. Bourque, et. al., "The kelp highway hypothesis: marine ecology, the coastal migration theory, and the peopling of the Americas," The Journal of Island and Coastal Archaeology. 2 (2): 161 (2007); Callaway, Ewen, "Plant and animal DNA suggests first Americans took the coastal route." Nature. 536 (7615), (August 11, 2016); Summer, Thomas, "Humans may have taken different path into Americas than through Arctic passage wouldn't have provided enough food for the earliest Americans' journey," Science News. (August 10, 2016).

The journey from the land bridge to the southern faces of the Cordilleran and Laurentian glaciers would have been no stroll in the park. The distance would have been in excess of 2,500 miles, a serious challenge even for experienced wilderness hikers and campers with the best high-tech equipment available…things the Beringians didn't have. It is also questionable whether resources along the corridor, in terms of flora and fauna that could provide food and shelter for the travelers, would have been adequate. One knowledgeable researcher has even expressed the opinion that, "even when open the corridor was probably biologically dead and difficult to traverse."
[Robert L. Kelly, "Maybe we do know when people first came to North America; and what does it mean if we do?" in www.science direct. com/Article/abs/pii/51040618202002094.]

However, the corridor would undoubtedly have attracted a variety of large and small animals that could have provided sustenance to the travelers. An herb and shrub tundra environment may have reestablished itself as the corridor was deglaciated, potentially providing both vegetarian foodstuffs and material useful for construction of shelters, although one group of researchers studying the issue have projected that the "biological productivity of the deglaciated landscape was gained slowly.
[Mandryk, Carole A.S.; Heiner Josenhans; Daryl W. Fedje; and Rolf W. Mathewes, "Late Quaternary paleoenvironments of Northwestern North America: implications for inland versus coastal migration routes," Quaternary Science Reviews. 20 (1): 301-314.]

Unfortunately, unlike Hansel and Gretel, the Beringians left no trail of breadcrumbs to let us know what route, or routes, they had taken. We don't even know how many made the trip. Information on the size of the groups is vague, from "small bands of Stone Age hunters," to "500 or so."
[George Gaylord Simpson, "Mammals and Land Bridges," mentioned by Vine Deloria, Jr., Red Earth, White Lies, p. 106;

www.smithsonianmag.com/science-nature/how-humans-came-to-Americas-180973739].

One detailed, but surprisingly understandable, report in Wikipedia, based on sophisticated population genetics, concluded that, "The overall pattern that is emerging suggests that the Americas were recently colonized [pre-Columbian] by a small number of individuals (effective size of about 70–250), and then they grew by a factor of 10 over 800–1,000 years.

The data also show that there have been genetic exchanges between Asia, the Arctic, and Greenland since the initial peopling of the Americas.
[Wells, Spencer and Mark Read (2002). The Journey of Man – A Genetic Odyssey (Digitised online by Google books). Random House. pp. 138-140; Hey, Jody, "On the Number of New World Founders: A Population Genetic Portrait of the Peopling of the Americas," PLOS Biology. 3 (6), May 24, 2005.]

[Ibid.; Wade, Nicholas, "Ancient Man In Greenland Has Genome Decoded," The New York Times, (2010), Retrieved January 10, 2010.]

A study reported in 2018 suggested that the effective population size of the original founding population of Native Americans was only about 250 people. [The University of Kansas DNA sequences suggest 250 people made up original Native American founding population (May 1, 2018) and Fagundes, Nelson J. R. and Alice Tagliani-Ribeiro; Rohina Rubicz; Larissa Tarskaia; Michael H. Crawford, Francisco M. Salzano; and Sandro L. Bonatto, "How strong was the bottleneck associated with the peopling of the Americas? New insights from multilocus sequence data,"
[Genetics and Molecular Biology. 41 (1 suppl 1): 206-214.]

Those projections of the size of the founding populations in the Americas are almost unbelievably small—possibly just 250 to 500 individuals…or less. That's about the size of the crowd at one of my granddaughter's fifth grade basketball games! Another projection based on a very sophisticated combination of genetic analysis and computer modeling by Jody Hey, an evolutionary biologist at Temple

University, suggests that the founding population coming out of Beringia could have been as small as 70 individuals who contributed genes to the next generation.

If that's not enough to drive a researcher plum out of his mind, the number of migrations into Meso-America and South America and the routes taken by the migrants are even less clear. "Current genetic data suggests that the people who settled South America were related to those in North America, but less so than the North American settlers were connected to the people in Siberia." That is potentially a function of the "great distances between north and south, the possibility of different demographic, biological, and environmental processes...and the fact that Meso-America and South America have been studied far less than North America, including by geneticists. [Thomas D. Dillehay, "Probing deeper into first American studies," Proceedings of the National Academy of Sciences, January 27, 2009.]

CHAPTER 8

MYSTERIES WITH THE HISTORIES

Maybe we do know when people first came to North America.

—Robert L. Kelly

Science Direct

"But then there is South America," writes anthropologist Robert L. Kelly, in what seems to have been written in an almost exasperated tone. He goes on to explain his frustration and that of many researchers studying the settling of the Americas: "A reasonable guess is that North America has seen a far greater intensity of field research than South America. And yet a growing list of South American sites seems to be as old, if not older than Clovis…If the first inhabitants of North America came from Asia, then they had to pass through North America before arriving in South America. How do we explain the presence of people in South America at the same time or prior to their appearance in North America?" (Emphasis added.)

The extra distance that migrants would have needed to continue from North America to the far reaches of South America would be considered a relatively staggering undertaking for someone traveling by motor vehicle today. It is unlikely that anyone would tackle the distance on foot, especially in a family group. It is a trip of something in the neighborhood of 5,500 to 6,600 miles, depending on the starting and ending points. Archaeologist Todd Surovell of the University of Wyoming developed a model to estimate how long it might have taken coastal migrant groups to gradually spread from Seattle, Washington, to Monte Verde, at the southern limit of continental Chile. The model predicted that it would take 2,267 years. That's right, 2,267 years!

Professor Thomas Dillehay, author of The Settlement of the Americas and the primary archaeologist at the Monte Verde site, weighed some of the risks that would probably have confronted the migrants. “If they reduced their risks by keeping in regular contact with distant groups, then they would have markedly slowed their overall migration.” Given constraints of that nature, Dillehay concluded, “I would guess that it took several millennia for people to reach Tierra del Fuego and fill in the major regions of North America.” Several millennia—several thousand years!

At the other end of the “travel time spectrum,” Craig Childs, author of Atlas of a Lost World: Travels in Ice Age America, and an experienced long-distance hiker, canoeist, and kayaker, thought he could make the trip in only about two years…but traveling without the limitations that would have been present for migrants in family units.

Yes, we are comparing apples and oranges with our examples, yet they serve to establish that in all likelihood it would have taken migrants from Beringia a very long time to reach whatever destination they went to in North America or South America. Additionally, it underscores the fact that it should have taken a great deal longer to settle in South America than it did in North America, even though testing of sites does not reflect significant differences in settlement dates.

Professor Kelly offers a number of explanations for that puzzling incongruence: He believes there could have been earlier pre-Clovis sites in North American that have not been discovered yet. (He feels that probability is small.) There is also some possibility that South America was discovered and populated by migrants from somewhere other than Asia. (He feels “there is no good evidence to support it.) There could also be discrepancies between the radiocarbon dating used in North America and that used in South America that could have resulted in radiocarbon dates that are out of sync. (He recommends the construction of a Carbon-14 calibration curve for South America to test for possible discrepancies.)

Much to the chagrin of archaeologists like, Thomas Dillehay, Professor Kelly also suggests, carefully, that there could be problems with some early sites in southern South America as the result of stratigraphic contamination and interpretive difficulties that North American sites experienced previously. After closely studying dates for South American sites and the basis of each dating, Kelly concluded, "at the moment we appear to be left with an initial occupation of South American that appears to be at least contemporaneous with the earliest occupation in North America, if not earlier."

In conclusion, and possibly in some confusion, Professor Kelly raised the possibility that a Coastal Migration Route was used by those migrants who settled in South America. There is data now that suggests that the coastal area along the Bering Sea and Pacific Ocean were largely ice-free by at least 16,000 years before the present, and completely ice-free by 13,000 before the present. Kelly feels that those dates make it feasible for migrants to have moved south from Beringia along the west coast, then turn to the east and moved into the interior of North America and South America, producing occupancy dates that are similar.

With his article, Professor Kelly includes a map of the United States showing the locations of eighteen Clovis sites dated at between 9550 BP and 11,500 BP [Before the Present]. He also presents a map of South America, showing 24 prehistoric sites that are dated at more than 10,000 BP.

It is interesting to note that only one of the Clovis sites in the U.S. is along the West Coast. Eleven are located in mid-continent, and six are located along the Northeast Coast. While the map provided with Kelly's article doesn't include state lines, it appears that the sites in New England are in the area now occupied by Maine, Massachusetts, and New Hampshire. Studying the map, it appears that if the migrants followed the shoreline, they must have turned east as soon as they reached the southern limit of glaciation, about at the Canadian-U.S. border in British Columbia and Washington. If a route through a corridor between the Laurentian and Cordilleran glaciers was followed and the migrants continued south after they exited the corridor, five to eight of the sites would have been basically in their direct path.

Why six of the migrant groups would have gone all the way to the Atlantic Coast is hard to understand, given the attractiveness and desirability of much of the land they transited enroute. The only explanation this author can come up with is the six groups travelled east following the southern limit of glaciation. The recently uncovered area south of the retreating glaciers would undoubtedly have been resource rich in both flora and fauna, providing a supportive environment for the travelers. Nonetheless, why they traveled all the way to the Atlantic coast should be the subject of discussion and study.

The pattern of the twenty-four sites in South America raises just as many questions. Ten of the sites are along the Pacific Coast, between the ocean and the Andes Mountains, as if they entered South America via the Isthmus of Panama and followed the shoreline to the south. That makes sense in that the ocean provided a source of protein and other game animals were likely attracted to the water where they could be hunted. It also makes sense that the migrants would avoid entering the mountain range. One other South American site was located at Taima-Taima,Venezuela, east of the Isthmus of Panama where the migrants would have had to enter South America. Again, the area provided great sources of protein from the ocean and from the many Mastadons and other mega-fauna in the area. Three groups went all the way to the southern tip of South America and Tiera del Fuego. Three others headed north along the Atlantic Coast in Patagonia. Four others went a considerable distance north along the Atlantic shore to what would become northern Argentina. Three others were scattered throughout Brazil in the eastern portion of South America, clear across the continent from the majority of the settlements. One of those was along the Amazon River, while another was along the Rio São Francisco River. The route by which the three reached their ultimate locations is unknown, but all three traveled a great distance and through some difficult country.
[Robert L. Kelly, "Maybe we do know when people first came to North America; and what does it mean if we do?" in www.sciencedirect.com/Article/abs/pii/51040618202002094.]

CHAPTER 9

OLDER THAN CLOVIS?

> This was not the Monte Verde Land Rush, with a known destination, a timetable to meet, and wagons bulging with homesteading provisions.
>
> **—David J. Meltzer**
> Search for the First Americans

The earliest known settlers in both North America and South America appear to have traveled almost incomprehensible distances before they chose to settle down. It is difficult to understand what would have motivated the distances traveled. The common factors that are likely to have forced Indigenous groups to move include life-and-death issues like pressure from enemies, food shortages, unfavorable weather, and the lack of necessary resources like wood and water, among others. It is hard to imagine that any of those would have been enough of a problem for the early humans to motivate them to travel clear across a continent—2,800 miles—or down the shoreline of two continents—more than 9,000 miles. It couldn't possibly just be cases of "maybe the grass is greener on the other side of the hill," could it?

If the unanswered questions about the travels of the migrants from the North aren't enough to keep researchers busy, a small problem has developed with the issue of when those travelers arrived in the Americas. Improved dating techniques like Carbon-14, thermoluminescence, and archeaolinguistics—the study of ancient language patterns—have caused researchers to revisit a number of archaeological sites where previous dating had been problematic for some reason. The results have been rather shocking.

Chiquihuite Cave in Zacatecas, Mexico, located in central Mexico about 375 miles north of Mexico City, had been worked by archaeological teams for more than seven years. During that time, nearly 2,000 stone tools and associated pieces of stone were found, 200 of which were in an archaeological layer that corresponded to the peak of the last Ice Age—between 26,000 and 19,000 years ago—formally known as the Last Glacial Maximum. That's before the time when the first humans were believed to have arrived, those referred to as constituting the now-infamous Clovis Culture.

A team of experienced international researchers eventually visited the remote site and reviewed the site and the archaeological materials discovered. Members of the multi-talented group built a chronology of more than fifty radiocarbon and optical dates for the artifacts and arrived at the conclusion that humans inhabited the cave as early as 33,000 years ago. Humans were clearly in North America "before, during, and immediately after the peak of the last Ice Age," but "it was not until much later that populations expanded significantly across the continent." The findings of the panel of experts rocked the "Clovis First" proponents.
[Becerra-Valdivia, Lorena, "Humans inhabited North America in the depths of the last Ice Age, but didn't thrive until the climate warmed, July 22, 2020 on the conversation.com. and Ardelean, Ciprian F. and Lorena Becerra-Valdivia, Eske Willerslev, et. al., "Evidence of human occupation in Mexico around the Last Glacial Maximum," Nature, 584, 87-92, July 22, 2020.]

Only a matter of months later, archaeologists announced that they had "obtained radiocarbon dates for the [bones of dead animals] excavated from Coxcatlan Cave in the Tehuacan Valley of Mexico, about 130 miles southeast of Mexico City, that ranged from 33,448 to

28,279 years old." Once again, researchers produced results that indicated humans were in North America well before the Clovis settlements. They concluded that during the period the Coxcatlan Cave was being occupied, "Large parts of North America would have been inhospitable to human populations. The glaciers would have completely blocked any passage overland coming from Alaska and Canada, which means people probably would have had to come to the Americas by boats down the Pacific coast." (For some reason they were apparently incapable of walking south down the beaches.) ["Humans Arrived in North America More Than 30,000 Years Ago, Study Suggests," www.sci-news.com/archaeology/coxcatlan-cave.]

While Mexico was a hotbed of almost earth-shattering Clovis-busting archaeological finds, researchers weren't ignoring sites north of the border. In September of 2021, another large team of researchers announced they had found human footprints in an ancient shoreline at Lake Otero in White Sands National Park in New Mexico, just north of the Mexico border and about midway between the Gulf of California and the Gulf of Mexico. The footprints were dated by analysis of seed layers above and below the footprints that were radiocarbon dated at between 23,000 and 21,000 years ago, during the Last Glacial Maximum.

Professor Vance Holliday of the University of Arizona's School of Anthropology said, "For decades archaeologists have debated when people first arrived in the Americas. Few archaeologists see reliable evidence for sites older than about 16,000 years. Some think the arrival was later, no more than 13,000 years ago by makers of Clovis points. The human footprints at White Sands provide a much earlier date. There are multiple layers of well-dated human tracks in streambeds where water flowed into an ancient lake. This was 10,000 years before Clovis people."

According to lead author Matthew Bennett of Bournemouth University in England, "The footprints left at White Sands give a picture of what was taking place, teenagers interacting with younger children and adults. We can think of our ancestors as quite functional, hunting and surviving, but what we see here is also activity of play, and of different ages coming together. A true insight into these early people." Tracks of mammoth, giant ground sloth, dire wolves, and birds are also present at the site. Dan Odess of the National Park Service said the site provided "the first unequivocal evidence for human presence in the Americas during the Last Glacial Maximum."

Dr. Paulette F. C. Steeves of Algoma University in Ontario captured my reaction completely when she wrote, "It can be said that for the last century, many archaeologists in North America viewed the deep past with eyes wide shut. If most archaeologists had opened their eyes and viewed the published archaeological record of the Americas, they could not possibly have supported the tenets of the Clovis First hypothesis of postglacial initial human migrations into the Western Hemisphere."
[Steeves, Paulette F. C., The Indigenous Paleolithic of the Western Hemisphere, (Lincoln: University of Nebraska Press, 2023), p. 127.]

While the examples of human activity in the Americas earlier than the Clovis settlements surprised many in the scientific community, an announcement by scientists in 2015 really shook things up. Two different teams of researchers announced that they had discovered that "some modern inhabitants of the Amazon seem to share genetic ancestry with Australasian groups that include both the Papua New Guineans and Aboriginal Australians." The leader of the team of researchers, award-winning geneticist Eske Willerslev, linked the genome of a 10,400-year-old from southeastern Brazil to an Australasian lineage. The team's concluded that the occurrence meant that there had been a previously "unknown migration to the Americas that had vanished from all but the most isolated groups in the Amazon." (The term "Australasia is defined in a variety of ways. In the late 19th century, the term was used in reference to the "Australasian colonies". In this sense it related specifically to the British colonies south of Asia: New South Wales, Queensland, South Australia, Tasmania, Western Australia, Victoria (i.e. the Australian colonies) and New Zealand. Two Merriam-Webster dictionaries online (Collegiate and Unabridged) define Australasia as "Australia, New Zealand, and Melanesia." The American Heritage Dictionary online recognizes two senses in use: one more precise, being similar to the aforementioned senses, and the other broader, loosely covering all of Oceania. Oceania is a geographic region that includes Australasia, Melanesia, Micronesia and Polynesia, and takes in many of the islands in the Pacific Ocean.)

The possibility that Australasians had interacted with the early American Indians in Brazil gave root to another potential development that neither Willerslev nor any of his team mentioned: that individuals from Australia or the islands of the Pacific may have visited South America and mated with American Indians. It is even possible that the Australasians were there before the American Indians arrived from the North. Because their numbers were small, they could easily have been absorbed by the larger Indian population. It is a potentiality that should at least be considered.

Jennifer Raff, an anthropological geneticist at the University of Kansas, who was a member of Willerslev's team made the point that, "The emerging picture of the Americas is less a revision of the earlier models and more of an elaboration. It's not that everything we know is getting overturned. We're just filling in details."

Raff was referring to genetics and the use of DNA analysis to trace the relationships of humans more accurately and in much more detail than previously. For many, maybe all, it is possible to follow the individual's genetic trail all the way back to the person's "original

ancestor" in Africa. Genetics has a precision to it that is lacking in many of the tools and techniques that archaeologists and anthropologists have been using previously. [Raff, Jennifer, Origin: A Genetic History of the Americas, (New York: Twelve, 2022); Callaway, Ewen, "Ancient genomics is recasting the story of the Americas' first residents,"
[Nature, November 8, 2018; Willerslev, E. et al. "Diverse plant and animal genetic records from Holocene and Pleistocene sediments." Science 300, 791–795 (2003); and Reich, D. et al. "Reconstructing Native American population history" Nature 488, 370–374 (2012)]

Anthropological genetics have made great contributions to our understanding of human origins and human evolution. DNA sequences allow us to infer the evolutionary relationships amongst organisms and the times of divergence between them. The distribution of human genetic variation suggests that modern humans evolved recently in Africa and then quickly spread around the globe, largely replacing the human groups that they encountered during their dispersal. The Neanderthal genome project has clarified our understanding of modern human origins and suggests that low levels of interbreeding occurred between Neanderthals and modern humans early during the expansion of modern humans out of Africa. Genomic sequences from additional ancient humans, such as the Denisova finger bone, promise to further refine our understanding of human evolution.
[Hodgson, Jason A. and Todd R. Disotell, "Anthropological Genetics: Inferring the History of Our Species Through the Analysis of DNA," Evolution: Education and Outreach, Vol. 3, pp. 287-398 (2010).]

Walking to America

CHAPTER 10

"WE WERE ALWAYS HERE"

> Beliefs about Indian origins that are drawn from myths and legends that have been passed down by word of mouth from generation-to-generation contrast sharply with the story that emerges through the examination of artifacts unearthed by archaeologists or documents carefully studied by learned ethnohistorians. One is left to wonder, which version of history is correct.
>
> **—Charles E. Cleland**
> Rites of Conquest

The theories the scientific community has put forth as possible explanations for how the Western Hemisphere was populated are not well-accepted by many Native Americans. Among those troubled by the land bridge hypothesis was the late Vine Delorea, Jr., a Sioux from the Pine Ridge Reservation; professor of history, law, religious studies, and political science; and the articulate and creative espouser of a new and "more satisfactory" explanation for the roles of Native Americans in the history of the Americas and the world. Delorea made a reputation, or several reputations, as an advocate for Native Americans and their mythical explanations for complex worldly phenomena, such as the creation of humans and the origins of the numerous Indian tribes. At the same time, in order to baptize his explanations with some measure of legitimacy in the face of scientific "facts," DeLorea was an outspoken critic of scientists of every discipline, including any theory they presented that has American Indians migrating into the Americas from Siberia, regardless of whether they came via an ice-free corridor, a shoreline route, or a Boeing 747.

In his thought-provoking, imaginative, Zinn-inspired Red Earth, White Lies, Professor Delorea explains why he and so many other Indians go out of their ways to try to undermine any theory that has the Indians coming from someplace—any place—other than the Americas. "We've always been here," is a common mantra of Indians across the country; maybe the one thing that most Indian tribes can agree about. Delorea explains it succinctly: "By making us immigrants to North America they are able to deny the fact that we were the full, complete, and total owners of this continent. They are able to see us simply as earlier interlopers and therefore throw back at us the accusation that we had simply found North America a little earlier than they had. On that basis, I would suppose, no nation actually owns the land its citizens live on, with the exception, if we accept early archaeological findings, of the people of Africa, where human evolution is believed to have begun."
[Vine Deloria, Jr., Red Earth, White Lies, (New York: Scribner, 1995), pp. 83-84.]

Deloria goes on to explain, "American Indians, as a general rule, have aggressively opposed the Bering Strait migration doctrine because it does not reflect any of the memories or traditions passed down by the ancestors over many generations." There are tribes, he says, that migrated to the Americas by boat, others claim having been "created" in the Americas, while "some tribes even talk about migrations from other planets." [p. 97] Other tribal traditions speak of snow and ice, which Deloria notes are normal phenomena in the U.S., and they were certainly familiar phenomena to the Siberians, Beringians, and Alaskans who migrated to what are now North America and South America during the last Ice Age. Most of the stories told by modern Indians begin with the Indians already in North America when the glaciation began and "quite possibly were observers of some of the climatic events of the Ice Age." Deloria explains that "Since the memories of the American Indians clash directly with scientific speculation, there is little room for compromise here." "I can't tell you how many White people have told me that 'science' shows that Indians were just a bunch of interlopers," said Deloria. "If we're only thieves who stole our land from someone else, then they say, 'Well, we're just the same. We're

all immigrants here, aren't we?" According to Deloria, the Beringian theory, accepted by a majority of scientists, is a "White lie…something that exists only in the minds of scientists."
[Vine Deloria, Jr., Red Earth, White Lies, (New York: Scribner's, 1995), Chapter 4.]

Deloria and the other American Indians who argue so vehemently that the Indians "were always here" certainly don't find much, if any, support for their contention among the scientific community, particularly those who have studied aboriginal sites throughout the Americas. Their response to those claiming "always here," would have to be "where is the evidence?" The general consensus among demographers indicates that there were probably 1,850,011 Indians in what are now the coterminous United States when Columbus arrived in 1492 If there were that many people in North America prior to the arrival and settlement by Europeans, where is the evidence? Prior to 1492, there were at least 1,850,011 people scattered around what is now America, but we can't find their middens, fire pits, structures, or skeletons? There must have been a large indigenous population here prior to the last Ice Age, but we can't find any evidence of them. Simple explanation: They weren't here. The American Indians arrived here at the end of the Ice Age, around 12,000 years ago. [Douglas Ubelaker, "Prehistoric New World Population Size: Historical Review and Current Appraisal of North American Estimates," American Journal of Physical Anthropology, Vol. 45, pp. 661-666, cited in Russel Thornton, American Indian Holocaust and Survival: A Population History Since 1492, (Norman: University of Oklahoma Press, 1987), pp. 23-29.]

Professor Colin Calloway, highly respected chair of the Native American studies program at Dartmouth College, responded to Deloria with the opinion that, "Most scholars are more concerned with finding evidence than with perpetuating lies. Archaeological, dental, biological, and faunal evidence all suggest ancient links between Asia and America," noting that there may also have been other migration routes "If humans were here all along," he observed, "they would, presumably have left evidence of a presence that predated the retreat of the ice sheets." No such evidence has yet been found.

[Colin G. Calloway: One Vast Winter Count: The Native American West Before Lewis and Clark, (Lincoln: University of Nebraska Press, 2003), p. 31.]

The fact, of course, is that we are all immigrants here. The American Indians, however, clearly appear to have been the "First Immigrants," at least based on the evidence we have available to us now. A note to Professor Deloria: That makes them, and you, different than all the rest of us. Your ancestors discovered and occupied the Americas first, and that means the Western Hemisphere belonged to the American Indians. If anyone argues with you about that, tell them to come and see me.

Deloria isn't the only Native American trying to convince us that the Indians have always been here, or at least that they have been here since "time immemorial." In a brief article titled "Where did Indians Come From? How did they get to the Americas?" the Smithsonian publication Do All Indians Live in Tipis? seems to elaborate on Deloria's explanation: "Many American Indians reject the various migration theories, wary that they could be used to portray Native people as immigrant settlers who happened to arrive earlier than their European counterparts. Dismissing as unscientific the creation stories that spiritually bind Native communities to the land, non-Native scholars and educators reinforce the idea that Europeans were simply another wave of immigrants who had the right to displace the Americas' previous inhabitants."

The writers of the piece in Tipis go on to provide two examples of Native American tribal theories for the populating of Mother Earth: "Native communities throughout the Americas have affirmed the creation of each nation on its land." In the Northeast, for example, "the world began when Sky Woman fell from her home in the heavens." In the Northwest, little people living underground were enticed out of their hiding places by a Crow.
[Rico Newman and Georgetta Stonefish Ryan, "Where Did Indians Come From," Do All Indians Live in Tipis? (Washington, DC: Smithsonian Institution, 2007.]

It should be noted, however, that many Native American tribes are no longer occupying the same lands they did in the past, having moved by choice, perhaps to find better hunting grounds, or they were driven out of their lands by another more powerful tribe. Those common situations would obviously complicate the belief that each Indian nation was created on its own unique piece of land.

My favorite mythic description originated with the late D'Arcy McNickle, a member of the Flathead tribe with Native American credentials as long as your arm. McNickle was both a novelist and a respected storyteller. When the Beringian migration into the Western Hemisphere took place in one of his books, McNickle took his readers along for the ride: "The world was full of rumors just then, a marvelous thing had happened: a new land had been discovered, and just when it was needed. The people had wandered to the end of the world, in quest of food and safety." Then, "over many thousands of years, wandering bands of people drifted toward the end of one world and crossed over into another."
[Colin G. Callaway, One Vast Winter Count, (Lincoln: University of Nebraska Press, 2003), pp. 25-26, quoted from D'Arcy McNickle, The Came Here First: The Epic of the American Indian, (Philadelphia: J. B. Lioppincott, 1949), pp. 15-19.]

Other descendants of those First Americans had other explanations of how the hemisphere was populated. According to the traditional Kiowas, "The Kiowas came one-by-one into this world through a hollow log. There were many more than now; but not all of them got out. There was a woman whose body was swollen up with child, and she got stuck in the log. After that, no one could get through, and that is why the Kiowas are a small tribe in number...They call themselves Kwuda, 'coming out.'"
[Ibid, quoted from N. Scott Momaday, The Way to Rainy Mountain, (Albuquerque: University of New Mexico Press, 1969), p. 17.]

The late archaeological anthropologist and linguist John Alden Mason recounted a number of origin stories, including one from the Cherokee that was quite unique: "It said the Earth is a great island floating in a sea of water, and suspended at each of the four cardinal points by a cord hanging down from the sky vault, which is of solid

rock. When the world grows old and worn out, the people will die and the cords will break and let the Earth sink down into the ocean, and all will be water again." According to Mason, "The Indians are afraid of this."
[John Alden Mason, The Ethnology of the Salinan Indians, (Berkeley: 1912), pp. 191-192.]

Noted anthropologist James Mooney, who spent a season living among the Eastern Band of Cherokee said that, "In daily life, the Cherokee acknowledged the spiritual significance of their local rivers, streams, and ponds with a ritual called 'going to water.' Each morning at daybreak, Mooney wrote, a party of Cherokee would be led by a healer down to a running stream, where the group would face the rising sun and immerse themselves completely in the flowing water, enacting a kind of rebirth. This ceremony of communion touched on nearly all spheres of social life."
[https://www.neh.gov/article/rivers-held-spiritual-place-lives-cherokee#]

A Wichita storyteller told an ethnographer studying early American Indian cultures the Wichitas' creation story. Originally, he said, the land was floating on the water and everything was dark. "Man Never Known on Earth" was the only man that existed at the time, and he created all things: "He made a man whose name was "Having P:ower to Carry Light" and a woman named "Bright Shining Woman. After the man and the woman were made they dreamed that things were made for them and then they woke they had the things of which they had dreamed...New villages sprang up; there were more people, but the people knew neither where they had come from nor how to live. Having Power to Carry Light and Bright Shining Woman went from village to village, teaching the inhabitants how to use the things they had. Having Power to Carry Light taught the men to make bows and arrows and to hunt, then disappeared to become the early morning star. Bright Shining Woman showed the women how to plant and raise corn, then disappeared into the sky and became the moon."
[George A. Dorsey, The Mythology of the Wichitas, 1904 reprint, (Norman: University of Oklahoma Press, 1995), pp. 25-29.]

Pawnees from the Plains said "the world was sung into being…" and they had come from the stars and they would return to them. Osages who live north of the Arkansas River in the middle of the continent "traced there origins to a meeting of heaven and earth and their clans honored the Sky and the Earth, and together they merged to become "The Children of the Middle Waters. The Navajo people traveled a long and complex road from First Man and First Woman to Dinétah, the Navajo homeland, bordered by four sacred mountains. [Ibid, and quoted from Howard Harrod, The Animals come Dancing (Tucson: University of Arizona Press, 2000), 38-40; John J. Mathews, The Osages: Children of the Middle Waters, (Norman: University of Oklahoma Press, 1961), pp. 7-10; and Aileen O'Bryan, The Diné: Origin Myths of the Navajo Indians, Bureau of American Ethnology, (Washington DC: Government Printing Office, 1956), pp. 1-13.

"The Hopi origin story has it that Hopis used to live beneath the Earth. When it came time to emerge into the world, that Hopi met Maasaw, Caretaker and Creator of the Earth, and promised him they would help take care of the world as a trade-off for staying." [www.gaia.com/article.native-american-creation-myths-uncovered-explained.]

As for the many wonderful origin stories that exist within the American Indian tribes, I see them as often highly creative explanations for something early humans could not know or understand—how humans, the flora and fauna, the Earth, the sky, and the stars came to be. Think of the questions you would ask, or that your children would ask—Where did we come from? What are the stars made from? Who made the Earth? How did we get fire? They are the types of questions a group of young Cub Scouts might ask their leader when they were sitting around a campfire on a starry night. In responding to those questions so central to our being, the scout leader probably wouldn't be as creative as the Indian chief, elder, medicine man, or priest.

The Indian origin stories were often finely crafted in sophisticated detail, largely from the elements the storyteller had around him—the land, the sky, rivers, streams, and lakes, stars and

planets, caves, mountains, rocks, the creatures that inhabit the Earth and the sky—especially those that played important, even critical, roles in daily Indian life—deer, fish, bison, eagles, etc. Humans often rose out of the water, out of caves or holes in the ground, or came from the sky. The Yakama origin story tells us that the Great Chief Above fashioned man out of a ball of mud, in one of several Apache origin stories gods Tepeu and Quetzalcoatl "think everything into being," the Lakota humans lived underground in the Wind Cave, and in the arctic region of North America the Eskimo tell tales of the moon god and tricksters who created the world as it is now. The stories of creation often included warnings or lessons, similar to those commonly found in fairy tales.
[medium.com@robert.f.williams/three-native-american-creation-myths; gaia.com/article/native-american-creation-myths-uncovered-explained; Craig Childs, Atlas of a Lost World: Travels in Ice Age America, (New York: Vintage Books, 2019), pp, 115-117.]

In his thought-provoking and instructional Atlas of a Lost World, Craig Childs told the story of Nikki Cooley, a Navajo woman who had graduated from Northern Arizona University and worked as a river guide in the Grand Canyon. Like many Indians, she believed "we came from here." According to Childs, "Cooley believes that the people came from the ground—her people's story." Vine Deloria, Jr. would be pleased. Not all Navajo agree with that "fundamentalist" explanation, however. Many accept the origin explanations shared by most scientists, and the simple fact that no evidence has been found to support the thesis that the Indians, or any other peoples, have always lived in the Americas. No evidence. None. As many researchers will tell you, "If you can't find evidence of a groups presence, it's probably because they were never here." The archaeologists and anthropologists, and all the other cadre of Indiana Jones wannabes have diligently been looking for evidence of anything faintly suggesting permanent occupation in the Western Hemisphere. So far, they haven't found anything.
[Craig Childs, Atlas of a Lost World: Travels in Ice Age America, (New York: Vintage Books, 2019), pp. 115-118.]

Members of those tribes would undoubtedly tell you that the story of the origins of their tribe date to the beginning, to the first days. In fact, the name of their tribe may have translated as "First Man," "Original Human," or something like that. If you are not an American Indian, you may accept the story of their tribe's beginnings, but it is more likely that you may consider the story to be a myth, or as a symbolic creation story, or…you may discount it as oral history gone awry, or a typical creation myth with little, if any, semblance to worldly reality.

Professor Thomas Dillehay, who made his name as the successful proponent of the Monte Verde pre-Clovis site in Chile, noted that "Traditional leaders of some North American groups state that no matter what the archaeologists may think, their stories and myths tell them that their people have always been in North America after having emerged from the underworld. Many South American groups, on the other hand, see their ancestors as having come from the west, across the Pacific Ocean.
[Dillehay, Thomas D., The Settlement of the Americas: A New Prehistory, (New York: Basic Books, 2000), p. 292.]

Vine Deloria, Jr., always trying to be helpful, casts some light on the issue: "The problem with Indian traditions is that hardly any open-minded scientist has heard them, and an even lesser number know how to listen to Indian elders, catch the nuances of meaning, and be prepared to elicit the proper information from the story." There are apparently a lot of nuances of meaning in Indian stories and explanations that are believed to be beyond the intellectual capacities of non-Indians for some undefined cultural or genetic deficiency. [Deloria, Jr., Vine, Red Earth, White Lies: Native Americans and the Myth of Scientific Fact, (New York: Scribner, 1995), p. 232.]

That is a fairly common claim: if you are not Indian, you can't understand our stories or our oral histories. (Dr. Paulette F. C. Steeves recently made the same claim in more detail in her The Indigenous Paleolithic of the Western Hemisphere.)

Neither Deloria nor Steeves bothers to define "Indian" for us, however. Most American Indians today are not full-blooded. My cousins, for example, have less than 5% Indian DNA, yet they are, or are qualified to be, members of the Sault Ste. Marie Tribe of Ottawa and Chippewa Indians. Would an individual who is genetically only 5% Native American be capable of understanding the "nuances" of Indian stories and oral histories? If not, what is the "magic quotient" at which an Indian begins to understand the tribal stories and histories?

When news came out about the finds of pre-Clovis occupation at White Sands, it made a lot of Indians happy. High Country News, an online monthly news magazine that covers issues in the western U.S. and seems to strongly advocate for Native Americans, ran the headline, "The White Sands discovery only confirms what Indigenous people have said all along," with the tag, "Once again, the media has excluded Indigenous peoples from our own story." The first line of the article by Nick Martin was, "We have been here since time immemorial." The article continues: "There might be no phrase more ubiquitous in Indian Country than this…The meaning of the phrase is clear: Indigenous peoples have existed on and stewarded these lands for far longer than modern conceptions of time or human history have ever acknowledged. This truth—this fact—is enshrined through our stories, through our bodies, and through our natural relatives. (Author Martin is going to have to explain that sentence to me!) "So why is it," he asks, "that Indigenous findings and voices continue to be ignored, even when they are proved correct?"

Gosh, Nick, the article you are referencing is all about early Indigenous peoples. I don't remember whether the members of the archaeological team referred to them as "Native Americans," or not. Of course, "Native American" wouldn't really have been accurate because "America" didn't exist yet. As an Indian, I'm sure you would be aware of that. Or, are you an Asian Indian, a Siberian Indian, or a Beringian Indian? Those would be accurate names for the Indigenous peoples who first migrated to what is now America. We all know, however, exactly who the people were that the authors were talking about…and we know that the Indigenous peoples have "been here since time immemorial." Really, we know that. As far back as any Indian can remember, and as far back as their origin stories reach, the Indians were here in the Americas. What we don't know is exactly how far back that was. When did the first Indians come here? By what route did they come? Did they interact with any other cultures? It's part of our history; it's part of your history. I would have thought that you would be interested in the finding. It is a step toward improving our knowledge of the past. You quoted Ciprian Ardelean, one of the experts who made up the archaeology team at White Sands. He's Romanian. Eske Willerslev, was one of the leaders of the team. He's Danish. Quite a few of the other members of the team are Mexican, and I'll bet a few of them have Indian roots. I'm an American historian and interested in all our country's cultures. For the sake of clarity, I am a mix of French, German, Scotch, Scandinavian, and several other nationalities, including almost five percent Neandertal. Lighten up a little, Nick, you'll catch more bees with honey than with vinegar. You wrote, "This discovery and the knowledge accompanying it, you see, is entirely owned and framed by people who, in the grand scheme of history, have only known this land for a blink of time." I'm 78-years-old Nick, and I'll bet that I have known this land longer than you have. Second, nobody "owns" history, kid. And your claim that, "Anyone who reads only mainstream coverage would walk away without a clue that this is actually an Indigenous story…" is insulting. Almost all of us are smart enough to know exactly who the article is about.

Nick Martin's article promoting Dr. Paulette F. C. Steeves' book also claims that she has "worked tirelessly within the colonial structures of the academy to enter indisputable claims [emphasis added] of Indigenous life and culture that extend far beyond the 23,000-year mark set by the team of 15 researchers on the White Sands footprints study. He also reports that, "In a profile of Steeves published in the Vancouver Sun in 2016, for example, she describes how archaeology's subservience to the 'Clovis first' hypothesis has acted as a firewall against Indigenous archaeologists" and discrimination against Native Americans."

It may, however, not be a matter of discrimination at all, but a matter of professional standards. When making claims about things like settlement dates, investigators need a lot of proof to satisfy experts around the world who have strong professional interests in

such things. Hell, those international standards have acted as a firewall against all archaeologists who espouse any claims of pre-Clovis settlement. To put some numbers on the process academics, go through to just to get their ideas into reputable journals, since 2010 there have been 4,459 articles submitted that deal with "whole-genome date." Of those, 711 had been published, as of November of 2017. The other 3,748 had not been selected for publication at that time. Only about 19 percent of the articles submitted were selected for publication, so 81 percent were rejected. Some had undoubtedly been submitted by Indigenous academics or researchers, but the overwhelming majority of those rejected had undoubtedly been submitted by non-Indian researchers. It is not an issue of bias against American Indian academics or researchers, it is more likely a reflection of the standards of the publications and the academic communities.
[www.sas.upenn.edu/~jesusfv/PEEA_2_PreColumbian_America.]

The Indigenous Paleolithic of the Western Hemisphere is advertised as a "reclaimed history of the deep past of Indigenous people in North and South America during the Paleolithic." Paulette F. C. Steeves mines evidence from archaeology sites and Paleolithic environments, landscapes, and mammalian and human migrations to make the case that people have been in the Western Hemisphere not only just prior to Clovis sites (10,200 years ago) but for more than 60,000 years, and likely more than 100,000 years.

Steeves discusses the political history of American anthropology to focus on why pre-Clovis sites have been dismissed by the field for nearly a century. She explores supporting evidence from genetics and linguistic anthropology regarding First Peoples and time frames of early migrations. Additionally, she highlights the work and struggles faced by a small yet vibrant group of American and European archaeologists who have excavated and reported on numerous pre-Clovis archaeology sites.

In this, marketed as "the first book on Paleolithic archaeology of the Americas written from an Indigenous perspective," The Indigenous Paleolithic of the Western Hemisphere includes Indigenous oral traditions, archaeological evidence, and a critical and decolonizing discussion of the development of archaeology in the Americas.

Steeves' research focuses on the Pleistocene history of the Americas. Her research supposedly indicates that artifacts and sacred sites show that Indigenous people were in North America more than 130,000 years ago. Her research supposedly "decolonizes" historical narratives about Indigenous people and settlement of the Americas.

What I hope people will come to understand from The Indigenous Paleolithic of the Western Hemisphere, Dr. Steeves wrote, "is that Western education has erased Indigenous histories and identities through violent processes of colonization. In gaining an understanding of the history and development of American archaeology I hope readers will come to understand the human cost of colonization and the power of education as a tool of empire, which often crafts social memories acceptable to the nation-state.

"The Indigenous Paleolithic of the Western Hemisphere provides evidence of (archaeological sites, mammalian migrations, paleoenvironmental data, oral traditions) a much longer timeframe of Indigenous history in the Western Hemisphere. Hundreds of stories held in the land (archaeological sites) attest to over 130,000 years of history. The complex part of this work was in recounting the colonial history of racism in American archaeology. Perplexing, because racism in American archaeology has been in plain sight for over a century yet was often ignored in discussions of the framing of history." [Paulette F. C. Steeves, The Indigenous Paleolithic of the Western Hemisphere (Lincoln: University of Nebraska Press, 2021).]

Not all readers of The Indigenous Paleolithic were thrilled with the claims made by Dr. Steeves and the evidence she presents to support her assertions. An individual identified as YossarianWWII visited Steeves' website and entered the following comments: "So, I went and found her database. It basically contains all claimed sites of pre-Clovis occupation, regardless of how controversial the claim is. Her citations are disappointing too, as many of these (especially the controversial ones) have had a lot written about them, but most entries have only a single citation, and only the author's [name] and year [of publication] at that."

Author Shepard Krech III spoke to the issue in The Ecological Indian: (New York: W. W. Norton & Company, 1999), p. 30.

Among American Indians outside the scientific community [the idea that the Indians had wandered eastward into North America from northeastern Asia] has not met with universal acceptance. Some have taken issue with the idea that their ancestors came initially from Asia. Asked about the origin of the world and human beings, or about the migrations of their ancestors, Indians have sometimes responded that their communities were never anywhere other than where they were at the moment the question was posed. Their ancestors, they said, came into the present world from worlds preceding and beneath the current one, through mouths of caves or from holes in the ground. Other native people believed they had migrated from the east, west, or elsewhere. Some living in the interior of the continent thought that their ancestors once lived far away on the shores of salty seas. In days before, they had incorporated European ideas of origins into their own. American Indians answered questions about their origin and historical movements in as many different voices as there were nations with separate cultures. (Emphasis added.)

To overcome the existing bias accepted by many American Indians—whether they actually believe in them, or not—archaeologists are going to have to present indisputable evidence to cadres of their associates, many of whom will approach the new "evidence" with a negative attitude. Some will never accept any "truth" that does not confirm their preferred explanation for where their ancestors came from. Shepard Krech III strives to explain how the process works in The Ecological Indian: Myth and History: "The nature of science is to debate theories and to test and confirm or falsify hypotheses spawned by theories. As with evolution, a long period of shared understanding may be suddenly punctuated by "fresh" insight fitting more seamlessly both new data and broader historical context in which all scientific thought exists, and a new consensus begins to build. One recent example of this process is illustrated by debates concerning mass extinctions before the

Pleistocene, for which there is widespread agreement that asteroids—a radical theory when initially proposed—and climate change spelled the end of the major orders of living things."

The case of the White Sands footprints, for example, shows that solid evidence can overcome long-held "facts" within the scientific community, and it has nothing to do with being American Indian or not-American Indian. Finding sites as old or older than Clovis has simply proven to be a challenge. Finding "indisputable" evidence within such a site requires even a higher standard, as everyone in the archaeological community knows. While Native American oral histories are interesting and potentially valuable at times, they are probably never going to be accepted as the sole basis for "indisputable claims," and for good reason.
[Shepard Krech III, The Ecological Indian: Myth and History, (New York: W.W. Norton & Co., 1999), pp. 30-31.]

CHAPTER 11

OTHER CLAIMS OF "DISCOVERY"

> Archaeological sites are histories held in the land, places where ancestors left us stories about their lives… It is essential for archaeologists to keep an open mind, as so often we are shown that we did not know what it was we thought we knew.
>
> —**Paulette F. C. Steeves**
> Indigenous Paleolithic of the Western Hemisphere

You can't really stop anyone from making claims about such things as who might have discovered the Americas. James W. Loewen, author of the popular Lies My Teacher Told Me, presented his readers with a list of fifteen explorations of the Americas that might have preceded that of Christopher Columbus, widely accepted as the "discoverer" of the Western Hemisphere. (Most people today know that Columbus didn't really "discover" the Americas, but it was his four voyages that led to development "Columbian Exchanges," trade and regular commerce between the Americas and Europe that continues uninterrupted today.)

Three of the pre-Columbian explorations on Loewen's list are actually the three groups of Siberian, Beringian, and Alaskan groups that reached the Americas via the Beringian land bridge and spread throughout the hemisphere. Absent any contradictory evidence, many of us believe they were the ancestors of most of today's American Indians, both those in North America and South America.

Other possible early visitors to the Americas cited by Loewen include the well-documented visits by Vikings and their establishment of trading settlements at L'Anse aux Meadows in Newfoundland; Montreal, Trois Rivieres, and Quebec in today's

Canadian province of Quebec; as well as a trading center at Norembega in Rhode Island. Between 30 and 160 people may have lived at the Vinland settlement of L'Anse aux Meadows, discovered in 1960 and now a Canadian National Historic Site, as well as a UNESCO World Heritage Site. There is strong archaeological evidence that the site was occupied in 1021. How long it remained in use is unclear, but it is thought to have been abandoned as a result of internal strife or conflicts with local Indigenous "Skraelings," or Indians. There is a growing body of evidence that at one time the Vikings had traders located throughout New England and as far east as Minnesota and they carried on a regular commerce in fish, furs, and timber for many years. The first known Viking visit to North America was by Leif Eriksson in 970 and they continued to trade there until sometime after 1356. However, knowledge of their involvement in the Western Hemisphere was probably not widely known outside of Norway, Sweden, and Denmark, and may have been totally forgotten by 1492 when Columbus claimed to have found a New Land. [Johnson, Robert G. and Janey Westin, The Last Kings of Norse America, (Edina, MN: Beaver's Pond Press, 2012); Skelton, R. A., The Vinland map and the Tartar Relation, 2nd ed., (New Haven, CT: 1995); Seaver, Kirsten A., Maps, Myths, and Men: The Story of the Vinland Map, (Stanford, CT: 2004).

The other possible visitors that Loewen found mentioned in the textbooks he reviewed include the possibility that Indonesians visited South America between 6000 and 1500 B.C.; Japanese visited Ecuador around 5000 B.C.; Chinese reached Central America around 1000 B.C.; Phoenicians may have visited England 500 B.C.; St. Brendan and Irish Monks reached New England around 600 A.D.; Polynesians may have visited Chile between 1304 and 1424 AD; Basque from Spain might have visited the Newfoundland coast between 1375 and 1491; English may have visited Newfoundland around 1481-1491; and the Portuguese may possibly have been to Newfoundland around 1460.

One of the more interesting possibilities that Professor Loewen mentions has to do with West Africans visiting Haiti, Panama, and possibly Brazil between 1311 and 1460. While he rates the likelihood that actually took place as only "Moderate," there's a lot more to the story.

[James W. Loewen, Lies My Teacher Told Me (New York: The New Press, 2018), pp. 39-42.]

In 1324, while Mansa Musa, rule of the wealthy Mali Empire, was visiting in Cairo, he reportedly told an Egyptian official that he had come to the throne when his predecessor led a fleet in an attempt to cross the Atlantic and never returned. Historians commonly attribute the risky attempt to a Mansa Abu Bakr II, or Abubakari II. Interestingly, however, no such Mansa every reigned and it is believed that it was Mansa Muhammad ibn Qu.

Mansa Muhammad was reportedly interested in exploring whether the Atlantic had another "bank." In 1311, he resigned and handed his throne to his brother, Kankou Moussa and set off from the Gambia coast with a fleet of 2,000 boats loaded with sailors, their families, and enough supplies to support the flotilla for at least a year. Mansa Muhammad and his entourage were never heard from again.

Researchers in Mali working on a book about the undertaking say there is evidence that Muhammad and his fleet reached Recife, Brazil. Written accounts of the expedition were reportedly also found in Egypt in a book written in the 14th century. One of the researchers also pointed out that Columbus even reported that there were Black traders present in the Americas when he reached there. People on the island of Hispaniola are also reported to have said that black people had come to their island who had spears made of a metal called guanin, an amalgam of gold, silver, and copper that was quite commonly used in Mali.

Most pre-Columbian scholars say "there is no evidence of any such voyage reaching the Americas," and "there are insufficient evidentiary grounds to suppose that there has been contact between Africa and the New World at any point in the pre-Columbian era." A book on the subject, The Saga of Abubakari II was released in 2021 by Malian scholar and author Gaoussou Wiawara.
["Atlantic voyage of the predecessor of Mansa Musa," at Wikipedia.org/wiki/Atlantic_voyage_of_the_predecessor_of_Mansa_

Musa; Joan Baxter, "Africa's 'greatest explorer'" BBC News Online, December 13, 2000.; C. R. Gibbs, "The Mystery of Abubakari II's Voyage," portofharlem.net/snippets21/mar102021-abubakari.html; and C. R. Gibbs, "Abubakari II: Africa's Greatest Explorer? And Mansa Musa: The Richest Man Who Ever Lived? portofharlem.net/snippets21/feb242021-abubakari.html.]

Professor Loewen also rated the chances that the Chinese had visited Central America around 1000 B.C. as having a "Low" likelihood of having actually occurred. While the date given for the possible visit may be a little too early, I believe there is now some very strong evidence that several Chinese fleets visited in the early years of the fifteenth century, followed by an unparalleled armada of Chinese ships, sailors, and government bureaucrats that explored much of the world between 1421 and 1423. The recent discoveries that seem to strongly legitimize can be credited to Gavin Menzies, a former Canadian Navy submarine commander whose interest in and knowledge of marine operations and navigation led to the "startling rediscoveries" of ancient, but forgotten, knowledge about the geography of the New World and historical navigational achievements.

That ancient knowledge had almost certainly paved the ways for Christopher Columbus to "discover" the Bahamas and Caribbean, for Bartolomeu Dias to transit the Cape of Good Hope, for Vasco da Gama to cross the Indian Ocean, and for Ferdinand Magellan to brave steering his ship into the Strait of Magellan. All braved unfamiliar shores and shoals, as well as the possibility of falling off the end of the world. In reality, the way for each of those famous mariners who once basked in the glory associated with their heroic maritime accomplishments had been paved by the Chinese mariners who preceded them, the brave Chinese mariners who risked their ships, their crews, and their own lives to pioneer vital maritime highways.

Captain Menzies' discoveries were pieced together in scores of libraries and document collections around the world, pouring over scores of old maps and sailing directions, rather than at the helm of a ship. They will almost undoubtedly be of more interest to generations of historians and academicians from countries around the world, than to the generations of Chinese sailors who pioneered those danger-ridden routes. It will be interesting to see whether knowledge of Menzies' discoveries will affect the reputations of those infamous mariners, like Columbus, who made their reputations primarily by clandestinely voyaging in the wakes of Chinese sailors and their red-sailed ships. In the future, I wonder if we will celebrate the unique historical accomplishments of the now-anonymous Chinese mariners? [Menzies, Gavin, 1421: The Year China Discovered America, (New York: Harper Perennial, 2002). See also his 1434: The Year China Discovered America.]

I'm certain that Professor Loewen isn't planning to hold his breath until archaeologists, historians, and biologists confirm or disprove the voyages we have promoted as having possibly resulted in pre-Columbian discoveries. After all, researching such evidence is a lot of work. (Remember Clovis! Change doesn't come easily.) To tell about earlier explorers, textbook authors would have to familiarize themselves with sources such as those cited here and elsewhere. It's easier to just retell the old familiar Columbus story!
[James W. Loewen, Lies My Teacher Told Me (New York: The New Press, 2018), pp. 41-42.]

At the present time, the only pre-Columbian, trans-oceanic contact with the Americas widely accepted is that of the Norse, or Vikings, who visited what is now northeastern Canada around the beginning of the eleventh century. Even though there was an oral history remembrance of the visits, as well as mentions in the Icelandic Sagas, it wasn't until 1960 that researchers actually found the L'Anse aux Meadows site in Newfoundland. L'Anse aux Meadows is a proverbial "needle in a haystack," as are most other sites that are a millennium old. They're out there, but it takes a literal miracle to find them, confirm their age, and interpret the sites. The process has gotten a little easier in recent years with tools like DNA analysis and LiDAR—Light Detection and Ranging sensors, but dedicated researchers are still searching for the proverbial "needles."

I believe that it is entirely possible that people other than the Vikings may also have visited the Americas at some time in the distant past. Whether they came before or after the Indians is questionable. They may even have remained in the Americas and may even have mated with other early arrivals, possibly even with American Indians.

Based primarily on similarities in the points they manufacture, there are scientists who believe members of the Solutrean culture from the Iberian Peninsula of France and Spain may have arrived in the Americas 25,000 to 13,000 years ago. The possibility that the earliest settlers in the Americas had arrived by boats, traveling along the coastlines and faces of glaciers, got people thinking in that direction in the 1970s when scientists began to find serious problems with the Ice-Free Corridor route.

While there were problems with this hypothesis, too, it began to grow legs when American archaeologists attended an exhibit in France showing the similarities between Clovis and Solutrean cultures. The Solutrean culture, located along the southeastern Iberian Coast of France and Spain had been dated between 18,000 and 25,000 years earlier. The possibility that the Solutreans and not the Beringians had been responsible for the Clovis points found in the Americas had been discussed, but dismissed the idea because it was not believed that Paleolithic people of that period had boats capable of carrying them to the Americas. However, the Solutrean peoples had lived along the ice age coastline of the North Atlantic that connected Europe with the Grand Banks off Canada, and it was assumed that they would have developed a skill set tailored to life along the ice, including boats that would have given them access to the rich marine environment.

Evidence presented to support the hypothesis, however, is not based on any evidence that the Solutreans had developed boats capable of transiting the North Atlantic during the glacial period. The promoters of the Solutrean hypothesis provide extensive details on other diverse cultures from around the world that had developed maritime abilities by, or during, the LGM (Last Glacier Maximum) period. They also suggest that "Solutrean sailors would have known from the behavior of polar bears, as well as birds and foxes that scavenge seal kills made by the bears, that they would find land to the west. They would have noted driftwood floating eastward in the sea current; perhaps the search for a wood source was itself a motivation to find the land to the west." They also explain the superior mirage, or Fata Morgana mirage, phenomenon that resulted from temperature inversions over water that sometimes made it possible to see things far beyond the horizon. The promoters suggest that the "mirages" might have allowed Solutrean sailors to have seen the mountains of Newfoundland or Greenland's ice cap and that might have prompted them to sail toward the unknown west.

The incentive for Solutrean sailors to sail into those unknown waters isn't explained. Seeing a mirage, in fact, might have generated exactly the opposite action by the sailors, a group known to be quite superstitious and unlikely to go charging into unknown waters. The authors also fail to take into consideration the weather conditions that would have existed along the face of the glaciers in the North Atlantic. Writing about the glaciers that covered the Great Lakes during the LGM, I asked a geographer friend of mine what weather conditions would have been like in the vicinity of the glaciers. He said that the ice of the glacier would have created an extreme low-pressure system and spawned very strong winds that would have circulated in a counter-clockwise fashion. My geographer friend, who was not known for exaggerations, said the weather to the east of the glaciers would have been "among the most brutal in the world." That would definitely have been another factor that would have reduced the likelihood that Solutrean mariners, or any mariners along the Atlantic Coast, would have been eager to explore the unknown waters to the west.

While I question some aspects of the hypothesis of Stanford and Bradley, I would not totally dismiss it. Their detailed analyses of points and flaking techniques, the fact that the Solutreans may have had the capacity to sail across the Atlantic well south of the glaciers, and the fact that the presence of Solutreans along the East Coast of North America would explain several of the mysteries that now haunt our knowledge of the peopling of the Americas, deserve careful analysis by the archaeological community. Let's not repeat the arrogant and frustrating failures of Clovis First.

[Stanford, Dennis J. and Bruce A. Bradley, Across Atlantic Ice: The Origin of America's Clovis Culture, (Oakland, CA: University of California Press, 2013).]

The researchers behind the Cell study, led by Max Planck Institute geneticist Cosimo Posth, found evidence for two previously unknown populations that also entered South America. Both are closely related to the main line of Southern Native Americans, but they are distinct enough to show up separately within ancient peoples' DNA.

One of those groups is represented by Andean peoples who seem closely related to ancient Native Americans who lived in California's Channel Islands. The other connects ancient Native Americans who had arrived in Brazil and Chile by 9,000 years ago to Anzick-1, a baby boy who lived in Montana about 12,800 years ago. Anzick-1 is especially important because he's associated with the North American Clovis culture. While this is the first genetic hint of possible Clovis influence in South America, current evidence firmly rules against this group being the main ancestors of today's South Americans.

The Science paper, led by Natural History Museum of Denmark researcher J. Victor Moreno-Mayer, shows another unexpected dispersal. While his team also saw migrations into South America 14,000 years ago, they found signs that a group living in Mexico or Central America spread out 8,700 years ago into South America and northward into what is now the U.S. Great Plains.

"When you try to include present-day South Americans into the picture, what you need is an extra population movement," Moreno-Mayer has said. "We have very little idea of which population represents the gene flow; the only thing we know is that it's on the Native American side."

The third new study, published in Science Advances, zooms in on the Andes, the mountainous spine of western South America. Archaeological evidence shows that people started living permanently in the Andean highlands about 9,000 years ago. But these aren't the easiest places to live, since it's cold and the air is thin, which makes it harder for human bodies to absorb oxygen. So how did Andean peoples move into this region, and how did they adapt to the harsh conditions? (Also, why did they move into a rather inhospitable place? Forced by other tribes? Shortages of food?)

To find out, researchers led by Emory University anthropologist John Lindo sequenced the whole genomes of seven Natives who lived in Peru's highlands between 1,600 and 6,100 years ago. The team also collected dozens of DNA sequences from two modern Native populations: the Aymara in Boliva's highland, and the Huilliche-Pehuenche, who live in Chile's coastal lowlands.

Comparing the DNA sequences revealed that the Andes' lowland and highland people split about 8,750 years ago, give or take a few centuries. The team also found signs of evolution acting on the highland Andeans' DNA, such as an uptick in gene variants linked to stronger hearts. If this is an adaptation to high altitudes, then the Aymara's bodies took a different approach than other high-altitude groups. Native Tibetans, for instance, more commonly have gene variants that affect blood's ability to carry oxygen.

"That was a bit of a surprise to me," says study coauthor Mark Aldenderfer, an Archeologist at the University of California, Merced. "What we see is convergent evolution: Here's an environmental challenge that people are confronted with in their genomes, and there appear to be multiple ways to [solve] the problem.

Andean DNA also bears the scars of disease that Europeans brought to the region in the 1500s. When compared to pre-contact Andeans' DNA, modern Aymara genomes show shifts in two immune genes, one of which is linked to smallpox. Lowland populations don't show this change, which may help explain another grim result: how much each population collapsed after European contact. The authors estimate that the highland Aymara lost about 27% of its population post-contact, but lowland groups shrank by 95 %.

"The fact that these populations adapted to such harsh environments, like the high-altitude environment of the Andes, may have provided some protection against either the European explorers themselves or protection from the pathogens [they] brought in," says study coauthor Anna Di Rienzo, a human geneticist at the University of Chicago.

While the three studies add new details, they also raise new questions. For one, there's still some tension between the archaeological and genetic records, particularly over the rapid move into South America around 14,000 years ago. "The implication is that if you're moving that far, that fast, there wasn't anybody home…and yet we have people in the Americas prior to that time," says Southern Methodist University archaeologist David Meltzer, one of the Science study's coauthors. "The next obvious question is, what is the relationship between the groups that we're mapping here, and the ones that we only have hints of genetically and archaeologically?"

To know more, scientists say they'll need even more data. To do that, teams are working closely with Native groups both to collect DNA from today's populations and to sample the ancient remains of living Natives' likely ancestors.

"We are unfortunately taught many incorrect ideas about them both in history classes and also implicitly in the media: that indigenous Americans are all but extinct, that their great cultural achievements are only in the past or should be attributed to anyone other than their ancestors," Jennifer Raff has stated. (Who thinks Indians are all but extinct? I have heard this claim many times over, yet in all my research and all my travels I have never met anyone who believes that the American Indians are going extinct. I question the validity of the claim.) "An understanding of the history of indigenous peoples, from both scientific and indigenous perspectives, is one way of seeing past these messages and recognizing the incredible resilience and achievements of the peoples of the Americas."

The North American climate was unstable as the Ice Age receded. The unstable climate led to widespread migration, with early Paleo-Indians soon spreading throughout the Americas, diversifying into many hundreds of culturally distinct tribes. At any one time there were probably 500 to 1,000 tribes in the Americas. In his definitive Atlas of the Indian Tribes of North America, Nicholas J. Santoro lists the names of 4,700 tribes. That isn't the number of tribes, however, because many tribes were known by a variety of names, sometimes at the same time, sometimes over a period of time. In fact, the name or names a tribe is known by may well not reflect what the tribe was called by members of the tribe, obviously a confusing situation. [Nicholas J. Santoro, Atlas of the Indian Tribes of North America, (New York: IUniverse, 2009), p. viii.]

For example, the Chippewa, one of the largest tribes in the region of the Great Lakes, were more accurately known as the Ojibwa, sometimes spelled and pronounced as Odjibwa, Odjibway, or Ojibway. Chippewa, which was apparently easier for non-Indians to pronounce, was also spelled and pronounced as Chippeway or Chippewas. Chippewa is also supposedly a derivative of Ojibwa, although I have difficulty making that transition.

The Ottawa are another major tribe from the Great Lakes region, today their lands generally adjoin those of the Chippewa in Michigan's Upper and Lower Peninsulas. While descendants of the Ottawa today refer to their tribe as the Odawa, which one Indian scholar insists is a mispronunciation of the original name. The earliest translations of the tribe's language were into French by Jesuit missionaries like Father Marquette and Bishop Baraga. Most French translators translated the sounds of the first and third syllables of the name as the French sound "ou," or, in English, "ew." As a result, the common French spellings were Outaoua, Outaouois, or Outaouat. Several of the key figures stationed at Fort Michilimackinac, guardian of the straits between Michigan's two peninsulas, used the spelling Outawas in their communications. That included John Porteous, a trader there in the 1760s, and Captain George Etherington, British commander there at the time Chippewa attacked the fort and massacred many of the soldiers and traders.

[Timothy Kent, Rendezvous at the Straits, (Ossineke, MI: Silver Fox Enterprises, 2004.]

If variations in spelling aren't confusing enough, many tribes are simply known by a variety of names. In his Handbook of American Indians North of Mexico, F. W. Hodge explained:

During the early exploration and settlement of North America, a multitude of tribes were encountered, having diverse customs and languages. Lack of knowledge of the aborigines and of their languages led to many curious errors on the part of the early explorers and settlers: names were applied to the Indians that had no relations whatever to their aboriginal names; sometimes nicknames were bestowed, owing perhaps to personal characteristics, fancied or real; sometimes tribes came to be known by names given by other tribes, which were often opprobrious; frequently, the designation by which a tribal group was known to itself was employed, and as such names were oftentimes unpronounceable by alien tongues and unrepresentable by civilized alphabets, the result was a sorry corruption, varying according as the sounds were impressed on Spanish, English, French, Dutch, German, Russian, or Swedish ears. Sometimes, again, bands of a single tribe were given distinctive tribal names, while clans were often regarded as independent autonomous groups to which separate tribal designations likewise were applied…thousands of such names are recorded, the significance and application of which are to be understood only after much study. [Hodge, F. W., Handbook of American Indians North of Mexico, Part 1, House of Representatives, 59th Congress, 1st Session (Washington, DC: Government Printing Office, 1906).]

The Paleo-Indians were hunter-gatherers, likely characterized by small, mobile bands consisting of approximately 20 to 50 members of an extended family. These groups moved from place to place as preferred resources were depleted and new supplies were sought. During much of the Paleo-Indian period, bands are thought to have subsisted primarily through hunting now-extinct giant land animals such as mastodon and ancient bison. Paleo-Indian groups carried a variety of tools, including distinctive projectile points and knives, as well as less distinctive butchering and hide-scraping implements.

The vastness of the North American continent, and the variety of its climates, ecology, vegetation, fauna, and landforms led ancient people to coalesce into many distinct linguistic and cultural groups. This is reflected in the oral histories of the indigenous peoples, described by a wide range of traditional creation stories which often say that a given people have been living in a certain territory since the creation of the world.

Over the course of thousands of years, Paleo-Indian people domesticated, bred, and cultivated an impressive number of plant species, including crops which now constitute 50-60% of worldwide agriculture. In general, Arctic, Subarctic, and Coastal peoples continued to live as hunters and gatherers, while agriculture was adopted in more temperate and sheltered regions, permitting a dramatic rise in population.

After the migration or migrations, it was several thousand years before the first complex societies arose, the earliest emerging about seven to eight thousand years ago. As early as 6500 BCE people in the Lower Mississippi Valley at the Monte Sano site were building complex earthwork mounds, probably for religious purposes. This is the earliest dated of numerous mound complexes found in present-day Louisiana, Mississippi, and Florida. Archeologists have found that they were built by hunter-gatherer societies who occupied the sites on a seasonal basis, and who had not yet developed ceramics.

Mound building was continued by succeeding cultures, who built numerous sites in the Middle Mississippi and Ohio River valleys as well, adding effigy mounds, conical and ridge mounds, and other shapes.

During the Woodland Period—1000 BCE to 1000 CE—there were no substantive changes but continuous development in stone and bone tools, leatherworking, textile manufacture, tool production, cultivation, and shelter construction. Some Woodland peoples continued to use spears and atlatls until the end of the period, when they were replaced by bows and arrows.

CHAPTER 12

THE FIRST AMERICAN RESIDENTS

Theirs are shapes only dimly seen, a shadowy people who came on stage on tiptoe when the lights were low.

—Thomas Y. Canby
National Geographic, 1979

We know very little about the Siberian-Beringian-Alaskan wanderers who found their ways south to the Americas near the end of the last Ice Age and eventually scattered throughout North America, South America, and Mezo-America. They seem to have been, the "First Americans." Their children who were born anywhere east of the Bering Strait and south all the way to Tierra del Fuego, then, were the first "Native Americans" and, necessarily, the ancestors, or partial ancestors, of all of today's Native Americans.

It's hard to imagine what it must have been like for the First Americans to break out of cold, ice-covered terrain they had potentially known for their entire lives onto the lush, green post-glacial tundra that would be their new homes. As they moved south away from the shrinking glaciers, they might have experienced warm weather, possibly for the first time in their lives. The variety and numbers of animals would also have exceeded anything they had known in their prior homelands. It must have been a hunter-gatherer's paradise of species of all sizes, from mammoths, wooly rhinoceros, bison, musk ox, reindeer, moose, fish of species that had been unknown to them, and every sort of smaller fauna, many of which would prove to be very tasty when grilled over an open fire.

These were epic journeys in every sense of the word "epic," and the stories of their travels should have been documented in a number of historical volumes. Books documenting the journeys would have been "bestsellers" by any standard. Unfortunately, there are no such books. In fact, the astounding journeys of the people that we refer to today as American Indians or the First Americans predated both books and written languages by thousands of years. The stories existed only in the reminiscences of those who made the long, arduous trips, and then in the recollections of those they shared their stories with, perhaps sitting around a campfire thousands of miles from Beringia, and in the tales passed on through the generations of American Indians. Some vestiges of those stories may still reside in the oral traditions of today's Indians, but it may well be impossible to ever link them with those days so long ago. Those collecting the oral histories of America's Indigenous peoples should be on the alert for any ancient stories that may go back to the days of the Bering Ice Bridge, the Kelp Highway, the Ice-Free Corridor, the Coastal Marine Route, or, quite possibly, some route that we haven't even considered yet.

It appears that the First Americans were entering upon a virgin continent, and they were the first humans in the Western Hemisphere to see a truly natural environment unspoiled by the machinations, the creations, the exploits, the enterprises, and the shameful behaviors of mankind. I wonder if they were constantly on the lookout for other humans, not knowing that they could walk for thousands of miles without coming across any sentient, upright beings. If they did make contact with other humans, those humans would probably have also been refugees from the icy North. There is no way that they could have understood that for the next 12,000 years, or so, they and the other refugees from the north and their descendants would be the only humans on the incalculable, seemingly boundless expanse before them.

In the beginning—undoubtedly for thousands of years—the First Americans were almost universally hunter-gatherer groups living off the resources of the lands they occupied, or the lands they traveled through. We really don't know how mobile they might have been, or how soon they would have given up traveling and become static or territorial. We don't know how long it took for family groups to transform, or expand, into "tribes" or "clans." Our knowledge of those early periods of occupancy have primarily been assembled from the study of archaeological remains, usually combined with a lot of hypotheses, theories, and other forms of guesstimations, including Native American oral histories.

May the Great Spirit of the American Indians, or the God—or Gods—of many of us non-Indians, bless the archaeologists, anthropologists, geologists, and individuals of all the other academic disciplines—and thousands of non-academics— who have dedicated much of their lives to trying to unravel and make some sense of the past—our past. In their outstanding North American Archaeology text, Timothy R. Pauketat and Diana DiPaolo Loren use the term alternative histories. My history is different than your history, the histories of Whites are different than those of American Indians, the histories of recent immigrants are different than the histories of those who can trace their family histories back for generations. Nonetheless, as Americans we all share in the totality of the past. In fact, we are all affected to some extent by that all-encompassing past. Sadly, we have a very limited knowledge of the majority of that past. Try as we might, much of that past will always evade us…but not because we are not trying to discover the sum total of all our alternative histories, and the alternative histories of all our ancestors. We know, or we think we know, bits and pieces of that incredible story.

We know, for example, that the First Americans, and their Native American descendants, would eventually scatter across both North American and South America, from what is now Canada to Tierra del Fuego at the southern tip of Chili and Brazil. Why they moved to such extremes is unknown. Historically, American Indians, and other groups as well, generally moved to find improved habitat or improved resources—food, firewood, water, etc., to escape their enemies, or out of curiosity—the desire to see what is over the next hill, to see if there are greener pastures. With the sparsity of the original populations, it would seem that the pressures to move would not have been very strong for many years—perhaps thousands of years.

Archaeologists differ in their estimates of how fast the populations of the First Americans might have grown or how long it might have taken them to spread across the continent or reach locations in southern South America where sites of early occupations have been identified. Todd Surovell of the University of Wyoming feels that population diffusion could have been quite rapid, although he is less clear on what might have instigated the First Americans to continue moving to the south. Nonetheless, he constructed a computer model designed to estimate the time it might have taken for the early arrivals to move from the area near what is now Seattle, "the maximum southern limit of the Cordilleran Ice Sheet," to the Monte Verde site along the southern coast of Chile. His model starts with a group of 175 people that increased at a rate of three percent, as they leap-frogged south as their group began to deplete food supplies. At that rate, Surovell's model projected that it would have taken 2,267 years for the migrants to reach Monte Verde.

If the First Americans travelled by boat for all or part of the trip, however, it would probably have taken them much less time. Craig Childs met Kanaan Bausler, a young man from Juneau, Alaska, in his early twenties, who made the trip from Alaska to southern Chile by kayak and bicycle—mostly by kayak—in two years, covering a distance of 8,400 miles. Bausler stopped about a thousand miles short of his original destination of Tierra del Fuego when he reached a site that proved to be very close to the important Monte Verde. He stopped there, he said, because the area's weather, it reminded his home thousands of miles to the north and the attraction was so strong that he abandoned the remainder of the route to Tierra del Fuego.

Bausler eventually returned to his home in Alaska, a fact that Childs thinks was noteworthy. "He was able to tell his family and friends about his journey. Unless the traveler returns, no knowledge can be passed on; no map will be laid out, no later migration of families will occur." He told his family and friends in Juneau "he'd passed beyond countless horizons, and at the far end of the world he found a familiar place with unfamiliar stars and an upside-down moon…Who could resist such a call?" Childs asked.
[Craig Childs, Atlas of a Lost World: Travels in Ice Age America, (New York: Vintage Books, 2018), pp. 95-98; Surovell, T. A.,

"Simulating Coastal Migration in New World Colonization," Current Anthropology New Series 36 (2003), 44 (4): 580-591.]

What undoubtedly began as small groups, probably family groups or extended family groups, eventually grew in size, due primarily to generational reproduction, acceptance of new members from other groups, additions due to marriages, and conquests over other tribes. Somewhere along that path, many of the groups became what we would refer to as "tribes," although they would never have called themselves that. Google defines a tribe as "a social division in a traditional society consisting of families or communities linked by social, economic, religious, or blood ties, with a common culture and dialect, typically having a recognized leader." That definition seems totally adequate for our purposes. In time, as the Native American populations increased, more and more tribes were organized throughout the Americas and some became very large, a number with thousands of members.

While this was going on, weather conditions were steadily improving, largely as the result of the end of the Ice Age. The melting of the mile-or-more-thick glacial ice resulted in dramatic increases in water levels throughout planet Earth beginning in about 19,000 BP and continuing for several thousand years. Warmer weather and an increased supply of water led to a dramatic shift from hunter-gatherer cultures to agricultural cultures. It is almost unbelievable but some of those agricultural settlements would grow into communities that were the equal of the largest cities in the world at those times. [Yusuke Yokoyama, Kurt Lambeck, Patrick De Deckker, Paul Johnston, and Keith Field, "Timing of the Last Glacial Maximum from observed sea-level minima," Nature, Vol. 406, August 17, 2000, pp. 713-716.]

It can be argued that the most astounding factor in the development of the Americas is the growth in the pre-Columbian population. Remember, scientists who have devoted their best efforts in an effort to predict how large the original groups of migrants were, all came up with figures between 70 and 500. Even if they entered North America in three or four groups of that size, the total individuals would still be only 280 to 2,000—280 to 2,000 First Americans. I'm sure that we could find a number of respected scientists who would have predicted that populations that small couldn't possibly have survived! It definitely wouldn't have taken much to wipe them out.

I guess the factor in the equation that I wrestle with is that the population growth took place over thousands of years, certainly 13,000 to 15,000 years, or maybe more. Maybe even 40,000 years! It all depends on when the first of the migrants moved onto the continent. All of those time periods seem to me to be beyond the comprehension of most humans.

Population estimates for the Western Hemisphere at the time of Columbus range widely, from 8.4 million to 112.5 million people. The total estimate for the coterminous United States is 1,850,011 If the original population was only in the neighborhood of 70-250 for a group, or 280-2,000 for four groups, the fact that they survived would probably be an indicator that there were not many threats to the lives of the individuals and there must have been an adequate supply of food wherever they wandered.
[Russell Thornton, American Indian Holocaust and Survival: A Population History since 1492, (Norman: University of Oklahoma Press, 1987, pp. 23-29.

In a paper presented in 2000, archaeologist Todd Surovell noted, "It is possible that the initial colonizers of the New World, occupying an empty niche and being highly residentially mobile, had unusually high rates of population growth.
[Surovell, T., "Early Paleoindian women, children, mobility and fertility," American Antiquity, 65, pp. 493-508, cited in Robert L. Kelly, "Maybe we do know when people first came to North America; and what does it mean if we do?" p. 140.]

For immigrants from frigid Siberia, Beringia, and Alaska, the Americas must have seemed like the Garden of Eden. At the same time, the pre-Columbian combined populations of Mexico, Central America, and South America has been estimated at about 37 million. As summarized in the Wikipedia article "Population history of Indigenous peoples of the Americas," there is so little pre-Columbian data available that most "experts" feel that it is impossible to come up with any meaningful estimates that can be used for comparison

purposes…but the "experts" do anyway. Russell Thornton of the University of California, after studying the issue extensively, wrote, "We do not know exactly how many American Indians were in the Western Hemisphere, or even parts of it, when Columbus came. The Indians themselves left no records of their total numbers and no European took a census in 1492, and even if someone had, it would surely not have been very accurate." Despite those conclusions, Thornton felt it would be possible to come up with a "reasonable estimate" of the American Indian population at that time.
[Snow, D. R. (16 June 1995), "Microchronology and Demographic Evidence Relating to the Size of Pre-Columbian North American Indian Populations," Science. 268 (5217): 1601–1604. and Dobyns, Henry (1983). Their Number Become Thinned: Native American Dynamics in Eastern North America. (Knoxville: University of Tennessee Press); "La catastrophe démographique" (The Demographic Catastrophe"), L'Histoire, July–August 2007, p. 17.]

Interestingly, the U.S. Bureau of the Census tried to do that in 1894. They concluded, "Investigation shows that the aboriginal population within the present United States at the beginning of the Columbian period could not have exceeded much over 500,000, that portions of families or stocks of Indians were given as original tribes, and that many small bands of the same tribe were given as separate tribes." They found few supporters for their estimate.

Professor Thornton "massaged" the sparse available data on Indian populations in the Americas at the time Columbus arrived, looking at figures promoted by artist George Catlin, Mexican Jesuit Priest Francsico Javier, Scottish writer William Robertson, Colonel Garrick Mallery of the Smithsonian Institution, and a variety of other academics. In the end, Thornton, faced with estimates ranging from a low of 500,000 to a high of 16,000,000, settles on what he refers to as a "conservative total" of 7,000,000 "for the area north of Mexico." His methodology, however, appears to have been more "pooled guesstimates" than "scientific."
[Russell Thornton, "American Indian Holocaust and Survival: A population history since 1492, (Norman: University of Oklahoma Press, 1987), pp. 15-32.]

William M. Denevan, the Carl O. Sauer Professor of Geography and Environmental Studies at the University of Wisconsin-Madison, also played around the with the available figures for a number of years and he has written one of the more thought-provoking books on the subject. His revised projection is 54 million, which falls just about in the middle of the range by all the experts who wanted to play the guessing game. Estimates from five "knowledgeable sources" collected by Denevan ranged from a low of 8.4 million to a high of 112.55 million. What do you do with those sorts of numbers? To categorize them as "unusable" without making any sarcastic comments might have been appreciated by those distinguished scholars who participated in generating the widely scattered population projections. As shaky as the estimates are, they continue to play roles in today's discussions of how many Indians were in the Americas in 1492 and at other important dates in the past. [William M. Denevan, "The Native Population of the Americas in 1492," 2nd Rev. Ed, (Madison: University of Wisconsin Press, 1992).]

CHAPTER 13

WHOOPS, NO INDIANS HERE!

> There was no shortage of imaginative philosophers trying to prove that the Mound Builders had been Israelites, Phoenicians, Malays, Irishmen, or members of some other immigrant group.
>
> **—Robert Silverberg**
> The Mound Builders

Use of the term "Indian" with respect to the American Indians was totally the fault of Admiral Columbus. He sailed for the West Indies in hopes of discovering riches that would make him a wealthy man. He needed a better map, however, because he pulled up well short of the Indies and parked the Santa Maria on a beach in the Caribbean. While referring to the Natives as "Indians" was understandable given the circumstances, it still ranks as an unfortunate error. If the old Admiral had studied his navigational charge a little more, he might have realized his error and made a mid-voyage correction, saving millions of humans in the Western Hemisphere from being misnamed. They are used to being called "Indians" now, but we all know that it's not correct. Most of our American Indians have never been to India, and it is likely that very few of them have ever met a real "Indian."

The best efforts of the various scientists and scholars notwithstanding, long before Columbus appeared on the scene the First Americans in Mesoamerica had transitioned from hunter-gatherers to hunter-gatherer-farmers during what has been referred to as a "second, independent Neolithic Revolution. That transformation undoubtedly represented a major step in the evolution of the many American Indian cultures, but not one that was shared in by all Indian cultures. Interestingly, the cultural change appears to have begun in

South America and worked its way through Mesoamerica and, finally, spread north to involve some of the tribes in North America, primarily southern North America.

[Charles C. Mann, 1491, 2nd ed. (New York: Vintage Books, 2011), pp. 19-20.]

It had long been believed that there was a limit to how large a hunter-gatherer tribe could grow, depending in large part on the resource base that was available to them. At the same time, that cultural change was believed to be a necessary step in a culture's progress toward becoming a "civilization." "A static society had both the incentive and the opportunity to build permanent dwellings, fortifications, and religious structures. These became important to society, not only for their function but also as symbols of prosperity and power."
[Martin J. Dougherty, The Astec, Inca, and Maya Empires: The Illustrated History of the Ancient Peoples of Mesoamerica and South America (London: Amber Books, 2018), pp. 17-18.]

The roots of the Neolithic Revolution, or the Agricultural Revolution, were planted in the Fertile Crescent region of Europe and Asia about 10,000-11,700 years ago with the domestication and cultivation of various plants and animals and the partial and gradual abandonment of the hunter-gatherer lifestyles in favor of more sedentary agriculture-based lifestyles. That facilitated the formation of villages, which led to all sorts of things that are still part of our cultures today: government administrations, dense populations, specialization, the division of labor, widespread distribution of knowledge, and so on. These were followed by the development of the wheel, steel tools, written languages, and books. About 5,000 years ago, the Sumerians put all these revolutionary factors together and created what has been called "the first great civilization."
[Wikipedia, "Neolithic Revolution;" Charles C. Mann, 1491, 2nd ed. (New York: Vintage Books, 2011), pp. 20-21.]

Our First Americans and our Native Americans, isolated in the Western Hemisphere, some struggling to find new homelands south of the glaciers, missed the Neolithic, or Agricultural, Revolution and all its "civilizing" features that were spreading across the known

world at that time. Long before 1492, however, apparently without any intervention or direction from the world's other continents, residents of the Mesoamerican regions of the hemisphere began cultivating vegetables like squash and corn, or "maize," and organizing into cities and towns. They, too, soon developed religions, civic leadership structures, writing systems, calendars, and even "books" on bark paper made from fig trees.
[Charles C. Mann, 1491, 2nd ed. (New York: Vintage Books, 2011), pp. 21-22.]

The best efforts of the various scientists and scholars notwithstanding, long before Christopher Columbus appeared on the scene many of the First Americans had transitioned from hunter-gatherers-fishers to hunter-gatherer-fishers-farmers during what has been referred to as a "second, independent Neolithic Revolution," or the "Agricultural Revolution," separate from the change that had occurred in Europe and elsewhere in the world. That cultural change, as basic as it might seem to us today, was unquestionably a major step in the evolution of the American Indian cultures. To say that it was a form of cultural "modernization" would not be unreasonable.

It had long been believed that there was a limit to how large a hunter-gatherer tribe could grow, depending in large part on the resource base that was available. That limit was largely lifted when a culture became agrarian. In fact, that cultural change, from being a hunter-gatherer society to one that had adopted agricultural practices, was believed to be a necessary step in a culture's progress toward becoming a "civilization." One author explained, "A static agricultural society had both the incentive and the opportunity to build permanent dwellings, fortifications, and religious structures. These became important to society, not only for their function but also as symbols of prosperity and power."
[Charles C. Mann, 1491, 2nd ed. (New York: Vintage Books, 2011), pp. 19-20; Martin J. Dougherty, The Astec, Inca, and Maya Empires: The Illustrated History of the Ancient Peoples of Mesoamerica and South America (London: Amber Books, 2018), pp. 17-18.]

CHAPTER 14

DISCOVERY OF THE MOUND BUILDERS

> Carl Haub has observed that "there are, of course, absolutely no demographic data available for 99 percent of the span of the human stay on earth.
>
> **—David Henige**
> Numbers from Nowhere

A dramatic cultural shift in American Indian lifestyles began "not with a bang, but a whimper." (My apologies to T. S. Eliot's The Hollow Men.) If anyone had been paying careful attention, the "whimper" would have been first heard around 6500 years before the present when two mounds were constructed at the Monte Sano Site near what is now Baton Rouge, Louisiana. The whimper was heard again 5400 years ago when a second complex of eleven mounds was built at Watson Brake, in the floodplain of the Ouachita River, near what is now the city of Monroe in northern Louisiana. Both sites were close to the "Queen" of American rivers, the mighty Mississippi, or on bayous spawned by it, but if you haven't traveled through northeastern Louisiana, it is unlikely that you have heard of either Monte Sano or Watson Brake. In fact, Monte Sano was deemed to be of such little significance that its mounds were annihilated in 1967 to facilitate a construction project.

If only a "whimper" had been heard when the mounds at Monte Sano and Watson Brake were built, a much louder, earth-shattering, and history-altering explosive "bang" was heard many years later when those sites were eventually identified as mounds built by humans—American Indian humans. In this instance, "eventually" means a very, very long time. It is difficult to imagine, but the mound sites, most of which were very obvious to the human eye, seemed to have avoided widespread discovery and identification until around

1900—more than 3,000 years after they had been constructed in the rural area northeast of New Orleans. For most of the intervening years, they were just hills and mounds, hills and mounds that apparently appeared to most people to simply be the natural products of Mother Nature. When the mounds were finally identified as having been constructed by humans, archaeologists who investigated the newly found sites of mound builders identified them as an example of what they have identified as being associated with the "Adena Culture." Other "Cultures" or "Traditions" include the Hopewell, Troyville, Baytown, Coles Creek, Mississippian, Caddoan Mississippian, Fort Ancient, and Plaquemine. Assignment of a mound site to one of the Culture or Traditions appears to be largely a function of proximity; in other words, they are close to each other. Many archaeologists will argue that the assignments or associations are on their basis of factors like the similarity structures, uses, age, construction techniques, rather than just proximity. To some extent, however, that becomes a question of "putting the cart before the horse." Most of the mounds were not identified or examined by competent archaeologists until they were hundreds of years old, in some cases more than a thousand, and by then they were subject to weather damage and damage by grave robbers, or gangs of 10-year-old boys looking for something to do on a hot summer day.

On September 19, 1997, researchers led by Joe Saunders, Professor of Geoscience at the University of Louisiana in Monroe, Louisiana, and archaeology student Reca Jones, announced the discovery of what they labeled as "the oldest reliably dated human-made structure in North America, a 5,400-year-old earthen mound at Watson Brake, Louisiana. The report described "a circular mound, as tall as a two-story house, forming an enclosure nearly 300 yards in diameter." According to Professor Saunders and Ms. Jones, they had not determined the purpose of the massive mound.
[Maugh, Thomas H. II, "Oldest Man-Made structure in N. America Found," Los Angeles Times, September 19, 1997; The Monte Sano mounds, older than those at Watson Brake, had not yet been explored by archaeologists at the time Watson Brake was first being studied.]

The impressive complex at Watson Brake was developed 5,400 years ago, 3,908 years before Columbus! The site contained a total of eleven mounds connected by ridges that are situated on the edge of an alluvial terrace known as Macon Ridge, that overlooked a swampy area along the Watson Brake, a minor tributary of the Ouachita River, not far west of the Mighty Mississippi. The mounds appeared to have been occupied most of the year by "fisher-hunter-gatherers." "The discovery of this and other mounds in Louisiana and Florida suggested that the earliest Americans, long thought to have been simple hunter-gatherers who roamed the countryside in small, mobile bands, were actually fairly sedentary people capable of organizing and executing large civil engineering projects."

The builders of the mounds were undoubtedly the descendants of early American Indians who settled in the area about 11,000 years ago, after making the long, arduous trip south from Beringia. It was likely that they remained in the area until after the arrival of the Spanish in the 1500s.

Watson Brake was a product of the American Indians' "Neolithic Revolution" during the Archaic Period...with no help from the Sumerians or any of the classical cultures. The site was being developed about the same time that the Sumerians were creating their cuneiform writing system and when the Egyptians were first using hieroglyphs. It was the period of the First Dynasty in Egypt, when their first kings were ruling over the largely unified country. In England, Stonehenge was probably being built on England's Salisbury Plain at the same time that the mounds at Watson Brake were under construction.

The Watson Brake mounds are excellent examples of the resident Indians working together communally in order to improve their habitat. Living on the high mounds got them up out of the damp, steamy bayou, protected them from floods that were probably common in the area, likely supplied a cooling breeze, allowed them to see enemies approaching and put them in a favorable defensive position if they were attacked. Mounds have served many different purposes, based on the needs of the people who built them. In addition to habitat improvement, it was common for them to have important ceremonial functions, sometimes they served as trade centers, or were territorial markers that indicated where the tribe's border was. Many mounds served religious or mortuary functions, while people frequently lived on top of mounds.

The massive project at Watson Brake provided strong evidence that the Indians who lived there had become relatively sedentary and developed an organizational structure that allowed them to take on and complete major projects spanning many years while still basically a fisher-hunter-gatherer culture. Such projects have not normally been associated with hunter-gatherer cultures that generally tended to be nomadic.
[Thomas H. Maugh II, "Oldest Man-Made structure in N. America Found," Los Angeles Times, September 19, 1997.]

Norte Chico

While the Egyptians were building the pyramids and a large Indian settlement was developing at Watson Brake in what would eventually become Louisiana, what has been described by archaeologists both as a "complex pre-Columbian society" and a "civilization," was taking root along the Pacific Coast of Peru. That widespread culture is known by a variety of names: Norte Chico civilization, Caral civilization, and Caral-Supe civilization. "Norte Chico" is translated as "Small North." "Caral" is a city in the Supe Valley. "Supe" is a major river in a river valley in which a large archaeological site was developed.

The culture, or civilization, dates to around 5500 years ago, and it survived until about 3800 years ago. The community of Aspero, on Peru's Pacific Coast and one of the culture's population centers, was identified as early as 1905, but the first extensive documentation of the civilization didn't occur until the late 1990s. The full significance of the settlements in the three river valleys along the central Peru coast wasn't documented until a 2001 paper in Science and a 2004 article in Nature described the archaeological finds and provided radiocarbon dating to determine the ages of the sites.
[Wikipedia: "Norte Chico civilization"]

While it lacked ceramics and visual art, characteristics normally associated with "civilizations," the most unique achievement of Norte Chico was its "monumental architecture," which included "large earthwork platform mounds and sunken circular plazas." There was also some evidence of textiles, the possible worship of common deities, and a fairly sophisticated governmental structure. Information gathered at the Norte Chico sites focused research attention on coastal sites along Peru's Pacific Coast, rather than the mountain and inland valley sites that were previously the focus of most attention.

The coastal region of Peru had always seemed to be an improbable locus for the presence of important archaeological sites, primarily because the region is severely arid, cut off from rain by the Pacific trade winds and the Andes Mountains. Researchers, however, must have overlooked the fact that the strip of land along the coast is riddled with more than fifty rivers that bring snow melt from the Andes down to the Pacific. Explorations have shown that irrigation was critical to communities in the Norte Chico culture. The coastal zone appears to also have been a primary route used by American Indians on their initial entry into the Southern Hemisphere, a fact verified by numerous archaeological sites there that are at least 10,000 years old. The oldest verified city in the region is Huaricanga, in the north of the region, that dates to 5500 before the present.

The Caral-Supe, or Norte Chico civilization, began to decline about 3800 years ago. While the precise causes have not been identified, it may be that residents were moving to more fertile farmlands farther north, the farming of which was made feasible by knowledge of irrigation that had been gained at Norte Chico.

With the progression of the Norte Chico culture down the Peruvian coast, it largely marked the completion of the diffusion of American Indians throughout North America and South America, a landmark event that went totally unheralded. It would be thousands of more years before residents of the Americas would understand the scope and nature of the continents, the complexity of their populations, and the fact that they all had the same origins in the ice-covered North.

The mound sites at Watson Brake and Poverty Point in Louisiana had both been abandoned by 3350 years ago. Watson Brake had been populated for about 600 years, while Poverty Point was only in use for about 380 years. They were not the last of the mounds, however. In fact, Indigenous mound cultures would continue to exist throughout much of North America until 1751, long after the Europeans arrived. After Poverty Point was abandoned around 3350 years ago, there appears to have been a lengthy break in the use of mounds as none of any significance appear until the Adena culture developed in Ohio and the surrounding areas of Kentucky, southeast Indiana, southwest Pennsylvania, and a small portion of West Virginia around 2500 years ago.

A number of "Proto-civilizations," or communities that were classified as being on the "Early Horizon" of civilization development, appeared in the aftermath of Watson Blake and Poverty Point, mainly in Peru. Among the first was the Chavín culture, which arose around 2,900 years ago, headed by local religious leaders. It was a common religion and religious practices that bound the Chavin communities together and encouraged the construction of monumental religious sites. Those sites were often open only to the priests and the elite members of the community. There is some indication that the Chavín religious practices may have involved the use of psychotropic drugs. The Chavín also "domesticated animals, such as llamas, and practiced fairly sophisticated agriculture in addition to fishing in the rivers of the region." The culture began to decline around 2300 years ago and it had completely disintegrated by 1800 years ago.
[Martin J. Dougherty, The Aztex, Inca, & Maya Empires, (London, England: Amber Books, 2018), pp. 29-31.]

Poverty Point

It wasn't until 3730 years ago, about 1900 years after the construction of Watson Brake—still 1000 years before Columbus—that the Poverty Point Culture constructed what still ranks as the largest known American mound site. Poverty Point is located along the Mississippi River in northeastern Louisiana, near today's city of Monroe. As in the case of Watson Brake, the Indians who built and occupied Poverty Point are believed to have been hunter-gatherers, rather than sedentary farmers, which makes their construction project unique. One of the websites about Poverty Point explains that the site's "American Indian inhabitants moved by hand about 750,000 cubic meters (nearly 981,000 cubic yards) of dirt to construct five earthen mounds as well as a set of six nested, semi-elliptical earthen ridges and a large flat, 43-acre plaza. Archaeologists estimate that a similar amount of earth was also moved in preparing the landscape prior to construction and in ongoing maintenance of the site."

"Poverty Point's inhabitants also imported great quantities of raw materials, particularly stone, over great distances; these materials were used to make tools and other objects. It is impressive that such achievements were attained by a people who depended on hunting and gathering, not farming, as a means of survival. For many years, archaeologists believed that earthen monuments like those at Poverty Point could only have been built by people who relied on farming to survive. It was assumed that people who depended on hunting, gathering, and fishing did not have sufficient resources to support such activities as mound construction." As in the case of Watson Brake, the Indigenous peoples at Poverty Point lived on top of the mounds.

It has been estimated that it took around 600 years—about 25 generations—to build the complex that was home to 4,000-5,000 individuals. When it was completed, it was the largest settlement in North America. Evidence of the Poverty Point mound culture has been found at more than 100 sites in the surrounding area along the Mississippi River in the Mississippi Delta of Louisiana and Mississippi. The mounds at the original Poverty Point site were abandoned about 3,000 years ago, when Queen Nefertiti was ruling Egypt. Why it was abandoned is unknown. Its only drawback was that there was no stone available in the surrounding area, an important element to these Stone Age people. Whether that was a factor in abandonment of the site is unknown. Poverty Point is now a UNESCO World Heritage Site.

The mounds, or, in some cases the remnants of the mounds, were eventually discovered by the European immigrants that began arriving in 1492. Sites like Watson Brake and Poverty Point were probably first seen by Spanish immigrants, or "invaders," in the early 1500s, and then by the French who acquired the Gulf Coast and a large chunk of North America in 1682. The Europeans were undoubtedly puzzled by the mounds, temples, and other massive structures they found. Their initial reaction could definitely have been not to attribute them to the local American Indians, who many Europeans viewed as "savages" and "uncivilized." Some felt the Vikings had probably built the mounds, while others attributed them to "Asians," which, of course, the American Indians were originally. Others reportedly felt the mounds and other structures had been built by people from Atlantis, or even aliens from space, which, in the case of the Nazca Lines in Peru, is still believed by quite a few people even today.

There were those who attributed the mound-building to the Romans, the Lost Tribes of Israel, Danes, Belgians, Saxons, Phoenicians, Hindus, or Africans. Quite literally, anyone but the Indians.
[64parishes.org/entry/poverty-point-7; Stacy Pratt, "The History of Indigenous Mounds in America," at www.ranker.com.]

The American Indians received little, if any, credit for mound building until publication by the government of the ground-breaking 730-page paper "Report on the Mound Explorations of the Bureau of Ethnology," written by Cyrus Thomas, head of the bureau and leader of the country's research into mound building. While his work was not without some factual errors, he strongly believed that Indians were responsible for most of the mound construction, but he erroneously felt that Europeans in the post-Columbian period had been involved in construction of many of the later mounds. "It is true that when we stand at the base of the great Cahokia mound (in Illinois) and study its vast proportions," Thomas wrote, "we can scarcely bring ourselves to believe it was built without some other means of collecting and conveying material than that possessed by the Indians." At the same time, he added, "But what other means could a lost race have had? The Indians had wooden spades, baskets, skins of animals, wooden and clay vessels, and textile fabrics; they also had stone implements…As a general rule the labor necessary to build them could not have exceeded that which has often been performed by Indians. It is also likely that all the people of a tribe, both men and women, aided in the work, and that the large works were built by additions made during successive generations." Continuing research on the mounds would support most of Thomas's conclusions.

In his book about the Archaic Earthworks of the Lower Mississippi Valley, Jon L. Gibson wrote that, "Radiocarbon assays reveal that the six known upper Louisiana Middle Archaic multi-mound complexes were erected successfully over a period of about seven and a half centuries." The six sites included mounds at the Contemporary Caney site, Frenchman's Bend, Watson Brake, the Hillman/Nolan Mounds, Hedgepath Mounds and Bush Mounds.

Thomas's observations about both Indian men and women being involved in construction of the mounds were later proven to be true. It appears that mound construction was more of a "community-wide project" than one built around a tribe, or tribes. Archaeologist Gibson, wrote that, "The Poverty Point culture is a prehistoric manifestation in the southern United States…that participates in the American Formative shift from Archaic band existence to a village-regional center-great ceremonial center complex." He went on to state, "Poverty Point's earthwork was not constructed in a single all-out effort by thousands of laborers…Individual mound stages, or in some cases entire mounds and rings/ring segments, were built rapidly…but the whole earthwork complex took about five centuries to complete."

We don't know how many generations of workers were involved in construction at Poverty Point, they could easily have been involved for 300 to 500 years, some ten to twenty generations. If so, major construction there possibly ended about 2700 years ago, around the time that Columbus and the other early European explorers and settlers were discovering the Americas. Data on Indian tribes, tribal locations, and tribal memberships from that period are very sparse, so it is just about impossible to accurately calculate how many Indians participated in construction and what tribes they were from. After 1492, what data there was about tribes and tribal populations generally came from White immigrant sources that arrived in 1492, or later, and is often of questionable accuracy.

Several published studies have provided estimates on the numbers of tribes that might have existed at one time or another. In his Atlas of the Indian Tribes of North America, Nicholas J. Santoro, author and archivist, lists 1,300 "separate" tribal names, and 30 different language families speaking 600 different dialects. In 500 Nations: An Illustrated History of North American Indians, Alvin M. Josephy, Jr., lists 600 distinct languages and 500 tribes. Population data for American Indians during the early periods vary greatly. In his American Indian Holocaust and Survival: A Population History Since 1492, Ethnologist Russell Thornton concluded that, "in the nineteenth century a considerable range was established for the size of the aboriginal population—from 500,000 for the United States to 16 million for North America. For Holocaust and Survival, Professor Thornton collected "Twentieth-Century Aboriginal population estimates" from fifteen reputable academic "scholars." They range from a low population of 8,400,000 to a high of 112,554,000. The range of populations can probably best be viewed most realistically as the inverse of the reliability of the data.
[Santoro, Nicholas J., Atlas of the Indian Tribes of North America, (New York: iUniverse, 2009), pp. vii-4; Josephy, Alvin M. Jr., 500 Nations: An Illustrated History of North American Indians, (New York: Alfred A. Knopf, 1994), pp. 8-9; Gibson, Jon L., Archaic Earthworks of the Lower Mississippi Valley: Interpretations from the Field, (Baton Rouge: Louisiana State University Press, 2019), pp. 11, 19, 33, 38; Thornton, Russell, American Holocaust and Survival: A Population History Since 1492, pp. 17-23.]

Sechin Bajo

Some of the early advanced cultures were not in North America, but in South America. In 2008, a combined German and Peruvian archaeological team announced that remnants of an ancient culture had been found at Sechin Bajo along the Pacific Coast in Peru. The ruins included a large, six-foot-tall platform built of rocks and adobe brick adjacent to a small circular plaza that was also built of rocks and adobe bricks. Nearby was a six-foot-tall frieze showing what has been interpreted as a "ritual knife or ceremonial cane in one hand and a human head or a shield in the other." Radiocarbon dating indicated that the plaza had been built about 5500 years ago; the frieze was about a hundred years older. Those dates meant, "the plaza and the frieze are the two oldest examples of monumental architecture discovered thus far in the Americas." In announcing the Radiocarbon dating results, National Geographic said that the site could also be the oldest urban site in the Americas.

["Oldest Urban Site in the Americas Found, Experts Claim," National Geographic News, February 26, 2008.]

Many years after Sechin Bajo was developed, around 3600 years ago, two other larger buildings were built over the original site, along with public squares, private areas, and many walls decorated with relief carvings. When those sites were abandoned, the area was used as a graveyard until the fifteenth century. This culture along the Sechin River Valley is usually referred to as the Casma/Sechin Culture, but it is not considered to have been an actual "civilization." Close, but no cigar. It has, however, been labeled as a "proto civilization," one of several that would exist in South and Central America. [Wikipedia-Sechin Bajo; Martin J. Dougherty, The Astec, Inca, and Maya Empires: The Illustrated History of the Ancient Peoples of Mesoamerica and South America (London: Amber Books, 2018), p. 21]

Sechin Bajo and other similar "cities and ceremonial centers were conquered about 3000 years ago, in 1000 BC, by invaders from the highlands. The purported invaders introduced maize, domesticated animals, warlike carvings, and different styles of ceramics and architecture. Many of those characteristics are associated with civilizations, although it has to be admitted that "experts" differ widely in what a civilization looks like. [Pozorski, Sheilia, and Thomas Pozorski, Early Settlement and Subsistence in the Casma Valley, (Iowa City: University of Iowa Press, 2006), pp. 127-131, and cited in Wikipedia, "Sechin Bajo."

The late V. Gordon Childe, of the University of Edinburgh and the Institute of Archaeology in London, wrote extensively on the

topic, and in 1950 he published a list of five primary characteristics and five secondary characteristics that could be used to identify a civilization. Childe's list of primary characteristics usually identifiable in communities that were civilizations included, a large, organized population, specialization of labor, collection and management of surplus production, a privileged ruling class of religious, political, and military functionaries, and a well-structured state political organization with membership based on residence instead of kinship. If a community had those five characteristics, it would also exhibit the following secondary characteristics: monumental public works, a long-distance trade network, monumental, symbolic artworks, written language, and science and engineering exhibited through the use of arithmetic, geometry, and astronomy.
[V. Gordon Childe, "The Urban Revolution," The Town Planning Review, Vol. 21, pp. 3-17, cited in Charles L. Redman, The Rise of Civilization, (San Francisco: W. H. Freeman and Company, 1978, p. 218.]

Defining what constitutes a civilization, compared to a community, culture, tribe, or clan that does not meet the standard, is one of those questions for which there is really no precise or specific answer, and it will seemingly always provide opportunities for academics to meet their "publish or perish" obligations by addressing the issue. Suffice it to say, if a large community has all, or most, of those characteristics, it is probably safe to label it as a civilization. Native American tribes or cultures were slow to meet the standards set forth by Professor Childe for several reasons: most were not densely populated, many were without hierarchical social classes, many were hunter-gatherer cultures, few constructed "monumental" public works projects, and most did not have a written language. Whether there was some unique benefit to members of a community that qualified as "civilized," rather than as a tribe or culture, is debatable. The historical record certainly broaches that question and there does not appear to be any clearcut answer even in late 2023 when we are in the midst of unbridled warfare between Jews and Palestinian adherents of the Hamas extremists that has impacted civilian populations of both Israel and Palestine. The behavior of both populations involved would be hard-pressed to be considered "civilized."

Nonetheless, Admiral Columbus and the other Europeans who found their ways to the Americas in his wake found an immense land occupied by cultures in almost unfathomably diverse stages of development.

Adena Culture

"Adena Culture" is one of numerous classifications used by archaeologists to categorize early cultures in the Americas, and it was the first "culture" identified. There is evidence that the people of the Adena Culture may have been the first mound builders. The Adena Culture was named after the "Adena" plantation at Chillicothe, Ohio, that had been owned by Thomas Worthington, Ohio's sixth governor. A mound located on the property had been "professionally excavated" by the state's Archaeological and Historical Society in 1900. After that, similar archaeological sites found in the area of Ohio, Indiana, Kentucky, West Virginia, and even into Pennsylvania were categorized as "Adena" to identify the common traits of the builders. Most of the sites were found along the major rivers in Ohio, including the Ohio, Miami, Kinnikinnick, and Scioto.

Researchers tell us that the Adena Culture, or the Adena Complex, existed in a time known as the Early Woodland period, from about 2800 years ago until about 1900 years ago. The Adena Culture refers to what were probably a number of related Native American societies that had all adopted the Adena burial practices and ceremonial system. Perhaps most significantly, the culture is known for its extensive trading network that stretched from the Great Lakes, where they acquired copper, to the Indigenous peoples of the Gulf Coasts of what are now Mississippi and Louisiana, who traded a variety of seashells that were used to make a variety of objects, such as spoons, beads, and other implements.
["Identifying Flint Artifacts/Early Woodland People". Retrieved 2008-09-12.; Silverberg, Robert, The Mound Builders, (New York: Graphic Society Ltd., 1968), pp. 76, 171-179.]

Lasting traces of Adena culture are still seen in the remains of their substantial earthworks. At one point, there were hundreds of the larger Adena mounds, but only a small number of the remains of the larger Adena earthen monuments still survive today. These mounds generally ranged in size from 20 feet (6.1 m) to 300 feet (91 m) in diameter and served as burial structures, ceremonial sites, historical markers, and probably gathering places for social activities or trade.

These earthen monuments were built using hundreds of thousands of baskets full of specially selected and graded earth. According to archaeological investigations, Adena earthworks were often built as part of their burial rituals, in which the earth of the earthwork was piled immediately atop a burned mortuary building. These mortuary buildings were intended to keep and maintain the dead until their final burial was performed. Before the construction of the earthworks, some utilitarian and grave goods would be placed on the floor of the structure, which was burned with the goods and honored dead within. The earthwork would then be constructed, and often a new mortuary structure would be placed atop the new earthwork." [wikipedia.org/wiki/Adena_culture.]

The Adena culture is frequently identified with members of the Anishinaabeg, Miami-Illinois, Shawnee, Kickapoo, Meskwaki, and Asakiwaki tribes who resided in the same areas and participated in the Adena traditions. The Adena Culture seems to have disappeared about 1900 years ago and it was followed almost immediately after its demise by the much larger Hopewell Culture that appeared about 2100 years ago, 200 years before the end of the Adena period, and lasted until around the year 500. In all likelihood, the Adena Culture was largely absorbed by the Hopewell Culture. [Wikipedia: Adena Culture]

The various mound-building cultures have been separately named, usually by their discoverers, the archaeologists that first reported on their existence, or the owner of the property on which they were found. Researchers have never been able to prove any direct descendancy between the various mound cultures, but they know that the cultures were definitely in contact with each other

through trade networks, a defining feature of the period. It would definitely be normal for members of one mound culture to informally "borrow" ideas from another mound culture and to apply them. The mound building practices employed by the Adena Culture are similar to those employed by Mexican Indians and some researchers believe that Mexicans who migrated north may have brought the tradition with them.
[Silverberg, Robert, The Mound Builders, (New York: Graphic Society Ltd., 1968), pp. 195-196.] Joseph, Frank, Advanced Civilizations of Prehistoric America: The Lost Kingdoms of the Adena, Hopewell, Mississippians, and Anasazi, (Rochester, Vermont: Bear & Company, 2010), pp. 10-63.]

Hopewell and Fort Ancient Cultures

The Hopewell Culture that seemed to replace the Adena Culture appeared around 2100 years ago. While the Adena Culture had been essentially a regional culture in what is now Ohio and portions of the states around Ohio, the Hopewell Culture, sometimes referred to rather appropriately as the Hopewell "tradition" or the Hopewell "exchange system," originated in Ohio and the surrounding area but grew to involve Indigenous people from the coasts of Florida and Louisiana north to the Great Lakes and northwest along the Rainy River into the Canadian provinces of northwestern Ontario and southeastern Manitoba. Participants in the culture in addition to those in Ohio were located in parts of what are now Florida, Georgia, Alabama, Louisiana, Texas, Oklahoma, Mississippi, West Virginia, Kansas, Michigan, Wisconsin, Indiana, Illinois, Iowa, Kansas, Pennsylvania, Iowa, North Dakota, South Dakota, Tennessee, Kentucky, Missouri, Arkansas, and New York, plus portions of Ontario and Manitoba in Canada—the heartland of North America. Most of the Hopewell concentrations were along major waterways that were important routes for the intensive trading that undoubtedly bound the participant groups together.

What Adena had been able to organize on a regional level, Hopewell accomplished in half of what would eventually become the United States. It is important to remember, however, that at the times of all these cultures that we have mentioned, all of the occupants of the Americas were Native Americans.

"Most of the items traded were exotic materials; they were delivered to peoples living in the major trading and manufacturing areas. These people converted the materials into products and exported them through local and regional exchange networks." [Wikipedia.org/wiki/Hopewell_tradition]

The inhabitants raised corn (maize) and possibly beans and squash but still relied upon hunting and fishing and the gathering of wild nuts, fruits, seeds, and roots. The amount of pottery and ornamental stonework and metalwork that has been found suggests some division of labor; moreover, the nature and size of the earthworks at many sites suggest that forms of public labor, whether voluntary or conscripted, may have been employed. The earthworks sometimes suggest defensive purposes, but more often they served as burial mounds or apparently formed the bases of temples or other structures.

Their best pottery was well made, with decoration applied by incised or stamped lines, often in naturalistic outlines. Even more notable were effigy pipes carved in stone and polished, representing birds, fish, and other animals. Their metalwork has been called the finest in pre-Columbian North America. Copper sheet was much used; some silver and meteoric iron, and occasionally gold, entered into various ornaments and utility pieces. Sheets of mica also characterize the culture.
[www.britannica.com-Hopewell Culture]

Like the Adena Culture, Hopewell settlements were stratified. In other words, members of the culture had different responsibilities to the culture as a whole. Many members were probably "specialists" who were good at performing certain functions—building mounds, hunting, trading, handling mortuary activities, farming, etc. Some individuals were also known "leaders," people able to get other members to agree with them on important issues. Some sociologists describe these individuals as "big men." They weren't "chiefs" who had the power to order members to perform certain duties, but they were definitely looked up to and probably had reputations as being good leaders. Based on the fact that their graves were almost always more elaborate and contained more valuable goods, it appears that hunters held a high status within the Hopewell settlements. Hunters were important people; they were relied upon to provide food for members of the community, particularly proteins. [Wikipedia.org/wiki-Hopewell Culture.]

About 1500 years ago, the Hopewell Culture went through a major and fairly rapid change. Mound construction, a hallmark of the culture and seemingly the central purpose of the community, ceased. The production of art objects and importations of exotic materials from often distant trading partners also declined dramatically. [Wikipedia.org/wiki-Hopewell Culture] At the same time, the bow and arrow were introduced. It is possible that improvements in hunting technology because of the new weapon stressed a food supply that was already stressed, maybe as the result of changes in weather conditions. It is also possible that the culture made the shift from hunter-gatherer-farmer society to an agrarian society organized largely around the production of maize. How exactly that might have affected the culture and its communities is unknown. Researchers have also indicated that around that time in the history of the Hopewell communities, they began to construct stockade walls, apparently to defend against attacks by their enemies. [www.livescience.com/58897_hopewell_culture.]

This might be a good time to remind readers, and myself, that the people we are talking about: Watson Brake, Norte Chico, Poverty Point, Hopewell, Adena, Olmec, Chimú, Sican, Moche, and any cultures that I might have forgotten, are American Indians! While these major cultures were developing, hundreds of other American Indian cultures, tribes, bands, and family groups were carving out lifestyles throughout the Americas. They fashioned lifestyles based on their own knowledge, the knowledge of the people they were traveling with, or people they came across in their travels, and the natural world in which they found themselves. Those who formed the sprawling Hopewell Culture, for example, had been in North America or South America for some 50 to 60 generations—12,000 to 15,000 years…or more. Most belonged to a tribal family, one of a thousand or more in the Americas, and they had carved out a homeland in which they were probably quite comfortable. We know very little about these Native Americans (All of the First Americans had died long ago.).

We also know very little about the languages spoken by the Siberians-Beringians-Alaskans who migrated into the Americas, or the unique languages that the various groups developed over the thousands of years that they were operating virtually independently. By the Hopewell period, there are reports that among the Native Americans there were speakers of the "Gulf" languages, the Caddoan, Siouan, and Iroquoian language families, the little-known languages of South Florida, and the Muskogean languages, along with four language isolates: Natchez, Tunica, Atakapa, and, possibly, Chitimacha. The actual list of all the languages spoken by the Native American tribes at that time would have been very much longer that what we have identified here. There could easily have been 1,000 tribes by the time of the Hopewell Culture, and they may well have spoken that many different dialects. Some that were from the same general areas may well have been able to understand each other to some extent, but most would not. [Wikipedia.org/wiki/Gulf_languages]

In the 15,000 years, or more, that passed after the relatively small groups of Siberians-Beringians-Alaskans moved south into North and South America, their numbers grew, potentially from a few hundreds of individuals to as many as 16 million in North America and as many as 112 million between North and South America. Spreading out across the Americas as they did, they gradually developed their own cultures—each of those cultures represented one of the tribes that existed at the end of the pre-Columbian period, or possibly even a group of associated tribes. By then the First Americans and the Native Americans had been spreading throughout the Western Hemisphere for around 15,000 years. That's 150 centuries! It's difficult for we humans to comprehend a period of time that long given that our life spans are seldom longer than 100 years, and there were periods in the past when the average life spans were much shorter. We really can't comprehend all that can happen in 15,000 years.

There had to have been considerable competition between the tribes at various times and in various locations—competition to control the best hunting or farming territories, competition to control limited resources, competition to increase the tribe's size, competition to dominate others, competition to demonstrate prowess in warfare, and so on. History has shown us that when competition existed between Native American tribes, it was not unusual for them to clash. Sometime those clashes were for show, counting coup or some other way in which one Indian could demonstrate to other Indians that he was a brave warrior, the goal of almost every male in most tribes. Other times, competition or conflicts led to serious warfare. The widespread construction of stockades around Hopewell settlements may indicate that hostilities existed between tribes in the region and that the probability those hostilities would lead to warfare was greater than zero.

In his authoritative study of warfare involving Indians, William M. Osborn included a chronological list of intertribal Indian wars that date back to the 1400s, based on the best available information. Unfortunately, little information is available prior to the arrival of Europeans in the 1400s and 1500s. Despite those limitations, Osborn's necessarily truncated list includes 235 tribe-on-tribe conflicts, beginning in the 1400s. That total does not accurately reflect the number of conflicts that occurred, however. His insertions in the 1400s and 1500s, for example, include entries like:

Some Indian villages in America were found to be palisaded or fenced, a sign of intensifying conflict;

Before 1492: There were "fierce intertribal conflicts: for several reasons, including fights over women, material possessions, hunting rights, plunder, adventure, revenge, and sometimes territory;

When Spanish explorer Hernán Cortés marched on the Aztec capital near Mexico City, he found "ever-warring" city-states in the empire;

Francisco Pizarro invaded Peru and found a civil war among the Incas;

Jacques Cartier sailed up the St. Lawrence River; the Algonquin tribes told him their Iroquois enemies had been driven out of that region several generations earlier;

The Iroquois invaded Algonquin territory before the settlers came. Many Algonquin lives were lost. The fighting continued after the settlers arrived;

The first explorers of the American coast and settlers as well found many Algonquin fighting one another and the Iroquois;

The Sioux were driven out of Minnesota and Wisconsin by the Chippewa; and the Sioux went west and took land from the Kiowa, Crows, Pawnee, and other tribes.
[Osborn, William M., The Wild Frontier: Atrocities During the American-Indian War from Jamestown Colony to Wounded Knee, (New York: Random House, 2000), pp. 281-291.]

About the year 1000, a progressive culture was developing on a hill above the Little Miami River, close to what is now the city of Lebanon in southern Ohio. Archaeologists believe that the site was originally built by Hopewellian people who had previously occupied the area. Generally referred to as the Fort Ancient Culture, it served people in numerous small farming communities in the Middle Ohio Valley and was thought to have been a ceremonial location, rather than as a military fort. Residents may have been responsible for introducing maize farming in the Ohio area. Perhaps the most enduring vestige of the Fort Ancient Culture is the nearby Great Serpent Mound, the country's largest effigy mound. [Wikipedia: Fort Ancient] As the result of conflicting Radiocarbon Dating results, there is some controversy over whether the colossal mound was built by the Fort Ancient people or the Adena Culture that previously occupied the area. [Wikipedia: Great Serpent Mound]

Mississippian Culture and Cahokia

About 200 years after the Hopewell Culture disintegrated, around 800 AD, or just over 1200 years before the present, another culture developed in the same basic area of the continent. Considerably larger than the culture it replaced, it does seem to have been greatly influenced by adherents of the Hopewell Culture that were still remembered. The Mississippian Culture was named for its central location along the Mississippi River Valley, and it included all or parts of the present states of Mississippi, Alabama, Georgia, Arkansas, Missouri, Kentucky, Illinois, Indiana, Ohio, Wisconsin, Wisconsin, and an area of the Great Plains to the west of Wisconsin.

While a major impetus for creation of both the Hopewell and Adena cultures had been development of a large trading system that improved the lifestyles of all involved; the communities participating in the Mississippian Culture were drawn together by their desire for a more complex, perhaps more rewarding, lifestyle. Trade was still extremely important, and the Mississippian trading network extended west to the Rocky Mountains, north to the Great Lakes, south to the Gulf of Mexico, and east to the Atlantic Ocean.

The thing we probably remember most about the Mississippian Culture, however, is the construction of the largest complex of earthwork pyramids, mounds, and platforms north of Mesoamerica. Many of those massive constructions still exist today and are visited by tens of thousands of tourists, most of whom are astonished by the sizes of the complexes, especially those around Cahokia, Illinois.

At one time there were more than two hundred packed-earth pyramids, or mounds, at Cahokia and its suburbs. More than half of these were built in a five-square-mile zone that was designed with reference to the four sacred directions and the upper and lower worlds. The pyramids were arranged around vast open plazas and were surrounded, in turn, by thousands of pole-and-thatch houses, temples, and public buildings. At its height, Cahokia had a population in excess of ten thousand, with at least twenty or thirty thousand more in the outlying towns and farming settlements that ranged for fifty miles in every direction…Centerpiece of Cahokia was "an open fifty-acre Grand Plaza, surrounded by packed-clay pyramids that was the size of thirty-five football fields."

The culture's agricultural system was based largely on the large-scale production of corn, or maize, that was capable of supporting larger populations than other agricultural or gathered products.

"For Cahokia's new government to work, some people must have accommodated it or been coerced by it. And since the latter is a costly short-term tactic, civilizations are almost always built on the formation of consensus or on ideologies that legitimize the rule of a few in the minds of the many." Political and social change happened quickly in Cahokia and throughout the culture, effected by visionaries who shaped events and influenced a group of people in a profound way. That influence spread to other areas at that time and to later cultures.
[Timothy R. Pauketat, Cahokia: Ancient America's Great City on the Mississippi, (New York: Penguin Books, 2009), pp. 2, 4, 7, 23.]

Many of the mounds at Cahokia covered burials. One of the small mounds, designated as Mound 72, was dug into by archaeologists in 1967. In the first year of digging, archaeologists found the spectacular "beaded burial" at the base of one end of the tumulus—the mound over the grave—two men-or at least their wrapped corpses—lying on the original (pre-mound) ground surface." One of the two corpses lay under a two-inch-thick layer of twenty thousand shell beads—more in one deposit than had ever been found before. Over the next four summers workers turned up pit after pit and tow after row of human skeletons in other parts of the mound. At the bottom of one pit were the "remains of fifty-three sacrificed women, forty-two of whom were young (most between the ages of fifteen and twenty-five). The fifty-third individual was an "elderly" (thirtyish) female," whom archaeologists thought of as "the matron," In a smaller nearby mound, referred to simply as Feature 229, archaeologists found a mass burial containing 16 males, 2 probably males, 3 females, 3 probable females, and 15 individuals of unknown sex. The average age of 26.2.

"Evidence of violence also distinguished these burials from the other mass graves. The individuals had been decapitated prior to being thrown into the pit and the heads were thrown in before the burials were covered. Another male appears to have been incompletely decapitated. The presence of two white chert (chipped stone) projectile points is also indicative of violence prior to interment. The broken tip of a point…lodged [in one body, and a] complete point…within the rib cage [of another]…could have resulted in immediate death…[or] could have been old wounds unrelated to the events leading to burial in the pit."

The archaeologists knew what they had discovered. There in the middle of North America, more than five centuries before European armies and diseases would arrive to take their own murderous toll, was evidence of large-scale acts of premeditated violence. Today, with newer theories in hand, the graphic violence seen in [the] accidental discoveries in Mound 72 has grown even more significant than it seemed at first.
[Pauketat, Timothy R., Cahokia, (New York: Penguin Books, 2009), pp. 72-77]

Aspects of the Mound 72 discoveries are also evocative of Mesoamerican customs and practices. Human sacrifice had occurred in North America before Cahokia…However, nowhere north of Mexico was their anything comparable to the scale of executions at Cahokia—4, 7, 19, 22, 24, 39, and 53 people at a time, on repeated occasions…The mortuary rites here were not done in secret. While Mound 72 sits at the southern end of the central city complex, over half a mile due south of Monk's Mound, the location is still highly visible. The hints of ramps to access the top of the various platform stages, and the clubbing to death of people in the open, not behind walls, also suggest staged public performances. This would be in keeping with practices of other Indian people. The sacrificial rites known from the Plains and South were all open, public affairs. These were not considered murders but formal public commemorations."
[Timothy R. Pauketat, Cahokia: Ancient America's Great City on the Mississippi, (New York: Penguin Books, 2009), pp. 80-81]

On the surface, it would seem that there are strong suggestions that the Cahokians, in building their vision into the landscape, drew on Mesoamerican models. "Their possible descendants or those of their allies or enemies practiced Mesoamerican-style human sacrifice, incorporated obelisk-like posts into their worship, relayed stories of superhuman men and women who wore distinctive garments and ear ornaments, used Mesoamerican-type flint daggers, and understood the cosmos in ways occasionally parallel to Mesoamerican notions."

"However, most archaeologists now believe that the Mississippian phenomenon as it emanated from Cahokia and its sister complexes was homegrown, and today's international border seems to have been an ancient boundary as well, stopping all but "beliefs and practices of a stylistic [aesthetic] sort." The only artifact found linking Mesoamerica and Cahokia is "a single, tiny chip of Mexican obsidian at the Spiro site in Oklahoma weighing only a little more than an ounce."
[Pauketat, Timothy R., Cahokia: Ancient America's Great City on the Mississippi, (New York: Penguin Books, 2009), pp. 7, 138, 141-142.]

The great expansion of Cahokia took place during what is referred to as the "Middle Mississippi Period," from 1200 to 1400, about a hundred years before Columbus. The Mississippian Culture was at its apex during that constructive, progressive 200-year period that saw a complex system of chiefdoms and religious-based art and symbolism spread through a large swath of what is now the central United States. Cahokia was the most populace city in North America at the time, although larger cities did exist in Mesoamerica and South America.

Things changed dramatically during the "Late Mississippian Period," from 1540 to about 1500, the hallmarks of which were "increasing warfare, political turmoil, and population movement." More defensive structures were built, often in conjunction with a downturn in the construction of mounds or large-scale ceremonial structures. By 1500, "the population of most areas had dispersed or were experiencing severe social stress." While the dramatic changes occurred at the same time that Europeans first visited the Americas, "scholars theorize drought and the reduction of maize agriculture, together with possible deforestation and overhunting by the concentrated populations, forced them to move away from major sites. [Wikipedia-Mississippian Culture]

Mississippian peoples were almost certainly ancestral to the majority of the American Indian nations living in this region in the historic era. The historic and modern day American Indian nations believed to have descended from the overarching Mississippian Culture include the Alabama, Apalachee, Caddo, Chickasaw, Catawba, Choctaw, Muscogee, Creek, Guale, Hitchiti, Ho-Chunk, Houma, Kansa, Missouria, Mobilian, Natchez, Osage, Quapaw, Seminole, Tunica-Biloxi, Yamasee and Yuchi.

By the time more documentary accounts were being written, such as those by Hernando de Soto following his expedition through the American South in 1539-1543, the Mississippian way of life had changed irrevocably. Some groups maintained an oral tradition link to their mound-building past, such as the late 19th century Cherokee. Other Native American groups, having migrated many hundreds of miles and lost their elders to diseases, did not know their ancestors had built the mounds that dotted the landscape. This contributed to the myth of the Mound Builders as a people distinct from Native Americans, which was rigorously debunked by mound expert Cyrus Thomas in 1894.
[Wikipedia.org-Mississippian Culture]

Not long ago, archaeologists with new techniques unraveled the tragedy of Cahokia. Despite there being substantial evidence of their power, Cahokia' rulers seem to have been setting themselves up for future trouble. By mining the forests upstream for firewood and floating the logs downriver to the city, they were removing ground cover and increasing the likelihood of catastrophic floods. When these came, as they later did, kings who gained their legitimacy from their claims to control the weather would face angry questions from their subjects.
[Charles C. Mann, 1491: New Revelations of the Americas Before Columbus, 2nd ed., (New York: Vintage Books, 2011), p. 29.

Olmec Civilization

The earliest known major Mesoamerican Civilization were the Olmecs who flourished in the period beginning about 3500 years ago and lasting until 400 AD, what is termed Mesoamerica's "formative period." The Olmecs were located in the tropical lowlands of the modern-day Mexican states of Vera Cruz and Tabasco and evolved from earlier cultures in the surrounding area. "The Olmecs, as we call

them, left behind no written records. What is known of them comes from archaeological evidence or secondary sources, such as other, later cultures. Even the name we give them comes from outside their culture. It is an Aztec word meaning 'rubber people,' referring to their use of rubber for a number of purposes, including the creation of balls for the ceremonial ball game.
[Martin J.Dougherty, The Aztec, Inca, & Maya Empires, (London: Amber Books, 2018), pp. 50-59.]

The Olmec civilization seems to have been the first Mesoamerican civilization, beginning around 1600–1400 BC and ending around 400 BC. Mesoamerica is considered one of the six sites around the globe in which civilization developed independently and indigenously. This civilization is considered the "mother culture" of the Mesoamerican civilizations. The Mesoamerican calendar, numeral system, writing, and much of the Mesoamerican pantheon seem to have begun with the Olmec.
[Mann, Charles M., 1491: New Revelations of the Americas Before Columbus, 2nd ed., (New York: Random Books, 2011), p. 236.]

The Olmec's distinctive style of art can be traced to 1500 BC, or 3500 before the present. The culture then is contemporary with ancient Egypt, Babylonia, the earliest civilization in China, and they could have known people from the Watson Brake and Poverty Point cultures along the lower Mississippi and Gulf Coast of Louisiana, of at least heard that those cultures existed.

It appears that the Olmec developed ritualistic bloodletting, the ballgame played with a rubber ball, and their artwork, especially their stone-carved "colossal heads."

The Olmec population dropped dramatically between 400 and 350 BCE, about 2400 to 3350 years ago, although a few Olmec remained in the area into the 19th century. Archaeologists believe the population decline was the result of serious environmental changes that rendered the region unsuited to human habitation by the large group of Olmec farmers. Damaging changes may have occurred to the riverine system the Olmec depended on for agriculture, hunting and gathering, and transportation.

The Olmec religion was based on reverence for elements of the natural world. Among the animals revered were powerful animals like eagles, sharks, and jaguars, the most revered of all.

The oldest known Olmec site is San Lorenzo, which dated to 1200 BC, or about 3200 years ago. It was built on a natural plateau that was modified with earthworks. It was destroyed and abandoned about 900 BC and its large carved stone monuments were defaced, toppled over, and buried. Nobody knows who went to such an extent to wipe out traces of the Olmec Culture. The smallest of the heads weighed six tons; the largest were in the 40-50-ton range. Archaeologists have never figured out how the Olmec moved the heads. They had no wheeled vehicles and no beasts of burden that would have been capable of moving the massive stone. It was a challenge similar to the challenge the Egyptians faced in moving stone blocks for construction of the pyramids, or residents of Easter Island moving their massive stone heads, or the British moving the heavy stones for Stonehenge. Where there's a will, there's a way!

Between 800 and 400 BCE, the town of LaVenta, located on a swamp island about 40 miles away, replaced San Lorenzo and became the center of the Olmec civilization. The Olmec culture went into decline after about 400 BC and was soon replaced by other cultures. Like San Lorenzo, LaVenta was destroyed around 350 BC, ending what one historian describes as "one of the most exciting times in American history." Mann, p. 239. The cause of the precipitous decline has never been determined with any certainty. The possibilities include conflict, always a possibility; climatic changes, also always a possibility; ash from active volcanoes could have irreparably harmed their ability to farm and feed their residents; or civil unrest resulting from a long list of potential problems could have caused strife.

Maya Civilization

Cultures and civilizations developed, they flourished, and they disappeared…then there were the Maya! The Maya Civilization emerged around 750 BC, or about 2770 years ago and the civilization survived until 1697 AD, a continuous reign of about 2450 years, including having survived for a little over 200 years of the post-

Columbian period of European invasions. The unique civilization included what are today southeastern Mexico, all of Guatemala and Belize, and the western portions of Honduras and El Salvador. It also includes the northern lowlands of the Yucatán Peninsula and the highlands of the Sierra Madre, the Mexican state of Chiapas, southern Guatemala, El Salvador, and the southern lowlands of the Pacific littoral plain. "Maya" is a modern term used to refer collectively to the various peoples that inhabited the area. They did not call themselves "Maya," however, and did not have a sense of common identity or political unity.

Today, Mayan descendants number more than 6,000,000 individuals who speak more than 28 surviving Mayan languages. They reside in nearly the same areas as their ancestors. [Wikipedia: Maya Civilization] Remember, until sometime after 1492, they were all American Indians and the descendants of the First Americans. Forming a unified civilization would have been the equivalent of uniting as many as 28 different tribes spread over a large area under a common ruler, even though they didn't speak the same language.

The Mayan civilization was agrarian, cultivating crops that were staples in the diet of residents, including maize, beans, squashes, and chili peppers. The successful agricultural economy supported the construction of monumental architecture, particularly large temple pyramids with elaborate facades. Around 300 BC, the Maya also created a complicated system of hieroglyphic writing that has still not been completely translated. Eventually, the numerous city-states were linked by a complex trade network similar to that of the Hopewell and Mississippian cultures in North America north of what is now Mexico, but the city-states were governed separately and there was never a single ruler of the Mayan empire.

The beginnings of the written Mayan language possibly dated back as far as 750 BC, but the oldest surviving examples are from around 250 BC. Glyphs used were complex, sometimes representing syllables, some whole words, and others used for concepts, names of places, and gods. The writing could be carved into stonework or written on things like bark. The written version was probably based on "classic Mayan," used by officials and possibly some merchants, but not spoken by most people. That didn't make much difference, because most people never mastered the complexities of the glyphs.

The Maya writing system is considered by archaeologists to be the most sophisticated system ever developed in Mesoamerica. The Maya wrote using 800 individual signs or glyphs, paired in columns that read together from left to right and top to bottom. Maya glyphs represented words or syllables that could be combined to form any word or concept in the Mayan language, including numbers, time periods, royal names, titles, dynastic events, and the names of gods, scribes, sculptors, objects, buildings, places, and food. Hieroglyphic inscriptions were either carved in stone and wood on Maya monuments and architecture, or painted on paper, plaster walls and pottery.

Mayan culture was stratified with upper echelons that included military leaders, religious leaders, and middle-class officials that included warriors, merchants, engineers, administrators and other civic officials. Below that level were agricultural and unskilled workers who had somehow worked their way into the middle class. Ordinary citizens made up the bottom ranks of the stratification and included construction workers, maintenance people, and agriculture workers and hunters. "By about 300 BC, the Mayan social order was well established, along with the concept of hereditary positions." It was around that time that the first massive construction projects were undertaken, including Mayan pyramids. Most pyramids served as temples, but some were burial places for kings. Each temple had a variety of flat areas that were used for ceremonies and sacrifices.

The Mayans believed that there were nine levels to the underworld, where most people went after death. Many evil gods lived in the underworld, and they occasionally got out and caused trouble. The underworld was also a place of raging rivers, rivers of blood, monsters, jagged mountains, and sharp obsidian blades that would attack those who traveled within the underworld.

To help deceased friends and family members to negotiate the underworld, funeral goods of a useful sort, like tools, could be provided. Other funeral goods included food, or sometimes a real or representational dog. The only way to avoid the underworld was to be sacrificed, die in childbirth, or get killed while working on a temple.

Maya, of course, are infamous for their human sacrifices. Disemboweling or cutting out the heart was often used to dispatch captives taken during wars. Many times, the individual being sacrificed was pushed off the top of the temple pyramid by the priests. Captive soldiers were often required to play the Mayan "ball game." Sometimes, the members of the winning team were pardoned, but more often than not both losers and winners were sacrificed afterward, usually by beheading.

During the period from 250 AD to around 900 AD, Mayan city states frequently warred with each other and with non-Mayan opponents. War was frequently on a limited basis with less bloodshed and more negotiations between the parties over the tributes to be paid to the winning army. "The best-documented war between Mayan cities took place between the cities of Calakmul and Tikal, culminating in the defeat of Tikal in 562 AD and the capture of the king of Tikal. He was taken to the city of Caracol in modern Belize and "treated as an honored guest…until his sacrifice to the gods."

The demise of the Mayan civilization took place over a prolonged period of about 150 years. Depopulation was common and there were cases when all the cities in a region were abandoned at the same time. Martin J. Dougherty, author of The Aztec, Inca & Maya Empires, feels that the most likely explanation for the collapse was a downward spiral resulting from conflict, social unrest, and natural conditions. As a result, he posits, the population lost confidence in their leaders and warfare became more common. Soil exhaustion is also known that have been a problem in the primarily agricultural culture, the result of the intensive farming that was need to support the population. Warfare also became more savage, often leading to the total destruction of cities. There were problems of drought, earthquakes, and plagues that took tolls on the population, but those had been experienced before without leading to destruction or depopulation.

The final factor, according to Dougherty, seems to have been "disaffection among the general populace…Total collapse of the social order followed and with it any chance of weathering the hard years."

By the time the first Spanish explorers arrived in the region, there was no organized Mayan state to oppose them. Mayapan, the last great Mayan city, was destroyed around 1450 AD, possibly due to an epidemic or natural disaster. Its destruction marked the end of the longest-lived Pre-Columbian culture.
[Martin J. Dougherty, The Aztex, Inca, & Maya Empires, (London: Ambor Books, 2018), pp. 81-123.]

Inca Empire

About a century after the rise of the Mississippian Culture in what is now east-central North America, a civilization rose to power in Mesoamerica, filling the void created by the failure of the previous Olmec, Zapotec, and Teotihuacán cultures, most often by civil unrest within the cultures or conquest from outside. Between 1100 and 1200 AD, 800-900 before the present, the Killke "tribe" founded Cusco in the southeast region of what is now Peru. Historian and author Martin Dougherty described the Killke as "an indigenous tribe" and spoke of Cusco as a "kingdom" and "proto-state" that developed as the Sican and Wuari cultures went into decline. Around 1100 AD, the Killke began construction of massive cut and dressed stone structure, called Sacsayhuamán, that appears to have been designed and built to function both as a fortress and religious center. It seems that during the lengthy construction process, the Killke were somehow displaced by the Inca and, as a result, Cusco became the capital of the empire of the Inca, although exactly how and why that transformation occurred is still the subject of discussion and debate.

[Martin J. Dougherty, The Aztec, Inca & Maya Empires, (London: Amber Books, 2018), p. 125.]

The Inca Empire was based on a "labor tax." The "tax" required every able person between 15 and 20 to take a turn at working for the government administration. Most of the tax "volunteers" were engaged on major civic construction projects, like building roads or great monuments. Some were even assigned to work in the farm fields of families whose working-age members were assigned to other tasks or were sick or had been killed by war.

Most Incan families farmed, including even those who had a skill or craft that they worked at. The were subsistence farmers, however, and to maximize production the government allocated the available lands and organized planting and harvesting. The diet was largely vegetarian, although some seafood was acquired from the coastal areas and people in the highlands raised llamas for their meat or hunted wild llamas."

The importance of having sufficient food to satisfy the needs of the Incans was well understood by the empire's leaders and they had many rituals that were intended to ensure good harvests. Each year, the emperor personally prepared a maize field using a golden plow. A full-size golden replica of a maize field was also displayed in the great temple at Cusco. Because arable land was at a premium in the mountainous territory, government projects terraced slopes and drained wetlands. Despite these tactics, raising enough food was a challenge and government officials knew it was imperative to maintain the stability of the empire.

In the early 1400s, the Cusco region had been dominated by the Chanka people, who were extremely warlike and prone to great savagery toward captives. In 1438, their army marched against Cusco with the intent of capturing it. Initially, it seemed as though the people of the city wouldn't be able to resist, but Prince Yupanqui, inspired by a vision from the sun god, called for assistance from all the surrounding friendly states. "According to legend, the gods turned large stones into powerful warriors" and they helped the Inca to defeat their enemy. Yupanqui led a force to drive the Chanka our of the Cusco Valley and confiscate all of their holdings. He then became emperor, taking the title of Pachacuti Inca Yupanqui, usually shortened to Pachacuti, which meant either "world-shaker" or "reverser of the world." Pachacuti continued to lead the Incan army and successfully conquered a large region around Lake Titicaca, expanding the Incan's Empire.

Pachacuti's priority then shifted to the construction of new palaces and temples throughout his empire, replacing existing structures of soil with durable cut stone that would last for many centuries. "Since religion and political power were intertwined in Inca society, many of the new structures are referred to as temple-fortresses. It is not always clear whether they were primarily a religious building with a good set of defenses or a fort that contained a temple. In practice, the distinction may be meaningless; to the Inca they were the empire's strong places in both the mundane and the spiritual world." [Martin J. Dougherty, The Aztec, Inca & Maya Empires, pp. 139-165.]

Pachacuti's empire was unique in many ways. It lacked many of the features that might normally be associated with civilizations in the Pre-Columbian world. Anthropologist Gordon McEwan, author of The Middle Horizon in the Valley of Cuzco, wrote: "They were isolated in a forbidding landscape and lacking in what many would consider some essential components of progress (writing, iron, the wheel, trading markets). Yet the Incas created one of the most. influential and innovative empires the world has ever seen, demonstrating an astonishing mastery of engineering, mathematics, astronomy, agriculture, medicine, politics, and more...Notable features of the Inca Empire included its monumental architecture, especially stonework, extensive road network reaching all corners of the empire, finely-woven textiles, used of knotted strings (quipu) for record-keeping and communication, agricultural innovations and production in a difficult environment, and the organization and management fostered or imposed on its people and their labor." [Gordon F. McEwan, The Incas, (Santa Barbara, CA: ABC-CLIO, 2006, and www.Google.com – Gordon F. McEwan.]

"Pachacuti died in 1471, plunging the empire into a year of mourning that was ended with an empire-wide celebration that included many sacrifices. Several hundred llamas and a large number of children were sacrificed at places the emperor had visited." Pachacuti's carefully mummified body was occasionally displayed to the public during the period of mourning. (The mummified body was found by the Spanish when they conquered the area and it was destroyed.)

Mummification was used throughout the Andes, although it was not a universal practice. "Early cultures used alcohol and/or salt as preservatives, removing flesh and fluids to reduce decay. For the Incas, living at high altitudes with cold and dry conditions, freeze-drying was a viable option," with the mummy wrapped in cloth and tied into a fetal position with cords.

When rulers were mummified, their organs were removed and their skin was treated to keep them as lifelike as possible. The remains of the influential people were brought out of the burial places from time to time so that they could be consulted on state matters and to take part in rituals. They were ritually fed at those time. The mummies of children sacrificed acted as intermediaries between humans and the gods and were believed to be helpful in ensuring a successful growing season and a good harvest. [Martin J. Dougherty, The Aztec, Inca & Maya Empires, p. 147]

Incan military forces functioned to both protect and expand the empire. All men between the ages of 20 and 50 could be drafted into military service on a rotating basis, ensuring that empire's large military forces would be always well-manned. "Although this system allowed large numbers to be raised, it did not produce a particularly effective fighting force…the warriors themselves were not trained professionals. Inca men were not entirely untutored in the arts of war, however. They would receive some instruction with common weapons in their youth and might take part in ritualized combat from time to time. [Martin J. Dougherty, The Aztec, Inca & Maya Empires, pp. 139-165.]

In the fall of 1532, the army was fresh from perhaps its largest victory ever, having put down a bloody civil war that threatened the throne of the empire. As many as 80,000 of the emperor's valiant forces celebrated their enormous victory by parading through Cusco. It was during their victory parades that "they learned that pale, hairy people who sat on enormous animals had landed on the coast." The "pale, hairy people," of course, were the Spanish Conquistadors. [Charles C. Mann, 1491, 2nd ed., (New York: Vintage Books, 2011), p. 91.]

Iroquois Confederation

Most American Indian tribes, particularly those in North America, did not rise to the developmental level of "civilization," like the Maya or Inca, given the divergent standards attached to the classification through the eighteenth and nineteenth centuries. The possible exceptions were the five or six tribes of the "Iroquois Confederacy" or "Iroquois League" that first emerged in the mid-1400s in what now upstate and western New York State. They refer to themselves as the Haudenosaunee, or "People of the Longhouse." The original five member tribes of the Confederacy included the following:

Mohawk – "People of the Flint"

Oneida – "People of the Standing Stone"

Onondaga – "People of the Hills"

Cayuga – "People of the Great Swamp"

Seneca – "People of the Great Hills

In 1722, the Tuscarora—"People of the Shirt"—joined the Confederacy as its sixth member.

The Iroquois Confederation is sometimes described as "one of the world's oldest participatory democracies," and, some will argue, a model for the United States Constitution. In 1744, Canasatego, leader of the Onondaga nation and spokesman for the Iroquois Confederation, advised the British colonists: "…We heartily recommend Union and a Good Agreement between you, our Brethren. Our wise Forefathers established Union and Amity between the Five Nations; this has made us formidable; this has given us great weight and Authority with our Neighboring Nations. We are a Powerful confederacy, and by your observing the same Methods our wise Forefathers have taken, you will acquire fresh Strength and Power…Those who support the theory that the First Peoples influenced the drafting of the founding documents point to the words of founders such as Benjamin Franklin, who in 1751 wrote to his printer colleague James Parker that "It would be a strange thing if Six Nations of ignorant savages should be capable of forming a scheme for such an union, and be able to execute it in such a manner as that it has subsisted ages and appears indissoluble; and yet that a like union should be impracticable for ten or a dozen English colonies." [Wikipedia: "Iroquois and the Founding Fathers."]

While the Confederacy was obviously taken into consideration by at least some of this country's founding fathers, most historians, political scientists, and other scholars seem to downplay the impact. For example, the late Elizabeth Tooker, a professor and anthropology at Temple University and editor of the three volume Iroquois Sourcebook, has said that "it was unlikely the U.S. founding fathers were inspired by the Confederacy, as it bears little resemblance to the system of governance adopted in the United States. For example, it is based on inherited rather than elected leadership, selected by female members of the tribes, consensus decision-making regardless of the population size of the tribes, and a single group capable of bringing matters before the legislative body."
[Wikipedia: Haudenosaune, as found in Mayson Kirby, History of Civilization, p. 235.]

The Iroquois Confederacy was a unique and enduring form of government for the tribes who belonged to it. "The significance of this collaboration was not only to retain power, but also to prevent conflict between their respective groups. Each group had its own area of jurisdiction and its own culture and way of life." While, eliminating war between the six tribes was one of the key aspects of the Confederacy, it did nothing to limit war with other non-Confederacy tribes and the Iroquois were almost constantly at war with other tribes from what is now New York State down the Ohio River Valley, all the way to the western Great Lakes, and north into what is now the Province of Ontario, but which was part of New France until 1763. [Sam Bleiweis, "The Downfall of the Iroquois," Emory Endeavors in History, 2013, pp. 84-99]

This appears to be an opportune and meaningful time to remind readers that the people we are talking about: Hopewell, Adena, Olmec, Chimú, Wari, Sican, Nazca, Moche, Chavin, Norte Chico, Poverty Point, Sechin Bajo, Watson Brake, Inca, Maya, and numerous other cultures and tribal groups that haven't been mentioned, are all American Indians! They were here first, as far as we know they were alone, and they built the thousands of mounds!

However, that fact regarding the mounds was not readily accepted by most Americans until sometime after the 1890s. It is an amazing, maybe startling, certainly hard to believe fact that with literally thousands of mounds built throughout the Indian lands of the Americas, most White Americans simply could not believe that Indians had the capacities to construct them. "Who built all the incredible mounds?" "Well, anyone but the Indians," would probably have been the most common response.

In fact, another answer to the question would probably have been, "anyone but the Indians." For example, William Henry Harrison, a future president of the United States, published several widely accepted "scientific" studies in which he claimed that the Aztecs were the mound builders. Edward Everett, former governor of Massachusetts, wrote "scientific papers" claiming that "the land was once the province of a lost white race" and they had built the pyramids. That became one of the most popular explanations—the mounds were built by White people from Europe. The Democratic Party latched onto Everett's explanation and adopted the position that a "lost race or White people" had done the incredible building. Highly respected Indian Agent William Walker, voiced the opinion that the area around the Great Lakes had once been occupied the Aztecs, sometimes referred to as Tartars or Hebrews, and they built all the mounds…then disappeared. Newspapers around the country seem to have been convinced that the mounds had been built by a lost race of White people, and that opinion was widely shared by "clerics of every stripe."

Those disparate explanations, most with strong racial roots, were not strongly rejected for many years. In 1882, for example, in 1882, "the greatest American geologist of the era, Alexander Winchell of the University of Michigan," strongly endorsed a book that claimed, "The most plausible solution of all…is the admission of an antediluvian and high civilized people living in Atlantis." There was no longer any doubt about it, the White residents of Atlantis were the architects and builders of the mounds.

[Colavito, Jason, The Mound Builder Myth: Fake History and the Hunt For A 'Lost White Race,' (Norman: University of Oklahoma Press, 2020), pp. 178-284, with quotes about Atlantis from John T. Short's, The North Americans of Antiquity, (New York: Harper & Brothers, 1889), p. 197.]

Americans, including most members of the country's growing "scientific community," didn't begin to strongly move off their "lost White race" explanation until Cyrus Thomas, head of the Smithsonian's Mound Exploration Division, completed an intensive ten-year study of the country's mounds and he and his staff issued a voluminous report with definitive, irrefutable evidence that the mounds in America had been built by our American Indians. It has been "settled history" since then.

CHAPTER 15

AMERICAN INDIAN TRIBES

> What is little understood even today, however, is that almost every community in Canada, the UnitedStates, and Mexico was once an Indian community, and those communities before the arrival of the Whiteswere part of hundreds of unique Indian nations that blanketed the entire continent.
>
> **—Alvin M. Josephy, Jr.**
> 500 Nations

While the unique cultures, civilizations, even an "empire" were developing, hundreds of other American Indian tribes, bands, nations, pueblos, villages, and family groups were trying to carve out lifestyles throughout the balance of the Americas.

Probably most commonly referred to as "Indian tribes," our knowledge of these groups of varying sizes that arrived long before Columbus is extremely limited. We don't even have a good handle on how many tribes, or how many individuals, there might have been.

They fashioned lifestyles based on their own knowledge, the knowledge of the people they were traveling with, or people they came across in their travels, the natural world in which they found themselves, and the skills, abilities, and desires of those in their group. Most belonged to a tribal family, one of many hundreds that existed in the Americas, and most had carved out a homeland in which they were probably quite comfortable. Some of the tribes were quite large, while others were little more than small family groups. Some, like those who eventually formed the sprawling Hopewell

Culture, for example, had already been in North America or South America for some 50 to 60 generations—12,000 to 15,000 years…or more…and they were large, creative, and powerful.

We really know very little about these thousands of Native Americans that lived in the Americas during the long pre-Columbian period. Most of what we know has come to us from the oral histories of tribes or from the discoveries and interpretations of generations of archaeologists. Demographers tell us that there could have been between 8.5 million and 112.5 million Indians living in the Americas at that time. We also know very little about the languages spoken by the Siberians-Beringians-Alaskans who migrated into the Americas, or the unique languages that the various groups developed over the thousands of years that they were operating virtually independently. By the Hopewell period, there are reports that among the Native Americans there were speakers of the "Gulf" languages, the Caddoan, Siouan, and Iroquoian language families, the little-known languages of South Florida, and the Muskogean languages, along with four language isolates: Natchez, Tunica, Atakapa, and, possibly, Chitimacha.
[Wikipedia.org/wiki/Gulf_languages]

The actual list of all the languages spoken by the Native American tribes at that time would have been very much longer that what we have identified here. There could easily have been 1,000 tribes by the time of the Hopewell Culture, and they may well have spoken that many different languages and dialects. Some that were from the same general areas may well have been able to understand each other to some extent, but most would not.

In the 15,000 years, or more, that passed since the relatively small groups of Siberians-Beringians-Alaskans moved south into North and South America, their numbers grew, potentially from a few hundreds of individuals to as many as 16 million in North America and as many as 112 million between North and South America. Spreading out across the Americas as they did, they gradually developed their own cultures—each of those cultures represented one of the tribes that existed at the end of the pre-Columbian period, or possibly even a group of associated tribes. By then the First

Americans and the Native Americans born after they arrived in the Americas had been spreading throughout the Western Hemisphere for around 15,000 years. That's 150 centuries! It's difficult for we humans to comprehend a period of time that long given that our life spans are seldom longer than 100 years and there were periods in the past when the average life spans were much shorter than that. We can't comprehend all that can happen in 15,000 years.

There had to have been considerable competition between the tribes at various times and in various locations—competition to control the best hunting or farming territories, competition to control limited resources, competition to increase the tribe's size, competition to dominate others, competition to demonstrate prowess in warfare, and so on. History has shown us that when competition existed between Native American tribes, it was not unusual for them to clash. Sometime those clashes were for show, counting coup or some other way in which one Indian could demonstrate to other Indians that he was a brave warrior, the goal of almost every male in most tribes. Other times, competition or conflicts led to serious warfare. The widespread construction of stockades around Hopewell settlements may indicate that hostilities existed between tribes in the region and that the probability those hostilities would lead to warfare was greater than zero.

In his authoritative The Wild Frontier: Atrocities During the American-Indian War from Jamestown Colony to Wounded Knee, William M. Osborn included a chronological list of intertribal Indian wars that date back to the 1400s, based on the best available information. Unfortunately, little information is available prior to the arrival of Europeans in the 1400s and 1500s. Despite those limitations, Osborn's necessarily truncated list includes 235 tribe-on-tribe conflicts, beginning in the 1400s. That total does not accurately reflect the number of conflicts that occurred, however. His insertions in the 1400s and 1500s, for example, include entries like:

Some Indian villages in America were found to be palisaded or fenced, a sign of intensifying conflict;' before 1492: There were "fierce intertribal conflicts: for several reasons, including fights over women, material possessions, hunting rights, plunder, adventure, revenge, and sometimes territory; when Spanish explorer Hernán Cortés marched on the Aztec capital near Mexico City, he found “ever-warring” city-states in the empire; Francisco Pizarro invaded Peru and found a civil war among the Incas; Jacques Cartier sailed up the St. Lawrence River. The Algonquin tribes told him their Iroquois enemies had been driven out of that region several generations earlier; The Iroquois invaded Algonquin territory before the settlers came. Many Algonquin lives were lost. The fighting continued after the settlers arrived; The first explorers of the American coast and settlers as well found many Algonquin fighting one another and the Iroquois; The Sioux were driven out of Minnesota and Wisconsin by the Chippewa; and the Sioux went west and took land from the Kiowa, Crows, Pawnee, and other tribes.

CHAPTER 16

AMERICAN INDIANS MEET EUROPEANS

> Indigenous peoples have not been hapless uncivilized societies, recoiling the face of progress, as much of Western writing claimed before the 1960s. Nor has the encounter between newcomers and the indigenous cultures been characterized by malicious domination, and intentional destruction, as much of the writing after the 1960s has suggested. History is a more complex, messy, and multi-directional process than either argument would suggest.
>
> **—Ken S. Coates**
>
> A Global History of Indigenous People

From the time that the Siberian-Beringian-Alaskan people first entered what is known now as North America and South America, they seem to have had the incomprehensible vastness of the Western Hemisphere to themselves, shared only with what must have been an astonishing assortment of wildlife in staggering sizes and numbers, towering virgin forests, mighty rivers, and grassy plains that probably seemed to go on forever.

Depending on when they arrived, they might even have experienced the first warm weather of their lives. It would have been a dramatically different life for people who had just escaped what must have seemed like a permanently icebound world, probably the only environment they and their ancestors back hundreds of generations had ever known. One question worth asking is, "why would they even have thought that there was someplace better to live?" Were there cultural memories of a time before the Ice Age when their lands weren't covered with snow and ice and there were periods of the year when their homeland was largely green, things could be grown in the soil, and the light coming from the sun was warm, maybe even hot? Both DNA analysis and historical weather studies suggest that there would have been some warmer weather in their ancient past.

The transition from the polar climate zone into a temperate weather zone would obviously have represented a dramatic, and probably a pleasant change, for the travelers from the far north. And, if they walked far enough to the south, as many did, they would probably have experienced some subtropical or tropical weather conditions that would have required a lifestyle and wardrobe change. By then, they would have transitioned, unknowingly, from "Beringians" to "First Americans." As far as we can tell, virtually nobody knew that the Americas and the Western Hemisphere even existed—not the future First Americans stranded as they were in Beringia, not the people in Siberia where their families had come from, and not the people in Europe who would someday struggle with the American Indians to see who would rule the New World.

Over the 10,000 years, or more, that the First Americans considered the Americas to be their new homeland, they separated into hundreds of groups, maybe as many as a thousand, or more. Mile after mile, year after year, and generation after generation, the groups changed, and they differentiated. Groups—families, clans, tribes, etc., formed…and split. They settled in an area…and they moved. In time, they were scattered throughout most of the habitable areas of the Americas. Why they split and why they moved during the long pre-Columbian period is a mystery. Splitting up and moving to new locations must have been a continuous, ongoing process over 10,000 to 12,000 years for the entirety of the Americas to be even lightly settled. Some groups probably found permanent homes early on; for others it may have taken thousands of years before they found a site that suited them…or that they could defend. We just don't know.

Based on post-Columbian American Indian history, also "Native American history," we do have some pretty good ideas of why tribes have moved around in the post-Columbian era. Considerations included factors like security, pressure from other tribes, adequacy of water supply, availability of adequate game and other foodstuffs, weather conditions, "spiritual direction," curiosity, and government action. They are the reasons that Indian groups moved around during the historical period when there was a chance that some accurate record of the move might have been made. Many of those same factors were probably also the catalysts for earlier tribal movements, even dating back thousands of years, even back to the day when they decided to leave their homes in Asia. Interestingly, they were largely the same factors that would be responsible for many of the Indian movements in the years after 1776 when the Indians found themselves occupying lands in the United States of America.

Information about movements that predated written records would only be "recorded" in the oral histories of the tribes; possibly represented in petroglyphs or pictographs that may, or may not, be decipherable; or noted in a tribal "winter count" or some other mnemonic device that was intended to aid in the recall of past tribal events. "Winter Counts" were commonly used by tribes on the northern Great Plains. The "count" was kept on a large animal skin, probably bison at first, but more recently deer hide, caribou hide, or some other large animal hide, muslin, linen, or paper have all been used. Each year is represented on the skin by a painted symbol, usually agreed upon by tribal leaders. Some tribes added two symbols each year, one during the winter and one during the summer. The accurate interpretation of symbols used on the winter counts is highly dependent on the "keeper" of the winter count who had supposedly memorized the meaning of each symbol. That knowledge is passed from one keeper to another to maintain the oral history recorded on the winter count.
[Wikipedia/wiki/Winter_count.]

After regular contact commenced between Europeans and American Indians beginning with Admiral Columbus in 1492, many tribal actions were recorded in written form by Whites—explorers, traders, missionaries, Indian agents, military personnel, settlers, and so on. Their written impressions were not always accurate, however. They reflected the settler's understanding of events, which were easily misunderstood, and just as easily distorted, often to make the settlers “look good” and the Indians to “look bad.”

Even oral communications between Whites and Indians were filtered through the use of translators, almost always Whites, well into the nineteenth century. Many of the translators were only marginally qualified to translate what were often critical, detailed, complicated communications, the thorough understanding of which could make a difference between war or peace, life or death. I believe it is safe to say that on many instances, the views of the American Indians were probably not accurately communicated. The same can be said for the translation of the comments of White military leaders or traders when their translator was French or Spanish and only marginally fluent in English, which were common situations on the American frontier.

To some extent, our knowledge of early interactions with the country’s American Indians is based on reports in government documents, newspapers, and books—especially non-fiction ones—and firsthand accounts that are tainted by erroneous, often anti-Indian information. Frequently, there may not even have been a malicious intent on the part of those involved, it is just that the records available were distorted and it was difficult, if not impossible, to correct errors and distortions.

While Columbus didn’t really “discover” the hemisphere or “America,” his visits, and there were four of them, opened floodgates between the Americas and Europe, referred to today as the “Columbian Exchange.” After 1492, that led to widespread exploration, trade, migrations, and settlement of the Americas, almost exclusively by Europeans during the early years.

While the Native Americans in what are now Nova Scotia, Prince Edward Island, Newfoundland, New Brunswick, Quebec, Labrador, and the eastern regions of the St. Lawrence River, as well as Maine and some of the colonies along the New England coast, may have had some limited contact with Europeans as early as the years 1000 or 1100, regular contact began in the sixteenth century, following Columbus’s visit, and intensified during the first half of the seventeenth century. During that time, the Indians began to integrate

some aspects of European culture, such as trade goods, into their own lifestyles. The most popular items seem to have been things like tin pots, pails, hatchets, fishhooks, pipes, and knives that made the lives of Indians easier.
[Nativeamericannetroots.net/diary, “Maine Indians & Early European Contacts”]

In an effort to be completely accurate in our terminology, it actually wasn’t until 1501 that an Italian merchant and explorer by the name of Amerigo Vespucci determined that what is now known as the Americas was part of new continents—a new hemisphere--and not part of Asia, as had been claimed by Christopher Columbus in 1492. Vespucci simply referred to it as the “New World,” but in 1507 famed German cartographer Martin Waldseemüller labeled it as America—to honor Amerigo Vespucci—on one of his popular maps…and that name stuck. We are today, and will always be, in a country named for an Italian who really had very little contact with North America or South America.

Columbus, of course, was thoroughly convinced that he had found a new trade route to the riches of the East Indies. Given that, he began referring to the local natives as Indios, or “people of the Indus Valley,” even though Columbus was nowhere near India. “Indios” was later translated as Indians, which is still widely used today to refer to the Indigenous residents of the Americas, who are also referred to as American Indians or Native Americans. In Canada, the Indigenous peoples are known as First Nations; Inuit if they reside in Northern Canada, Greenland, or Alaska; or Métis, if they are of mixed Indigenous and European blood.

Until Columbus visited the islands of the Caribbean in 1492, it is unlikely that many people in Europe, Asia, or the other known, or unknown, continents on the planet would have had any significant suspicions that the lands of what are now the Americas existed. The only confirmed visitors were the Vikings, or Norse, who explored what is now northeastern Canada and Newfoundland about 1000 AD and established a small trading settlement at L'Anse aux Meadows on the coast of Newfoundland. That settlement was abandoned after several years, probably due at least in part to ongoing conflicts with

the Indigenous residents. For centuries it remained unclear whether the Icelandic stories, or sagas, represented real voyages by the Norse to North America. The sagas first gained serious historic respectability in 1837 when the Danish antiquarian Carl Christian Rafn pointed out the possibility of there having been a Norse settlement in, or voyages to, North America. North America, by the name "Winland," or "Vinland," first appeared in written sources in a work by Adam of Bremen from approximately 1075. The most important works about North America and the early Norse activities there, namely the Sagas of Icelanders, were recorded in the 13th and 14th centuries. Norse sites were also depicted on the Skálholt Map, made by an Icelandic teacher in 1570 and depicting part of northeastern North America and mentioning Helluland, Markland and Vinland.
[Wikipedia: "L'anse aux Meadows]

The Norse explorers would have encountered both Indians (the Beothuk, related to the Algonquin) and the Thule, ancestors of the Innuit. While reports of interactions between the Norse and the local Indigenous residents are virtually nonexistent, there is one report that in the spring of 1005, "Thorvald Eriksson attacked nine of the local people who were sleeping under three skin-covered canoes. The ninth victim escaped and soon came back to the Norse camp with a force. Later the same day, Thorvald and his men saw a swarm of canoes sailing down the fjord towards them. Outnumbered, they took refuge in their ship and, with the advantage of iron weapons, beat off the attack. However, during the fight Thorvald received an arrow wound in the armpit and died shortly afterwards." That would seem to have been the first bloody encounter between the Indigenous descendants of the First Americans and the European interlopers. Unfortunately, it would not be the last. Although brief hostilities reportedly ensued, the Norse explorers stayed another winter, but it was reported that they left the following spring."
[John Haywood, "Vikings in America: The Europeans Who Arrived 500 Years Before Columbus," www.historyextra.com; Wikipedia: Norse colonization of North America; Wahlgren, Erik, The Vikings and America. (New York: Thames and Hudson, 1986); Wernick,

Robert; The Seafarers: The Vikings, (Alexandria, VA: Time-Life Books, 1979).]

Clear evidence of the Norse presence west of Greenland came in the 1960s when archaeologist Anne Stine Ingstad and her husband, outdoorsman and author Helge Ingstad, excavated the Norse site at L'Anse aux Meadows in Newfoundland. The location of the various other lands described in the sagas remains unclear, however. Many historians identify Helluland with Baffin Island and Markland with Labrador. The location of "Vinland" poses a thornier question. The most recent scientific dating validates that the Vikings were definitely in residence at L'Anse aux Meadows in 1020.
[Riley, Carroll L., J. Charles Kelley, Campbell W. Pennington, and Robert L. Lands, eds., Man Across the Sea: Problems of Pre-Columbian Contacts, (Austin: University of Texas Press, 1971), pp. 446-448.]

In addition to continuing to look for other indications of Norse presence or settlements in North America and Canada, there are a few other cases of potential Pre-Columbian contact that seem to deserve our continued attention. If you are interested, you can find numerous research citations and further information at: "Pre-Columbian transoceanic contract theories" at Wikipedia.

First on my list of possible pre-Columbian contacts, however, are Polynesians and other Pacific islanders. There is evidence of a genetic link between American Indians and Easter Islanders, and between Easter Islanders and Native Americans from South America. South American Indians living in Brazil were found to have a genetic link to "Polynesians and other subgroups of Austronesians." Some Native Americans from Amazonia were found to be "more closely related to Indigenous Australians, New Guineans, and Andaman Islanders than to any Eurasians or Native Americans." Populations in the Mangareva, Marquesas, and Palliser islands and Easter Island had a "genetic admixture from indigenous populations of South America," most closely related to the Zenú people of the Pacific Coast of Columbia. In addition, "the sweet potato, a food crop native to the Americas, was widespread in Polynesia by the time European explorers first reached the Pacific." The potatoes could have been introduced by Polynesians who had made a round-trip to South America, or by South American Indians who traveled to the west, although there are also a few other possible explanations. Some of the other possible indications of contact would include some language similarities; skulls found on Mocha Island, off the cost of Chile, that had Polynesian features; and even a nautical chart belonging to a Javanese pilot that included parts of the Americas.

Pre-Columbian contact between Japanese and American Indians is also not out of the question. One American anthropologist claims that the Zuni Native American language bears similarities to Japanese, as well as sharing a number of unique cultural characteristics. It is also known that ocean currents carried several dozen Japanese ships to North America in the 17th, 18th, and 19th centuries, landing as far north as the Aleutian Islands and as far south as Mexico. In a number of the cases, Japanese sailors were reportedly assimilated into local Native American tribes. It has also been argued that there is no reason to believe that Japanese vessels didn't pay similar visits to the Americas during the Pre-Columbian period.

From the title of his most recent bestselling book, Who Discovered America? The Untold History of the Peopling of the Americas, you might think that researcher and author Gavin Menzies had the answer to that question. Unfortunately, he doesn't. Menzies uses "discover" in same way that people used to say that Columbus "discovered" America. It didn't necessarily mean that Columbus was the first to find the Americas, but that he did not previously know that the land area of the Americas existed. Menzies argues that Marco Polo, in Kublai Khan's Mongol fleet of 1297, "discovered" the Americas, which they didn't previously know existed…despite the fact that the Vikings had been there several hundred years earlier and the people we know as American Indians, or the First Americans, had bested the Mongols by 10,000 years or more. The title of Menzies' book is misleading, probably intentionally. After all, it enticed me to purchase it! I believe the book does have substantial value in documenting, or suggesting, early visitors to the Americas that most of us would otherwise not know about, including interactions they might have had with several of the American Indian tribes.

Menzies advocates for the First Americans having arrived by boat, a position strongly supported by Professor Jack Rossen of Ithaca College. In speaking about the First Americans, Menzies quotes Rossen as having commented, "What would people rather do? Try to find a meal in a world of ice or take a boat down the coast and help themselves to fish, oysters, and greens?"

In advocating for a Rossen's Pacific Coast route by boat, Menzies points out that "Sea travelers from Asia to North and Central America have a free ride and food along the way" due to currents in the Pacific. "This great clockwise, nearly rectangular, flow of water takes place all year long," Menzies notes, adding that "It appears certain that man reached the Americas by sea at least forty thousand years ago." He thought that date was likely to eventually be pushed back to 100,000 B.C. on the basis of future research.

Based on his extensive and meticulous research, Menzies has concluded that settlers arrived in the Americas by boat "in never-ending waves from 40,000 B.C. onward, settling initially along the coasts, then migrating inland. He also believes there is evidence that other "sea people" settled in Brazil, Florida, the Great Lakes, and other locations in North America.
[Menzies, Gavin and Ian Hudson, Who Discovered America? The Untold History of the Peopling of the Americas, (New York: HarperCollins, 2013), pp. 245-247.]

CHAPTER 17

EARLY INDIAN INTERACTIONS WITH EUROPEANS

When the first Europeans arrived, so various were the peoples of the Americas that continent-wide generalizations were risky to the point of folly.

—Charles C. Mann
1491: New Revelations of the Americas Before Columbus

In his summary of Columbus's diary, Bartolomé de las Casas, first Catholic Bishop to the Indians of the Americas, wrote, "It should be noted here that the natural docileness, simple, benign, and humble condition of the Indians, and their lack of weapons, together with their going naked, gave the Spaniards the audacity to hold them in low esteem, and put them to such harsh labor as they put them to, and to be relentless in their oppression and destruction of them."

In colonial times, Spaniards sought to control history by harnessing it to what may be the simplest trope ever invented to explain human behavior, differences between peoples. For example, the outcome of historical events was attributed to the trope of superiority. Colonial chroniclers and the modern historians who followed them found a satisfying simplicity and safety in the following circular argument: Spaniards conquered natives because they were superior, and they were superior because they conquered natives.
[Bartolomé de las Casas, A Short Account of the Destruction of the Indies, (New York: Penguin Books, 1992), pp. 104, 132.]

Spaniard Ponce de León first sighted the Florida coast near Mosquito Inlet at the southeast end of Timucua territory in 1513, twenty-one years after the first visit of Columbus. De León then sailed southward past the land of the Ais Indians, where native huts were sighted, perhaps fishing camps or small villages. Needing firewood and fresh water and probably anxious to see what the new land was like, Ponce sent men ashore. Skirmishes took place and two Spaniards were wounded by fishbone-tipped arrows. One Indian was kidnapped and taken to be used as a guide. Obviously, the first encounters between Florida Indians and people from Europe were less than felicitous.

Continuing down the coast, Ponce de León mapped the shore and recorded natural features, naming them in some cases. He probably sailed into Biscayne Bay, where he noted the location of the main town of the Tequesta Indians at the mouth of the Miami River. Sailing farther south, he traveled along and around the Keys and then turned back north, arriving in Calusa Indian territory. Names of two Calusa towns are recorded on the Freducci map, on which the depiction of the Island of Florida is thought to be based on Pence de León's discoveries.

In Ponce de León's encounter with the Calusa Indians more skirmishes took place. The Calusa used bows and arrows to attack the Spaniards aboard their anchored ships, fighting from canoes and catamarans, canoes hooked together like the toy one recovered by Cushing from the Key Marco site. Ultimately fatalities were suffered by the Spaniards and the Calusa. Even so, both groups of combatants sought to learn more about each other and to trade in order to obtain exotic goods.
[Milanch, Jerald T., Florida's Indians: From Ancient Times to the Present (Gainesville, FL: University Press of Florida, 1998), pp. 134-136.]

The Calusa weren't the only Indians who quickly demonstrated their dissatisfaction with the Spaniards who showed up uninvited on their shores. When a group led by Cabeza de Vaca and Pánfilo de Narváez was wandering around somewhere north of Tampa Bay—they weren't sure where they were, so we aren't either—they came across a group of about 200 Indians. Narváez reported he "went out to them, and after having spoken to them by means of signs, they gestured to us in such a way that we had to turn on them." The Indians were threatening the Europeans and a skirmish resulted, during which the Spaniards were able to capture five or six Indians who led them to their village, where they found plenty of food, mainly ripe corn. The Spaniards were near starvation at the time, and they feasted at the Indian village for several days.

Just prior to their contact with the agitated Indians, the Spaniards had crossed a river, thought to have possibly been the Withlacoochee River in what is now Citrus County, Florida. The river was apparently the boundary between the lands claimed by two different local tribes. By crossing that unmarked boundary, the Spaniards were essentially invading the lands of the Indians who met them on the north side of the river. It was one of numerous instances where the Spaniards' lack of knowledge about the territories they were passing through, combined with their inability to communicate clearly with the Indigenous population whose land it was, created dangerous situations. It was a situation that arose on at least five occasions during the wanderings of the Spaniards.
[Andrés Reséndez, A Land So Strange: The Epic Journey of Caveza de Vaca, (New York: Basic Books, 2007), pp. 92-93.]

Until the 1550s, despite the massacres and the exploitation associated with the system of the encomienda, the Spaniards had not completely disrupted the subsistence economies which they had found in the areas they colonized. Instead, they had relied, for the wealth they accumulated, on the tribute systems put into place by the Aztecs and Incas, whereby designated chiefs delivered them quotas of goods and labor supposedly compatible with the survival of the local economies. The tribute which the Spaniards exacted was much higher than that the Aztecs and Incas had ever demanded of those they conquered; but it was still not sufficient to satisfy their needs. By the 1550s, they were finding it difficult to obtain enough labor for both the obrajes (manufacturing workshops where goods were produced for the international market) and the exploitation of the newly discovered silver and mercury mines..."
[Sylvia Federici, Enduring Western Civilization, (Bloomsbury Publishing: Bloomsbury, England, 1995), p. 224.]

Along the Northeast Coast, European fishing boats were trading with the Micmac in Maine and the Maritime Provinces by 1519. By 1524, ships were crossing over from Europe in increasing numbers, first to fish offshore for the great schools of cod, and eventually to trade with natives for furs. During the early part of the seventeenth century, English ships scouted the coast from Maine to Cape Cod, trading with Indians and gathering sassafras roots which were prized in Europe as a treatment for syphilis. In 1602, off the coast of Maine, the crew of an English ship saw people in a European boat—described as a Biscay shallop—sailing toward them. They assumed that the eight men in it must be Europeans. However, all were Indians. The Indians, using a piece of chalk, drew a map of the Maine coast for the newly arrived English sailors.

Sailing shallops could be fairly large, up to 12 tons and forty feet in length. Many had more than one mast. Regarding the adaptation of this craft by Indian people, the Jesuit missionaries noted that the Souriquois handled them "as skillfully as our most courageous and active sailors in France."

There are a number of other reports of Indians using the European shallops. In 1606, for example, the Souriquois under the leadership of Membertou raided other Indian villages using sailing shallops. The following year, the English, on their way to establish their colony on the Kennebec River encountered two sailing shallops being used by Souriquois under the leadership of Membertou. The Souriquois offered skins for trade and the English noted that the Indians seemed to be using a lot of French words.

When Giovanni da Verrazano, an Italian working for the French, explored the North American coast from the Carolinas northward to Maine in 1524 he found that the Indians in Maine were not particularly friendly. They appeared to have already had some contact of an unpleasant sort with Europeans. The following year, a Spanish expedition led by the Portuguese pilot Estevan Gomes landed near the River of Deer in Maine and took 58 Indians captive. That obviously didn't improve the image of the Europeans amongst the Indians.

In 1580, the English adventurer, John Walker, landed in Penobscot Bay. He took about 300 moose hides from an unattended building. Such a large collection of moose hides in a single structure was a strong indication that they may have represented a year's collection and that the hides were intended not for local consumption, but were actually intended for export; that is, to be traded to Europeans.

In 1602, the English explorer Bartholomew Gosnold landed at "Savage Rock" [Cape Elizabeth, Maine] where he encountered some Micmac. The European explorers found that the Indians were wearing large copper breastplates and European costumes including shoes, waistcoats, breeches, and hose. The following year, English explorers under the leadership of Martin Pring encountered a group of Indians near present-day Saco [Maine]. They reported that some of the Indians had brass breastplates which were a foot long and about half a foot wide.

In 1604, the French explorer Samuel de Champlain sailed up the Penobscot River. Near the site of present-day Bangor [Maine], he made contact with Wabanaki under the leadership of Bashabes. From Bashabes the French learned a great deal about the interior of Maine. Bashabes, wanting French partnership in the fur trade, provided Champlain with guides. While the French were looking for the fabled Indian city of Norumbega, they found that the city was a myth. The French did, however, gain a great deal of information about the interior between Kennebec Basin and the St. Lawrence. Getting around the language barrier, the Indians drew maps on sand and bark for the French.

The French next explored Saco Bay [Maine] where they saw and recorded on their charts an Indian corn-growing settlement. On the Saco River they were met by Indians who painted their faces black and red. The Indians were farming people who raised corn, beans, squash, pumpkins, grapes, and tobacco. Champlain's Etchemin guides called the people of this village Archmouchiquois, and they called the village Chouacoit. The area surrounding the village contained many small hamlets.

In 1605, the English established a trading camp on the Kennebec River. The expedition was funded by Sir Ferdinando Gorges, captain of the Port of Plymouth. At the end of the trading season, the English kidnapped five Abenaki and took them to England to turn into guides and interpreters. The Abenaki captives were not to be sold into slavery, but they were exhibited as curiosities. They were also studied by Gorges, who wished to learn more about the new land to the westward and its inhabitants. Among those taken by the English was Tisquantum, also known as Squanto, who later became an important figure in Massachusetts history. [Nativeamericanroots.net/diary/729]

In 1607, the Virginia Company established the colony of Sagadohoc on the Kennebec River. The party included 120 men and Skidwarres, one of the Abenaki Indians who had been kidnapped in 1602. Skidwarres was supposed to serve as the trusted interpreter-liaison between the English and Abenaki. However, as soon as he made contact with the Abenaki he simply slipped into the crowd and returned to his people. In one instance, five Abenaki, including Skidwarres and the leader Nahaneda, showed up at the fort. They joined the colonists for both food and church services and had to endure public prayers both morning and evening. They told the English that King James was a good King and that his God was a good God, but that Tanto, their own deity, had commanded them to avoid contact with the English.

"Modern descriptions of the meetings between Indians and the English colonists generally agree that the English were abruptly dismissive of Indian culture, that they were either totally uninterested or else saw it as something to be shunned or even destroyed as the work of the devil. My reading of the early descriptions of the Indians yielded a very different result, and one which seemed to me to make better sense of this early cross-cultural confusion. Some English colonists were just not interested in an alien culture, though none of these dismissed the Indians as being cultureless. But many colonists were fascinated by the Indians, their government, social organization, and religion. Despite the language barrier, they struggled mightily to understand the culture. Moreover, they were writing for an audience in England which was hungry for such information and analysis.

"Thus, though the record could have varied in its details and the English record could have been more honorable, the domination of the Indians by the English is portrayed as virtually inevitable. I do not think this is the way the English saw it at the time. When they describe Indian technology, it is with admiration born of experience. In the American environment Indian technology was frequently superior to English and the colonists made no secret of their continuing dependence on Indian aid…Nor did the rank-and-file colonists have a much more sophisticated understanding of the operation of the universe than their Indian counterparts. They interpreted natural phenomena in very much the same ways. European disease, not European technology, conquered the Indians." [Karen Ordahl Kupperman, Settling With The Indians, p. vii-viii.]

The English soon managed to anger their Abenaki neighbors so that trade between the two groups had to be suspended. There were a number of minor skirmishes in which eleven colonists were killed. The English basically bungled their opportunity to establish influence with the Abenaki.

In 1608, the English abandoned their colony on the Kennebec River. The resupply ships from England found that the colonists had successfully traded with the Indians for furs, gathered the herbal cure-all sarsaparilla, and built and launched a 50-foot ship. However, the colony's leader, upon discovering that he was the heir to an immense fortune decided to return to a lavish castle in England and the other colonists went with him.
[Nativeamericanroots.net/diary/729]

In 1609, Henry Hudson met with Indians in Penobscot Bay. The Indians told him that they traded with the French. A few days later, two French shallops filled with Indians sailed into the harbor bringing many beaver skins and other furs for trade. Hudson was not equipped for trade, so he simply resorted to force to obtain the furs. His men captured one of the shallops and took the Indian furs.

In Alden T. Vaughan's New England Frontier: Puritans and Indians, 1620-1675, the author said that "he had originally been impressed by the Puritans' attempt to deal justly and peacefully with their Indian neighbors, but that approach, while successful in the early year, eventually failed. He opined that the Puritans had a paternalistic but genuine concern for the Indians. He noted, for example, that in 1638 Plymouth Colony hanged three Englishmen for murdering an Indian and that by mid-century Harvard College admitted Indian students, who were also welcomed by the colony's common and grammar schools for many years." The failure, Vaughan said, had to do with the colonists' "cultural absolutism," but not "color prejudice"—or racism, for they believed that Indians had descended from the ten lost tribes of Israel.
[They did see Indians as "White," based on the skin color of Indian babies being the same as that of White babies. They did see their culture as superior to "the non-Christian savages."] Vaughan was Professor Emeritus at Columbia. He wrote extensively, including The Puritan Tradition in America, 1620-1630; Transatlantic Encounters: American Indians in Britain 1470-1776; and Puritans Among the Indians.]

On July 30, 1676, tobacco planters led by Nathaniel Bacon asked for and were denied permission to attack the Susquehannock Indians, who had been conducting raids on the colonists' settlement. Enraged at Governor Berkeley's refusal, the colonists burn Jamestown and kill many Indians in what is known as Bacon's Rebellion, before order was restored in October.

After one hundred years of American Indians and Whites squabbling primarily over land ownership, Thomas Jefferson probably reflected the collective opinions of the White settlers when he referred to North American Indians as "merciless Indian savages whose known rule of warfare is an undistinguished destruction of all ages, sexes, and conditions," in the Declaration of Independence. That assessment and the fact that many Indians fought with the British during the Revolutionary War appear to have set the stage for U.S. government policies toward Native Americans. Most government officials saw the Indians as "enemies" who stood in the way of settling the vast and resource rich areas of the country.

An online history site included the following observation: "Despite some myths to the contrary, not all Native Americans were peaceful. Like Europe, the American continent faced tribal warfare that sometimes led to human and cultural destruction."

["Native American Society on the Eve of British Colonization," U.S. History: Pre-Columbian to the New Millennium, www.ushistory.org/us.]

"Writing in 1934, Alfred L. Kroeber, one of the founders of American anthropology, took the extreme position that the Indian in eastern North America could not develop—could have no history—because their lives consisted of "warfare that was insane, unending, continuously attritional." Escaping the cycle of conflict was "well-nigh impossible," he believed. "The group that tried to shift its values from war to peace was almost certainly doomed to early extinction." [Charles C. Mann, 1491: New Revelations of the Americas p. 16.]

Noted colonial historian Alden Vaughan reported, "Not until November 15, four days after the Pilgrims began exploring the cape [Cape Cod], did they catch even a distant glimpse of its Indian inhabitants. To the Pilgrims' relief, this meeting involved none of the torments they had imagined: the five or six Nausets took to their heels while still some distance away.

"The Pilgrims were certainly not looking for trouble with the Indians, and it was not in their nature to become over-confident, yet within a few days of their anchoring off Cape Cod the first Puritan settlers had given the Red Men cause for anger. When the Englishmen discovered some freshly concealed underground corn barns, they could not resist the urge to know what was inside. Once they knew, they could not pass up the chance to acquire food and planting seed. At the risk of jeopardizing the friendship of the natives, the Pilgrims carted off all the corn they could carry, vowing to repay the owners at the first opportunity. Bradford credited the stolen seed with saving the colony from possible starvation, but in the meantime, it undoubtedly added to the prevailing hostility of the Nauset."

"In December of that first year, the Pilgrims discovered two burial mounts and robbed them of their prettiest things, before reburying the corpse. When they found two wigwams, they relieved them of a variety of native crafts ware that they took back to their ship. They supposedly intended to return and leave some trinkets of European manufacture, but they ran out of time and didn't get back to the area. "Another link in the chain of unfriendly relations had been forged."

[Alden T. Vaughan, New England Frontier: Puritans and Indians, 1620-1675, pp. 66-68.]

Father Paul Le Jeune, a Jesuit missionary to the American Indian tribes in New France explained the Indians' proclivity toward violence in a report to his European superiors: "It begins with an individual who raises a band of young men who gather, so it seems, for the purpose of avenging a private quarrel and the death of a friend, rather than for the honor and preservation of the nation. Then, if they succeed in capturing some of the enemies, they treat them with all the cruelty they can devise."

[Allen Greer, The Jesuit Relations: On the Good Things Which Are Found among the Indians from Jesuit Relations 6:228-235, Paul Le Jeune, 1634, p. 33]

In its most extreme form, indigenous inferiority was expressed in terms that denied Native Americans their humanity. Juan Ginés de Sepulveda's comment is often cited because it suggests this image so candidly. The Spanish jurist and philosopher openly stated that natives "hardly deserve the name of human beings."

[Matthew Restall, Seven Myths of the Spanish Conquest (New York: Oxford University Press, 2003), 107, 131-132.]

"When Columbus and his contemporaries provided Europe with a first view of the Americas, the Inca and Aztec empires were as complex, urbanized, and internally diverse as the cultures of Europe. Ancient, but subsequently vanished, societies in the Mississippi valley were as large as the biggest cities of Europe. The Aztec capital city of Tenochtitlan had a population of close to 200,000, at a time when the largest European cities would have been around one-tenth the size. [Ken S. Coates, A Global History of Indigenous Peoples: Struggle and Survival, (New York: Palgrave Macmillan, 2004), p. 65-66.]

"The survivors of the Pánfilo de Narváez expedition were the first outsiders to have lived in the immense territories north of Mexico and to come in contact with many peoples across North America. It was an experience that neither the Spaniards nor their Amerindian 'hosts' would forget. At contact, both groups appeared strikingly different. The contrasts were so patent that many Europeans openly discussed whether the natives were human at all and vice versa." That unanswered question led the Spanish and other European explorers, traders, entrepreneurs, and settlers to consider themselves superior to the Indigenous peoples. The opinion was widespread and enduring. Andrés Reséndez, A Land So Strange: The Epic Journey of Caveza de Vaca, (New York: Basic Books, 2007), p. 139.

Alden Vaughan has concluded, "A persistent American tragedy has been the inability of European colonists and their descendants to live equitably with the aboriginal population…Our ancestors failed to solve the infinite problems of racial adjustment; perhaps modern America is not doing much better."

"My assessment of early Puritan attitudes and actions was on the whole favorable," said Vaughan, arguing that until 1675 the New Englanders generally respected the Indians (though not Indian culture) and tried sincerely to win them to English ways and beliefs. "The Puritans' ultimate goal," he said, "was assimilation of the natives into Anglo-American society. Accordingly, the colonists—especially those with political or ecclesiastical authority—sought peaceful and equitable methods of acquiring land and furs, administering justice, and recruiting converts." "The Puritans' effort was not flawless, and their goal was fundamentally presumptuous, but in the context of the seventeenth century," I contended, "the Puritan record deserved a more affirmative judgment than it had usually received."

[Alden T. Vaughan, New England Frontier: Puritans and Indians, 1620-1675, 3rd ed., (Norman: University of Oklahoma Press, 1995), pp. ix-xi, xiii.]

In public speeches, famed photographer Edward Curtis's theme, "consistent from the beginning, was that Indians were spiritual, adaptive people with complex societies. They had been massively misunderstood from the start of their encounters with European settlers and were passing away before the eyes of a generation, mostly through no fault of their own. For them, the present was all of decline, the future practically nonexistent, the past glorious."

"The average conception of the Indian is as a cruel, blood-reeking warrior, a vigorous huntsman, a magnificent paint-and-feather-bedecked specimen of primitive man...," wrote Curtis, "Of such we have no end of mental pictures, but to the wonderful inner and devotional life we are largely strangers."

[Timothy Egan, Short Nights of the Shadow Catcher, (Boston: Houghton Mifflin, 2012) pp. 210-212.]

[1607] "was also the year when the recorded history of the Indians of this part of America began, marked by the completion of Bishop Baraga's Chippewa dictionary. The history of these peoples before this period is entirely unknown, owing to the lack of historical documents of any kind."

[The Diary of Bishop Frederic Baraga, ed. and annotated by Regis M. Walling and Rev. N. Daniel Rupp, (Detroit: Wayne State University Press, 1990), translated from the original, p. 50.]

On July 29, 1609, Samuel de Champlain, accompanied by two other Frenchmen and sixty Algonquin and Huron Indians defeated a band of Iroquois near what is now Ticonderoga, New York, beginning a long period of French-Iroquois hostilities.

In 1611, a former Dutch lawyer named Adrian Block explored Manhattan Island in the ship Tiger. He returned to Europe with a cargo of furs and two kidnapped Indians, whom he named Orson and Valentine.

"It is unfortunate, but the stories of most Indian women have not been told. It is almost as if they didn't exist. However, one Indian woman who definitely received her share of recognition was Amonute, also known as Matoaka. We know her best as Pocahontas, daughter of Powhatan the paramount chief of a network of tributary tribal nations in the Tidewater region of Virginia at the time of earliest European settlement. She supposedly saved the life of Englishman John Smith in 1607, an event doubted by many historians. Pocahontas was captured and held for ransom by the English during Anglo-Indian hostilities in 1613. During her captivity, she converted to Christianity and took the name Rebecca. When the opportunity arose for her to return to her people she chose instead to remain with the English." [Wikipedia.org/wiki/Pocahontas]

"Among the Indians of the Great Lakes region, a tribe numbered from a few hundred to several thousand individuals. A tribe was a loose organization, which had little or no formal territorial claims. Although such a group might stay in one general area for centuries, it was often on the move with it, and sometimes, as occurred with the Ottawa after 1615, it might leave permanently.

"If a tribe had been in existence for several centuries, most or all of its members would be related by blood, and certain bodily characteristics, such as height and facial appearance, would become common. The members of the tribe all spoke the same language and were governed by one set of customs. Both language and customs might be unique for a given tribe or might be common to a number of separate tribes. Algonquins in Michigan all spoke dialects of the same language, but some dialects were so different their speakers could not understand each other."

[Emerson F. Greenman, The Indians of Michigan, (Lansing, MI: Michigan Historical Commission, 1961), p, 1.]

Between 1810 and 1825, most of the Spanish colonies that had been established in Mexico, Central America, and South America won their independence and established the independent nations that exist today in those regions.

The independence of Mexico triggered a "domino effect" throughout Meso-America and South America. Chili declared its independence from the Spanish Empire on February 12, 1818. Chile won its formal independence when San Martín defeated the last large Spanish force on Chilean soil at the Battle of Maipu on April 5, 1818. San Martín then led his Argentine and Chilean followers north to liberate Peru; and fighting continued in Chile's southern provinces, the bastion of the royalists, until 1826.

In 1822, Simón Bolívar and Francisco de Miranda led independence movements in Venezuela, Ecuador, and Columbia. Peru won its independence from Spain in 1824, led by the indomitable Bolívar and Antonio José de Sucre.

It seems that, for the most part, the initial Indian-European encounter was less of an intellectual shock to the Indians than to the Europeans. Indians were surprised when strange-looking people appeared on their shores, but unlike Europeans they were not surprised that such strange people existed.

According to many scholarly texts, Moctezuma II, Emperor of the Aztec (American Indian) Empire during the period 1502 or 1503 until 1520, believed that Spanish explorer Hernán Cortés was the Aztec god-hero Quetzalcoatl returning home in fulfillment of a prophecy. Similarly, American Indian tribes like the Wampanoag, Narragansett, and Haudenosaunee in eastern North America also initially thought that Europeans could possibly have supernatural qualities. These views were in part because Indians in both North and South America regarded Europeans as human beings exactly like themselves. In their view of the world, certain men and women, given the right circumstances, could wield more-than-human powers. If the Wampanoag and Mexica had shamans who could magically inflict sickness, why couldn't the British or Spanish?

"For the most part the initial Indian-European encounter was less of an intellectual shock to the Indians than to Europeans. Most Indians were surprised when strange-looking people appeared on their shores, but unlike Europeans they were not surprised that such strange people existed. (The Norse, French fishermen, and other temporary visitors may have been seen along the shore; they may even have interacted with natives, perhaps trading fish for meat or fresh water, but there is simply no record of any interactions, although word of them could have spread widely among the Indigenous communities.)

Many natives, seeking to categorize the newcomers, were definitely open to the possibility that they might belong to the realm of the supernatural. They often approached the strange visitors as if they might be deities, possibly calculating that the downside of an erroneous attribution of celestial power was minimal.

The Taino Indians, Columbus reported after his first voyage in 1492, "firmly believed that I, with my ships and men, came from the heavens…wherever I went [they] ran from house to house, and to the towns around, crying out, "Come! Come! And see the men from the heavens!"

[Charles C. Mann, 1491: New Revelations of the Americas Before Columbus, 2nd ed. (New York: Vintage Books, 2011), p. 160-161.]

Another Spanish entourage arrived along the coast of North America in the spring of 1528. Like Columbus, they claimed land for the Spanish royal family. Interestingly, lacking a qualified pilot on their voyage, the Spaniards who led the well-equipped and enthusiastic group had no idea where they were. That apparently didn't really make a difference. "Panfilo de Narváez, [commander of the expedition] lost no time in claiming the land for Spain and for himself. Even though the expeditioners did not know their exact location, at least they were certain to be within Narváez's enormous adelantamiento, somewhere between Florida and the Rio de las Palmas." Like Columbus, Narváez gathered his followers and raised the standard of Spain, taking possession of the land in the name of the royals.

[Andrés Reséndez, A Land So Strange: The Epic Journey of Caveza de Vaca, (New York: Basic Books, 2007), p. 84-85; Morison, Samuel Eliot, Admiral of the Ocean Sea: A Life of Christopher Columbus (Boston: Little, Brown and Company, 1942). pp. 228-229.]

While we have substantial records of what European explorers and settlers thought about the Indigenous peoples they met, unfortunately records of Indian reactions to the arrival of early Whites are scant. Without a written language, the Indians' versions of those first contacts with Europeans could only be preserved in tribal oral histories, with a character on a Winter Count or some other mnemonic device, or with the records of Europeans who observed the events. The earliest written records were often provided by missionaries who traveled with the explorers and groups of settlers. Among the religious observers, the Jesuits, Dominicans, and representatives of other Catholic orders have undoubtedly provided us with the most observations of the early interactions between Indians and Europeans as a result of the detailed reports they were generally required to provide to their superiors in Europe.

Part of the motivation for the European invasion of North America, in fact, was to acquire converts to their religions. The Jesuits, "Black Robe" Catholic Priests, were among the most active missionaries. Arriving in New France, now Canada, in 1611, they immediately began to learn the native languages as a way of carrying their message to the people. Unlike other Europeans, the Jesuits did not want land or furs, they asked only to live in an Indian household that they might study the language. While the Jesuits were well-liked because of their quiet manners, the Indians felt that these men were poorly educated because they had not learned that God made all religions, and they came to tell the Indians, who already believed in a Creator, that such a one existed. nativeamericanroots.net/diary/729]

Tisquantum, a Wampanoag Indian from New England who had been kidnapped by the British in 1614 and taken to England, returned in the spring of 1619, accompanying a British ship. "What Tisquantum saw on his return home was unimaginable. From southern Maine to Narragansett Bay, the coast was empty—utterly void." What had once been a line of busy communities was a mass of tumbledown homes and untended fields overrun by blackberries. Scattered among the houses and fields were skeletons bleached by the sun. Slowly, the crew realized they were sailing along the border of a cemetery two hundred miles long and forty miles deep. The Patuxet band of Wampanoag had been delivered a lethal blow. Not a single person remained, struck by a virulent epidemic, believed to have been viral hepatitis, probably spread by contaminated food. Beginning in 1616, the lethal pestilence took at least three years to exhaust itself and killed as many as ninety percent of the people in coastal New England.

The Wampanoag came to the obvious logical conclusion: "their deities had allied against them." Incredibly, the Pilgrims reached similar, but perverted, conclusions. Governor Bradford is said to have attributed the plague to "the good hand of God," which "favored our beginnings," by "sweeping away great multitudes of the natives…that he might make room for us." Indeed, more than fifty of the first colonial villages in New England were located on the former sites of Indian communities that had been emptied by disease.

[Charles C. Mann, 1491: New Revelations of the Americas Before Columbus, 2nd ed. (New York: Vintage Books, 2011), pp. 60-63.]

"At the time the French settled in Montreal, Au-tche-a, one of the Ottawa prophets, told his people there were some strange persons living in this continent, who were far superior to any other inhabitants upon the earth. So, Au-tche-a determined to search for these wonderful people, and he persuaded five of his neighbors to accompany him in his undertaking. When they came where the White men were, they first saw a vessel or ship anchored in the middle of the St. Lawrence, which they thought was a monster waiting to devour them as they came along. But as they neared it, they saw some people on the back of the monster. Ao Au-tche-a and his party were taken on board, and his little frail canoe was hoisted into the ship. They found some Stockbridge Indians there also, who spoke a dialect of their language.

After exchanging all they had and learning how to handle firearms, they started back again to the Straits of Mackinac. The tradition says they arrived at their village on an exceedingly calm day, and the water was in perfect stillness in the straits. The Indians saw the canoe coming towards the shore of the village, when suddenly a puff of smoke was seen, and a terrific clash of sound followed immediately. All the inhabitants were panic stricken, and thought it was something supernatural approaching the shore. But again, and again they witnessed the same thing, as it came nearer and nearer. At last, they recognized the great prophet Au-tche-a and his party coming back from his long trip, having found his "Manitou" that he was looking after.

The reader may imagine how it was, when Au-tche-a landed and exhibited his strange articles—his gun, his axes, his knives, his new mode of making fire, his cooking utensils, his clothing and his blankets. It was no small curiosity to the aborigines."

[Andrew Blackbird, History of the Ottawa and Chippewa Indians of Michigan, (Ypsilanti, MI: Ypsilanti Auxiliary of the Women's National Indian Association, 1887).

"Evidence suggests that [the Indians] tended to view Europeans with disdain as soon as they got to know them. The Wendat [Huron] in Ontario, a chagrined missionary reported, thought the French possessed "little intelligence in comparison to themselves." Europeans, Indians told other Indians, were physically weak, sexually untrustworthy, atrociously ugly, and just plain smelly. (The British and French, many of whom had not taken a bath in their entire lives, were amazed by the Indian interest in personal cleanliness.)

When Verrazzano and his crew visited the Maine coast, the Abenaki did want steel and cloth—demanded them, in fact. But up north the friendly welcome had vanished. The Indians denied the visitors' permission to land; refusing even to touch the Europeans, they passed goods back and forth on a rope over the water." When the transfer of goods was complete, the local Indians began "showing their buttocks and laughing." Mooned by the Indians! Unlike the Narragansetts, who had welcomed the visitors, the Abenaki had a long experience with Europeans…and were not impressed.

[Charles C. Mann, 1491: New Revelations of the Americas Before Columbus, 2nd, ed., (New York: Vintage Books, 2011), pp. 52-54.]

On the evening of October 12, 1492, the people in hundreds of progressive Indigenous settlements from the tip of South America to the Hopewell settlements north of Lake Superior, and from the Mayan and ancient Aztec settlements in in the highlands of South America to the snakelike mounds on Florida's Crystal River, to the urban and suburban sprawl of Cahokia along the banks of the

Mississippi River and the barely visible remnants of Watson Brake's ancient mounds, the oldest known in North America…those Indigenous people sought the sleep of the innocents, not aware that their world was in the process of undergoing what surely must have been the most dramatic changes in the history of planet Earth.

The old cultures were in the process of changing. The massive mounds built by the residents of their proud communities over hundreds of centuries had either abandoned or they were in the process of being abandoned. It was a change that was so dramatic and so confusing that scores of educated people are still trying to understand why it happened. Why did the people abandon what had taken so long to build, and which had brought such pride to their communities? Five hundred years later, desolate scholars would still be making statements like, "The end came. We do not know how and why." It is still one of the great mysteries of our time.

There are many possible explanations for the abandonments, but none that is universally accepted, or supported by a strong majority of scholars as being significant enough to have caused the abandonment of the Mound Builders' communities and dissolution of their communities. The communities had been built over many years by the residents themselves; as many as six hundred years! Massive mounds, buildings, courtyards, mortuary facilities, towers, and palisades that were built with less equipment than you use to cut your grass and maintain your garden.

CHAPTER 18

WHAT THE SPANISH THOUGHT ABOUT INDIANS

> I forbade that they be given things so worthless as bits of broken crockery and of green glass and lace- points, although whey they could get them, they thought they had the best jewel in the world.
>
> **—Christopher Columbus**
>
> Admiral of the Ocean Sea, p. 231

The legendary landing of Christopher Columbus in the New World took place on the coral sand beach of what would henceforth be known as Fernandez Bay in the Bahamas on October 12, 1492. To borrow the familiar words of President Franklin Delano Roosevelt, it was "a date that shall live in infamy." Details of the landing from Columbus's personal Journal were later provided by Bartolomé de Las Casas and Ferdinand Columbus, son of Christopher Columbus:

Presently they saw naked people, and the Admiral went ashore in the armed ship's boat with the royal standard displayed. So did the captains of Pinta and Niña, Martin Alonso Pinzón and Vicente Yáñez his brother, in their boats, with the banners of the expedition, on which were depicted a green cross with an "F" on one arm and a "Y" [for King Ferdinand and Queen Ysabella] on the other, and over each his or her crown. And all having rendered thanks to Our Lord kneeling on the ground, embracing it, the Admiral arose and gave this island the name San Salvador. Thereupon, he summoned to him the two captains, Rodrigo de Escobedo, secretary of the armada, and Rodrigo Sánchez of Segovia, and all others who came ashore, as witnesses; and in the presence of many natives of that land assembled together, took possession of that island in the name of the Catholic

Sovereigns with appropriate words and ceremony…Many Indians, having come together for that ceremony and rejoicing, the Admiral, seeing that they were a gentle and peaceful people and of great simplicity, gave them some little red caps and glass beads which they hung around their necks, and other things of slight worth, which they all valued at the highest price.

According to Las Casas, [who edited Columbus's journal after his death] in his journal for that auspicious day Columbus recounted: They remained so much our friends that it was a marvel; and later they came swimming to the ships' boats in which we were and brought us parrots and cotton thread in skeins and darts and many other things, and we sopped them for other things that we gave them, such as little glass beads and hawks' bells. Finally, they swopped and gave everything they had, with good will; but it appeared to us that these people were very poor in everything. They go quite naked as their mothers bore them; and also the women, although I didn't see more than one really young girl. All that I saw were young men, none of them more than 30 years old, very well made, of very handsome bodies and very good faces; the hair coarse almost as the hair of a horse's tail and short; the hair they wear over their eyebrows, except for a hank behind that they wear long and never cut. Some of them paint themselves black (and they are the color of the Canary Islanders, neither black nor white), and some paint themselves white, and others red, and others with what they have…They bear no arms, no know thereof; for I showed them swords and they grasped them by the blade and cut themselves through ignorance; they have no iron. Their darts are a kind of rod without iron, and some have at the end of fish's tooth and others, other things…I saw some who had marks of wounds on their bodies and made signs to them to ask what it was, and they showed me how people of other islands which are near came there and wished to capture them, and they defended themselves. And I believed and now believe that people do come here from the mainland to take them as slaves. They ought to be good servants and of good skill, for I see that they repeat very quickly all that is said to them; and I believe they would easily be made Christians, because it seemed to me that they belonged to no religion. I, please Our Lord, will carry off six of them at my departure to Your Highnesses, so that they may learn to speak. [Bartolomé de Las Casas, A Short Account of the Destruction of the Indies, (New York: Penguin Books, 1992).

When Columbus prepared to depart for Spain at the conclusion of his first trip to the Caribbean, he reportedly left the following instructions for his men: "They should greatly respect King Guacanagari and his chiefs and principal men…And they should avoid as they would death annoying or tormenting the Indians, bearing in mind how much the owe these people and why it is necessary to keep them content, since they are remaining in Indian land and under Indian dominion.

"I want the natives to develop a friendly attitude toward us," Columbus wrote in his logbook, "because I know they are people who can be made free and converted to our Holy Faith more by love than by force."

[Kevin Jones, "Critics of Columbus Day get history wrong, scholar says," Catholic News Agency, October 12, 2020.]

In his letter to the King and Queen upon his return to Spain, Columbus again described the Taino: "They are so ingenuous and free with all they have, that no one would believe it who has not seen it; of anything that they possess, if it be asked of them, they never say no; on the contrary, they invite you to share it and show as much love as if their hearts went with it, and they are content with whatever trifle be given them, whether it be a thing of value or of petty worth

In the "Introduction" to Las Casa's book, Anthony Pagden, Professor of History and Political Science at UCLA, speaking about Las Casa, wrote, "Columbus, whose diary he preserved and edited, had, in Las Casa's view, been chosen by God for his learning and virtue to bring the Gospel to the New World. It was for this, he wrote, "that he was called Christopher, that is to say Christum ferens, which means carrier or bearer of Christ."

According to Columbus biographer Samuel Eliot Morison, "These Indians of the Bahamas, and indeed all whom Columbus encountered on his First Voyage, belong to the so-called Taino culture of the Arawak language group. Their ancestors had emigrated to the Antilles from the mainland of South America, and within a century of Columbus's voyage had branched out from Haiti, overrunning Cuba, Jamaica, and the Bahamas, pushing back or enslaving an earlier and more primitive tribe known as the Siboney."

[Morison, Samuel Eliot, Admiral of the Ocean Sea: A Life of Christopher Columbus, (Boston: Little, Brown and Company, 1942), pp. 228-232.]

There never crossed the mind of Columbus, or his fellow discoverers and conquistadors, any other notion of relations between Spaniard and American Indian save that of master and slave. It was a conception founded on the Spanish enslavement of Negroes in Africa, which Columbus had observed and taken for granted, and which the Church condoned. It never occurred to him that there was anything wrong in this pattern of race relations, begun and sanctioned by that devout Christian prince, D. Henrique of Portugal. But Dominican friar Bartolome de Las Casas, who spent the better part of a noble life vainly invoking the words and example of Jesus against the cruel and inordinate greed of Castilian Christians, comments on the words of the Admiral in stern and measured words: "Note here, that the natural, simple and kind gentleness and humble condition of the Indians, and want of arms or protection, gave the Spaniards the insolence to hold them of little account, and to impose on them the harshest tasks that they could, and to become glutted with oppression and destruction. And sure, it is that here the Admiral enlarged himself in speech more than he could and that what he here conceived and set forth from his lips, was the beginning of the ill usage he afterwards inflicted upon them."

[Morison, Samuel Eliot, Admiral of the Ocean Sea: A Life of Christopher Columbus (Boston: Little, Brown and Company, 1942), p. 291.]

Bartolomé de Las Casas, who traveled with Columbus, eventually became a Dominican priest and the first Bishop in the New World. In 1552, long after the death of Columbus, he recounted his experiences with Columbus and in the days when Columbus and his sons ruled the island of Hispaniola (Now Haiti and the Dominican Republic).

“The indigenous peoples never did the Europeans any harm whatever; on the contrary, they believed them to have descended from the heavens, at least until they or their fellow-citizens had tasted, at the hands of these oppressors, a diet of robbery, murder, violence, and all other manner of trials and tribulations.

“The island of Hispaniola was the first to witness the arrival of Europeans and the first to suffer the wholesale slaughter of its people and devastation and depopulation of the land. It all began with the Europeans taking native women and children, both as servants and to satisfy their own base appetites; then, not content with what the local people offered them of their own free will (and all offered as much as they could spare, they started taking for themselves the food the natives contrived to produce by the sweat of their brows, which was in all honesty little enough. Since what a European will consume in a single day normally supports three Native households of ten persons each for a whole month, and since the newcomers began to subject the locals to other vexations, assaults, and iniquities, the people began to realize that these men could not, in truth, have descended from the heavens. Some of them started to conceal what food they had, others decided to send their women and children into hiding, and yet others took to the hills to get away from the brutal and ruthless cruelty that was being inflicted on them. The Christians punched them, boxed their ears and flogged them in order to track down the local leaders, and the whole shameful process came to a head when one of the European commanders raped the wife of the paramount chief of the entire island. It was then that the locals began to think up ways of driving the Europeans out of their lands and to take up arms against them. Their weapons, however, were flimsy and ineffective both in attack and in defense (and, indeed, war in the Americas is no more deadly than our jousting or than many European children’s games) and, with their horses, and swords, and lances, the Spaniards easily fended them off, killing them and committing all kinds of atrocities against them…

“They forced their way into native settlements, slaughtering everyone they found there, including small children, old men, pregnant women, and even women who had just given birth.”

[Bartolomé de Las Casas, A Short Account of the Destruction of the Indies (London: Penguin Books 2004), Nigel Griffin, ed., first published in 1552, pp. 13, 14-17.]

"From the very beginnings of exploration…Native Americans were identified as different from, and mostly inferior to, Europeans. Columbus's own words are revealing. In his Diaro, the first mention of Native Americans was a reference to their nakedness, a sign of their incivility. The Diaro also shows that Columbus immediately assumed a superior position toward the indigenous people, seeing them as natural subjects of Spanish power and religion. He gave the first Americans he met red caps and glass beads "because I recognized that they were people who would be better freed [from error] and converted to our Holy Faith by love than by force." The people were "very poor in everything," he noted; they were also primitive, never having seen iron weapons. "Although Columbus sometimes praised the native people and even recognized their intelligence, he did so—and this is telling—as part of his evaluation of their potential to be servants." [Christopher Columbus, The Diaro of Christopher Columbus's First Voyage to America, 149201493, trans. Oliver Dunn and James E. Kelley, Jr. (Normal: University of Oklahoma Press, 1989), pp. 65-68.]

According to Howard Zinn's revisionist narrative, "Columbus and his successors were not coming into an empty wilderness, but into a world…where human relations were more egalitarian than in Europe, and where the relations among men, women, children, and nature were more beautifully worked out than perhaps any place in the world." This narrative came to dominate the teaching of American history. Needless to say, even were this one-sided history true—and Columbus's personal treatment of the natives was exaggerated in extraordinary fashion by Zinn through selective quotation—this doesn't debunk the free-market principles that have animated America any more than pointing out that muggers victimize old ladies from whom they steal purses."

European intellectuals, and others, were startled when Christopher Columbus bumped into "Indians" in 1492. The new settlers encountered no wilderness: "In this bay wherein we live," one colonist noted in 1622, “in former time hath lived about two thousand Indians.”

[Mary Grabar, Debunking Howard Zinn, quoted in Shapiro, Ben, How to Destroy America in Three Easy Steps, p.183.; James W. Loewen, Lies My Teacher Told Me, (New York: The New Press, 2018), p. 85.]

CHAPTER 19

EARLY EUROPEAN IMPRESSIONS OF INDIANS

"A major part of the Europeans' attitude of superiority was religious. They believed the "Christians' conviction that they possessed an absolute and exclusive religious truth."

—Stephan Greenblatt
Marvellous Possessions: The Wonder of the New World

The impressions recorded by Roger Williams, William Wood, Thomas Morton, Daniel Gookin, and other prominent New England chroniclers are by no means uncritical, but neither are they fundamentally derogatory. All, for example, agreed that the Indians they knew were exceptionally hospitable to strangers, usually helpful to any in need, and about as pleasant as any people they had encountered. Roger Williams summed up the temperament of the Indians by noting that "the Natives are of two sorts, (as the English are). Some are Rude and Clownish…the general, are sober and grave, and yet cheerful in a mean, and as ready to begin a Salutation as to Resalute." He added that "there is a favour of civility and courtesie even amongst these wild Americans, both amongst themselves and towards strangers." This attitude on the part of the Indians would be important to the English colonists, for a persistently hostile native population might well [44] have changed the character of Puritan settlement. As it was, most of the Indians were happy—thought perhaps somewhat apprehensive—to see the white man arrive. Serious tensions later developed between some of the Indians and the Puritan community, but they did not grow from any innate hostility toward newcomers.

Not only were the Indians generally courteous and hospitable, they also were quick to lend a hand to colonists in distress...The Indians further served the English interest by disclosing the treacheries of the few who plotted against the colonists, and by acting as scouts and coastal lookouts in conflicts between the Puritans and their European foes. Other Indians attached themselves to colonial settlements as interpreters and guides.

Although the Puritans deplored the Indian's lack of formal schooling, most of the chroniclers did not permit this deficiency to prejudice their view of the native's basic intelligence. Williams insisted that "they are intelligent, many very ingenious," and Edward Winslow considered them "ripe-witted." Thomas Morton was of similar mind but noted that many of his compatriots thought otherwise.

On only two counts did the New Englanders condemn the native without reserve: his indolence and his drunkenness. The former was presumed to be either an inherited defect or the work of the Devil; in either case it was regrettable to all Englishmen...In terms of the Protestant work-ethic, the Indian men were perhaps guilty as charged, but certainly the Indian women were not...And the indolence of the men was only intermittent; in hunting and fishing seasons, in wartime, and when special tasks challenged the family or tribe, Indian men showed more energy and stamina than most Englishmen could muster. It is less easy to mitigate the charge of drunkenness, for it was voiced by Indian as well as by Puritan spokesmen. Within a short time after the arrival of the English, the Indians had become inordinately fond of alcohol. As early as 1637, Thomas Morton observed that "they will pawn their wits to purchase the acquaintance of it. In large part this weakness stems from unfamiliarity with intoxicants..." (The British were accessories to the intoxication because they were the source of the liquor. Every New England colony passed strict rules against selling alcohol to Indians, although such legislation was futile. Drunkenness persistently marred relations between Puritans and Indians.)

[Vaughan, Alden T., New England Frontier: Puritans and Indians, 1620-1675, 3rd ed. (Norman, OK: University of Oklahoma Press, 1995), pp. 41-42.]

"The problem for [the Europeans] was to explain the existence of a place and people that seemed to have been overlooked in the Bible. European thinkers ran through a number of explanations for the apparent omission of Indians, and quickly abandoned any that did not conform with Christian orthodoxy and concluded that since all humans were derived from Adam and Eve, and the Indians were human, then so too were Indian descendants of the first man and woman. Indians were most likely descendants of people mentioned in the Bible, possibly one of the Lost Tribes of Israel, and were not readily recognized as such because of cultural degradation due to long separation from the originating culture. This theory was fairly popular, and many European observers in North America used it to account for Indians and some of their practices."

[For a discussion of this problem and its resolution, see Robert Berkhofer, Jr., The White Man's Indian: Images of the American Indian from Columbus to the Present (New York: Alfred A. Knopf, 1978), pp. 33-69; Brandão, José António, ed., Mémoires of Michilimackinac and the Pays d'en Haut: Indians and French in the Upper Great Lakes at the turn of the Eighteenth Century (East Lansing: Michigan State University Press, 2019), p. 153.]

From the very first arrival of Europeans in the Western Hemisphere, the Whites marveled at what they saw and wondered where it had all come from. Who were the peoples of these Indian nations, they asked, and where did they originate? The question tantalized generations of non-Indian scholars and scientists, some of whom spent lifetimes trying to prove that the Indians were descendants of seafaring Phoenicians or Chinese, pyramid-building Egyptians, one of the Lost Tribes of Israel, Welshmen, or even survivors of Plato's legendary lost continent of Atlantis.

[Alvin M. Josephy, Jr., 500 Tribes: An Illustrated History of North American Indians (New York: Alfred A. Knopf, 1994), p. 9.]

"The curiosity of newcomers rested in the remarkable "otherness" of the newly encountered indigenous peoples." When they traveled outward from their territory in Europe or Asia, the people and societies they encountered "looked, in many respects, like their own." "This did not hold when they went overseas." They found people of different skin colors and people who did not hold to European norms of modesty and public comportment." Dress, demeanor, language, and religions were all different. They also found people they described as "strange" and "savage." "They seemed scarcely more advanced than the animals. Amerigo Vespucci wrote of the Brazilian Indians in a widely circulated 1503 description:

They have no laws or faith and live according to nature. They do not recognize the immorality of the soul; they have among them no private property, because everything is common; they have no boundaries of kingdoms and provinces, and no king! They obey nobody, each is a lord unto himself. [They have] no justice and no gratitude, which to them is unnecessary because it is not part of their code. They are a very prolific people but have no heirs because they hold no property.

Most European observers, like Carvajal, found little to admire among these societies, save for basic animalistic qualities such as bravery, ferociousness, and skills on the land, and occasionally they discovered ways of using these traits and knowledge to their advantage…It is incorrect, however to assume that the newcomers saw indigenous peoples in consistently negative terms. Although the Europeans found much wanting in the societies they encountered, they were nonetheless impressed with many aspects of the indigenous world. Jose Mariano Mozino, one of the first newcomers to visit the west coast of North America, wrote of the peoples he encountered:

A languid look is rather frequent among them, but rarely does one find a stupid-looking one. On the contrary, I noticed in many such a lively expression that, through it alone, one could guess many of their thoughts with little question…Either because it is natural among them or because they have eliminated all sentiments of modesty entirely, the men frequently abandon this clothing and appear stark naked, without so much as covering their private parts with their hands, even though they might be in a group of numerous women. The women, on the contrary, preserve more decency.

[Ken S. Coates, A Global History of Indigenous Peoples: Struggle and Survival (New York: Palgrave Macmillan, 2004), pp. 73, 76-77.]

Humanities scholar Stephen Greenblatt of Harvard, has noted that the first wave of European explorers "shared a complex, well-developed, and, above all, mobile technology of power: writing, navigational instructions, ships, war-horses, attack dogs, effective armor, and highly lethal weapons, including gunpowder...Little wonder that Europeans felt superior to Native Americans, people who were, in their eyes, obviously deficient. But what author and historian Tzvetan Todorov has described as the "European prejudice of superiority" extended beyond technology, for Europeans tended to view Native Americans as inferior even when they recognized their achievements.

[Tzvetan Todorov, The Conquest of America: The Question of the Other, (New York: Harper & Row, 1984), pp. 33, 165; Stephen Greenblatt, Marvelous Possessions: The Wonder of the New World (Chicago: University of Chicago Press, 1991, p. 9.]

"The first mariners who anchored on the coasts considered the natives as little less than wild beasts. They enticed them on board vessels, and carried them off to work in the mines, or to be sold as slaves. They were abused and deceived in various ways by the commercial class, who supplied them with deleterious liquor, in the shape of ardent spirits, which crazed their brains, paralyzed their exertions, and led them to commit crimes...Worst of all, it was the mistaken policy of the times to attempt to drive them, instead of persuading them into the principles of Christianity." [Henry Rowe Schoolcraft, Information Respecting the History, Condition and Prospects of the Indian Tribes of the United States, Part III, under the direction of the Bureau of Indian Affairs per act of Congress of March 3rd, 1847, (Philadelphia: Lippincott, Grambo & Co., 1853), illustrations by Seth Eastman. pp. 22-23.]

Thomas McKenney, chief administrator of Indian policy under three presidents, wrote: "Our Indians stand pretty much in the relation to the Government as so our children to us…Indians are children and require to be nursed, and counseled, and directed as such…Indians, I have found out, are only children and can be properly managed only by being treated as such."

[Sheehan, Seeds of Extinction, (Chapel Hill: University of North Carolina Press, 1973), p. 153; quoted in Osborn, The Wild Frontier, (New York: Random House, 2000), p. 41.]

Europeans "found positive elements that were worthy of emulation. In general, however, portraits highlighted the fact that more mobile societies, which newcomers assumed struggled daily for survival, were seen as uncivilized and were deemed an impediment to settlement and development…The expansionary powers assumed that their own military and technological prowess proved their superiority, blessed as it was by the hand of their God, and formed little understanding of the dynamics or complexities of the indigenous peoples."

"On occasion, however, the newcomers were impressed with the people they encountered. Travelers in the Arctic, for example, marveled at the ability of the Inuit to find sustenance in such a harsh and forbidding land, even though they were initially reluctant to adopt the Inuit lifestyle and material culture. Early French and Portuguese observers wrote favorably about the gentleness, generosity, and sharing cultures of the Brazilian indigenous peoples. Many of the first observers of the Indians feared their warlike nature and saw them, legitimately, as a worrisome but truly impressive military threat. There was, in fact, something of an idealization of the original inhabitants of the Pacific Islands, who seemed to inhabit a tropical paradise and were freed from the worries and struggles of northern countries. Visitors to the west coast of North America described positively the large well-organized salmon-based communities in the region. Many of the early European explorers among the peoples of the American Northeast described such groups as the Mohawk in favorable terms…Even in these cases, however, observers quickly identified social elements they described as distasteful—just as indigenous peoples often found newcomers customs disagreeable. Polygamous marriages, multi-deity world views, seemingly casual attitudes toward life and death, and the absence of material wealth, social stratification, or skills differentiation all provided evidence to outsiders that the indigenous peoples, however.

"From first contact through to the present, however, indigenous peoples have generally been viewed as 'the others,' not as variants on a central theme of humanity...Clearly, to the dominant powers, these were lesser societies, less 'advanced,' less technologically sophisticated, and by definition less 'civilized.' The indigenous peoples "were intellectual and social novelties, of interest more because of what they illustrated about the distant past of humanity..." [Ken S. Coates, A Global History of Indigenous Peoples: Struggle and Survival (New York: Palgrave Macmillan, 2004), p. 78-82.]

The Choctaws entered European historical records when the Spaniards of Herenando DeSoto's expedition encountered them in the 1540s—an unhappy encounter for both parties. DeSoto, who had been Francisco Pizarro's cavalry captain in Peru, came to the southeastern portion of North America seeking another civilization as rich in gold and silver as the Inca. When he demanded women and baggage carriers of Chief Tuscaloosa at the Choctaw town of Mom Bina, a battle ensured, and the Spaniards' baggage train was burned in a fire that also destroyed Mom Bina. The armored Spanish war horses struck terror in the Choctaws, who had never seen horses before, and Choctaw losses in the battle were heavy. The Choctaws nonetheless inflicted a reported 644 arrow wounds on the Spaniards, piercing their skin wherever armor did not protect it. After a period of rest and recovery, DeSoto's expedition passed through Choctaw country without further incident and wintered among the Chickasaw, who trapped them in a fire so hot that the Spanish had to build a force and re-temper the steel in their swords before crossing the Mississippi and leaving the lands of the southeastern Indians." [D. L. Birchfirld, www.everyculture.com/multi/Bu-Dr/Choctaws]

American Indians of the Mississippian culture got involved with the Spanish colonizers of the Juan Pardo expedition who built a base near what is now Morganton, North Carolina in 1567, that they called Fort San Juan. "The soldiers were at the fort about 18 months, during 1567-1568, before the natives killed them and destroyed the fort. They also killed soldiers stationed at five other forts as well; only one man of 20 survived. (This marked the first European colonization in the interior of what became the United States.) [Wikipedia: Juan Pardo Expeditions.]

"Evidence suggests that [the Indians] tended to view Europeans with disdain as soon as they got to know them…In about 1606, Sir Ferdinando Gorges—British, despite the name—tried to found a community in Maine. It began with more people than the Pilgrims' later venture in Plymouth and was better organized and supplied. Nonetheless, the local Indians, numerous and well-armed killed eleven colonists and drove the rest back home within months." [Charles C. Mann, 1491: New Revelations of the Americas Before Columbus, 2nd ed., (New York: Vintage Books, 2011), pp. 52-54.]

Father Paul Le Jeune, a French missionary who served the Indian tribes around the Great Lakes from 1632 to 1639, wrote an analysis of Native Americans for a 1634 report to his superiors in France that was published in Jesuit Relations: "If we begin with physical advantages, I will say that they possess these in abundance. They are tall, erect, strong, well proportioned, agile; there is nothing effeminate in their appearance…I see here upon the shoulders of these people, the heads of Julius Caesar, of Pompey, of Augustus, of Otto, and of others that I have seen in France, either drawn upon paper or in relief on medallions…

"As to the mind of the Indian, it is of good quality. I believe that souls are all made from the same stock and that they do not differ substantially. Hence, the well-formed bodies and well-regulated and well-arranged organs of these barbarians suggest that their minds too ought to function well. Education and instruction along are lacking. Their soul is naturally fertile soil, but it is loaded down with all the evils that a land abandoned since the birth of the world can produce. I naturally compare our Indians with [European] villagers because both are usually without education, although our peasants are slightly more advanced in this regard. Nevertheless, people who come to this country always confess and frankly admit that the Indians are cleverer than our ordinary peasants."

He went on to say that Indians are “free of both ambition and avarice, which torture so many Europeans.” The Indians also profess to never get angry, “though not because of the beauty of this virtue, for which they have not even a name, but rather for their own contentment and happiness.” With respect to patience, Le Jeune said, “The Indians surpass us to such an extent in this respect that we ought to be ashamed.” “They are very much attached to each other,” Le Jeune reported, “and cooperate admirably. You do not see any disputes, quarrels, enmities, or reproaches among them.”

[Paul Le Jeune, On the Good Things Which Are Found among the Indians (1634), p. 33-35.]

“The White settlers of Michigan were inclined to look upon the Indians as savages. Such has always been the relationship between people with a superior technology and those they have conquered. Neither side, until quite recently, have informed themselves in matters of history, folklore, and anthropology. The Indians of Michigan, and all Indians for that matter, were civilized in their own way, with strict rules of conduct and manners, and ideas that come under the heading of religion.”

In 1650, the Indians of Michigan and of all North America were in the early stage of the Neolithic Period, comparable to that in the mainstream of technological progress between 4000 and 3000 B.C. in the lands around the eastern Mediterranean.

[Emerson F. Greenman, The Indians of Michigan, (Lansing, MI: Michigan Historical Commission, 1961), pp.44-45.]

“Although Europeans sometimes saw the complex variety of Native life—as did Americans—Native Americans were, over time, reduced to two broad categories: the bloodthirsty barbarian and the romantic, sentimental Indian. Unfortunately for Native Americans, neither of these identities was an adequate conception of their cultures.” The difference in the two categories, however, “provided intellectual and moral support for the ongoing usurpation of Indian lands and a host of other anti-Indian polities to come.”

[Thomas D. Matijasic, "Reflected Values: Sixteenth-Century Europeans View the Indians of North America," American Indian Culture and Research Journal, November 2, 1987, pp. 31-50]

"No nation or people upon the earth have been more shamefully misrepresented than our American Indians, and perhaps this circumstance has operated more than any one thing to the injury of that unfortunate race. A popular writer of England has described them as 'animals of an inferior order, incapable of acquiring religious knowledge, or of being trained to the functions of social life. Writers of our own country may not have used this language, but they have endorsed the sentiment, and it is at this moment so popular, that the public mind is far from being disabused of it. Even the church feels it to some extent...There is naturally no difference between the innate propensities of the white and red man."

[Comments by Presbyterian Minister David Lowery of the Winnebago School in Prairie du Chien, Michigan Territory, in response to a questionnaire from Schoolcraft, Henry Rowe Schoolcraft, Historical and Statistical Information..., 1853, pp. 474-479.]

"By the early nineteenth century, the great assumption of many Europeans, and particularly of clergy, was that Native peoples were living in some remote age, in a kind of state of suspended cultural animation, and therefore needed assistance to "catch up" with European practices...Approaches toward Euro-Native consolidation were, it was suggested, to be both technological and spiritual. It was a logical enough vision of a closed system. If it was possible for one group of "others" to "catch up," it was just as possible for the "civilized" to revert back as "backsliders," to use the favorite term of many a clergyman."

[Editor's Introduction by Graham MacDonald who translated and edited the French manuscript of Frederic Baraga, Short History of the North American Indians, (Lansing, MI: Michigan State University Press, 2004), pp. 44-45.]

In public speeches, photographer Edward Curtis, who spent a great deal of time photographing the Indians of the American West, always expressed the opinion, "that Indians were spiritual, adaptive people with complex societies. They had been massively misunderstood from the start of their encounters with European settlers and were passing away before the eyes of a generation, mostly through no fault of their own. For them, the present was all of decline, the future practically nonexistent, the past glorious.

"The average conception of the Indian is as a cruel, blood-reeking warrior, a vigorous huntsman, a magnificent paint-and-feather-bedecked specimen of primitive man…Of such we have no end of mental pictures, but to the wonderful inner and devotional life we are largely strangers." In a speech to a group in New York City, Curtis said, "We cannot weigh, measure or judge [Indian] culture with our philosophy. For our analytical and materialistic viewpoint, theirs is a strange world. Deity…is everywhere present." "And off Curtis went on his oratorical flight, explaining the Great Mystery, the logic behind fasting and sweat lodges, the offerings to the sun, to snakes and to cedar. But it was wrong to see nothing more than primitive animism in these rituals. "It is often said of certain tribes that they are sun-worshippers," Curtis told his audience. "To call them sun-worshippers is, I believe, in most instances about as nearly right as it would be to call all Christian people cross-worshippers. In other words, the sun is but the symbol of the power."

[Timothy Egan, Short Nights of the Shadow Catcher: The Epic Life and Immortal Photographs of Edward Curtis, (Boston: Mariner Books, 2013), pp. 210-212, 267.]

"Thus, the Indian was declared equal in potential to Whites by reason of birth if not circumstances by many American thinkers from the 1780s to 1830 or so, even if he was not treated that way in policy or philanthropy. As Jefferson declared, 'I believe that Indian then in body and mind equal to the white man,' although his actions implied something else."

[Robert F. Berkhofer, Jr., The White Man's Indian, (New York: Vintage Books, 1979), p. 41; and Jefferson quote from Antonello Gerbi, The Dispute of the New World: The History of a Polemic, 1799-1900, translation. Jeremy Moyle (Pittsburgh: University of Pittsburgh Press, 1973, p. 261.]

"As Benjamin Franklin observed in 1764, after a major atrocity in western Pennsylvania: 'The spirit of killing all Indians, friends and foes, [has] spread amazingly through the whole country.' Two years later, Sir William Johnson reported to Whitehall that in the backcountry from Virginia to New York the settlers "murder, rob, and otherwise grossly misuse all Indians they could find…and [are] treating the Indians with contempt, much greater than they had ever before experienced." The settlers, Sir William lamented, "perpetrate murders whenever opportunity offers." The stereotypical frontier view that "the only good Indian is a dead Indian" was an American reality long before General Sheridan coined the infamous phrase. [Alden T. Vaughan, Roots of American Racism, (New York: Oxford University Press, 1995), p. 20, and, regarding quote from Sir William Johnson, see Labaree, et al, eds, Papers of Benjamin Franklin, 11:76-78.]

"The experience of Spaniard Cabeza de Vaca and his companions afforded Spain an opportunity to consider a different kind of colonialism. These four pioneers had revealed the existence of many native cultures north of Mexico and the availability of precious metals, buffalo, and other resources. But instead of advocating a conquest in the traditional mold, Cabeza de Vaca and the others proposed a grand alliance with the native inhabitants. Over the course of their long odyssey, they had come to recognize the natives of North America as fellow human beings. Their life-changing experience had persuaded them that a humane colonization of North America was possible—a far cry from the views held by most of their contemporaries in the Old World."

[Andrés Reséndez, A Land So Strange: The Epic Journey of Cabeza de Vaca, (New York: Basic Books, 2007), pp. 4-5.]

Largely as a result of the catastrophic decline in the Indian populations as a result of European diseases that rampaged through the Indigenous settlements after 1492, many Whites concluded that the Indians were a dying race and would soon disappear. Among those sharing that opinion were artists George Catlin and Edward Curtis.

Self-taught Philadelphia portrait painter George Catlin (1796-1872), desired to leave "a monument to a dying race" in his hundreds of paintings of Indians whom he met throughout the American West. Also a famed showman, Catlin toured North America and Europe with an exhibition that combined his paintings, extensive program notes, and dramatic lectures on Native American history and culture. He ventured west in 1830. Over the next six years, he visited—by his own account—forty-eight tribes to "(Lend) a hand to a dying nation (and snatch) from a hasty oblivion what could be saved for the benefit of posterity.

[George Catlin, Letters and Notes on the Manners, Customs, and Condition of the North American Indian, Vol. 2 (New York: Wiley and Putnam, 1844), p. 3.]

One other thing that Whites would soon come to believe about Indians was that they were vanishing, disappearing from the face of the earth, or at least the face of the Western Hemisphere. It was, of course, the result of the great variety of rampant diseases the European immigrants unknowingly brought with them and turned loose on an American Indian population that had little immunity to them. In a relatively short and definitely noticeable period of time the Native population plummeted. For those alive during that period of extreme infestation, the tragic results would have been horribly obvious, the path of the diseases littered with dead bodies. Some Indian tribes totally disappeared. Large tribes became small tribes. A commonly accepted feature of the Indian tribes was that they were disappearing. They were a dying race. Some misguided folks saw it as the hand of God at work; confirmation that Whites were God's chosen people, and he was making room for them in the New World.

The dramatic decline in the Indian population would also lead many well-meaning Whites to, including many government officials, to initiate programs they thought could save the Indians from disappearing. The acculturation of the Indians and the assimilation of them into White culture—usually forced assimilation—led to Indian education programs, the breakdown of tribes by distributing tribal lands to individuals, encouraging Indians to become farmers, even the removal of tribes from their traditional lands and segregating them from the White population, usually west of the Mississippi River. For a time, it appeared that efforts to save the Indians would speed up their disappearance.

CHAPTER 20

ARRIVAL OF THE SPANISH CONQUISTADORS

The Spanish conquerors had no intention of leaving. Instead, they consolidated their control over the region and overlaid their culture on its people.

—**Martin J. Dougherty**
The Aztec, Inca & Maya Empires

Beginning in 1492, American Indians who had occupied the Americas for 10,000-12,000 years, more or less, got unexpected company—a situation not altogether dissimilar from having distant cousins you have never met before drop by, ask if they could spend the weekend at your house, and then keep coming up with excuses for why they can't leave. Columbus, of course, arrived in 1492, then, after a quick trip back to Spain, he returned the following year with the first group of Spanish settlers, the second of his four trips to the Western Hemisphere. The Spanish expanded their interests in the Caribbean before they began establishing settlements in North America, Central America, and South America around 1500.

Spain also began to explore areas of Mexico, Venezuela, and the southeastern coast of what is now the United States. Their interests were certainly commercial, as were the interests of the French, Dutch, and English, but the Spanish approached it a little differently. Rather than trading with the locals to obtain products they could sell at a profit, they preferred to claim ownership of the productive land and "retain" the Indigenous workers necessary to produce the marketable commodities, whether it was an agricultural product, a valuable mineral—like gold, or something as pedestrian as bat guano. It probably goes without saying that when the Spanish government allowed it, "retain" meant to enslave.

Of all the local products Columbus and his crews hoped to find in the New World, gold was right at the top of the list. Columbus, never the luckiest guy around, soon discovered that only relatively minor amounts of gold would be found in the islands of the Caribbean. While many areas of the Americas were rich in both gold and silver, unfortunately that was not true of the Caribbean islands that Columbus and his crews had found. He and the Spanish colonists would benefit from the trifling quantities of gold that their "slaves" were able to extract from their property. Meanwhile, the Spanish monarchs and Spanish overlords in other locations throughout South America and Meso-America would get wealthy beyond all rational expectations from their shares of the extensive heavy cargoes of gold and silver from their lands that were being regularly shipped to Spain between 1566 and 1790 by the "Treasure Fleets."

A small unit of about 168 Spanish cavalry under the command of Francisco Pizarro arrived in South America in late 1531. Horribly outnumbered, Pizarro set an ambush for the Inca King who had agreed to meet with him. Reports of exactly how the meeting went down are reported differently. It is often said that the Inca King was suspicious of Pizarro, but he was overconfident and chose to show up for the meeting with only a small honor guard. Another report says that the emperor was carried "in his gilded and feather-decked litter, preceded by a squadron of men who swept the ground and followed by five or six thousand troops, almost all of whom bore only ornamental, parade-type weapons."

[Martin J. Dougherty, The Aztec, Inca & Maya Empires, (London, England: Amber Books, 2018), p. 166.]

At this point, the exact details of their meeting are inconsequential: the emperor of the Inca Empire, a god to his people, was summarily captured by the small cadre of Spaniards. The emperor bartered for his life, offering to give Pizarro a room twenty-two feet by seventeen feet full of gold and gold objects and two similar rooms filled with silver. Over the next six months, caravans bearing gold and silver arrived regularly and slowly filled the rooms with previous gold and silver. Pizarro melted the precious metals and cast the gold and silver into ingots to be shipped to Spain. The Inca watched the operation, transfixed and paralyzed by fear for their godly emperor.

When the rooms had been filled with the requisite amounts of gold and silver in 1533, the imprisoned emperor and the people of his empire waited for his promised release. Pizarro, instead, ordered his men to garrot the Incan god. The failure of the Spanish to uphold their end of the agreement set off a war between the Inca and the Spanish that would last for forty years, but it was the end of the Inca Empire.

There are numerous explanations for how a shockingly small group of Spanish soldiers could destroy the Inca Empire: the Spanish had guns, they had cannons, they had steel swords, they had horses that the Inca had never seen before, and so on. The most convincing may have been put forth in 1963 by Professor Henry Dobyns, who spent most of his academic career studying the size of Indigenous populations in the Americas. Dobyns felt the Inca were "not defeated by steel and horses but by disease and factionalism." In 1983, Dobyns claimed that "American Indians involved in the first smallpox epidemic suffered almost 75 percent mortality."

[Charles C. Mann, 1491, 2nd ed., (New York: Vintage Books, 2011), pp. 91-93, 104; Russell Thornton, American Indian Holocaust and Survival, (Norman: University of Oklahoma Press, 1987), p. 64.]

Smallpox broke out in the Inca Empire in 1524 or 1525, "so severe that more than 200,000 died of it, for it spread to all parts of the kingdom." Among those who perished from the dread disease was Wayna Qhapaq, sometimes spelled Huayna Capac. Regardless how you spell the man's name, he was the "Inca," the human god who ruled the empire that bore his name. In addition to killing Wayna Qhapaq, the initial outbreak of smallpox killed his son and heir, his brother, uncle, and his sister-wife (While Inka kings could have many wives, their first wife was always the king's sister, whom he married after his coronation.).

The virus struck the Inca Empire, was more important than armed combat in the European invasion. The conquest of America was "the most striking example of the influence of disease upon history, of which we can speak with any certainty..."

[Russell Thornton, American Indian Holocaust and Survival, (Norman: University of Oklahoma Press, 1987), p. 47.]

Hernan Cortés arrived in 1519 and began building alliances with local tribes who wanted to get rid of their Aztec overlords who were forcing them to pay significant tributes. Moctezuma II was killed by his own people in 1520. Moctezuma's brother Cuitláhuac then assembled 100,000 warriors and drove the Spanish out, but the empire was in tatters and rebellions were common. Cuitláhuac died of smallpox after only eighty days in power and leadership passed to a nephew, Cuauhtémoc, who had 200,000-500,000 warriors and fortified their island capital of Tenochtitlan by removing the bridges from the three causeways leading into the city.

The Spanish laid siege and eventually captured Cuauhtémoc, and he was executed when he wouldn't cooperate with the Spanish. The city surrendered in August 1521. Cortés took Cuauhtémoc on a trip to Honduras. On the trip, Cortés got word that a plot was being developed against the Spaniards and that the Aztec were massing a huge army with 200,000 to as many as 500,000 warriors. Angered, Cortés had the last Aztec Emperor hung. The emperor's war leader, Tlacotzin, was to have succeeded Cuauhtémoc, but he was killed on his way back to Tenochtitlan. "By that time, the fabric of the Aztec Empire had completely unraveled. The social structure that had permitted its unique culture to flourish and create an effective, vigorous, not-quite empire was gone."

[Martin J. Dougherty, The Aztec, Inca & Maya Empires, (London, England: Amber Books, 2018), p. 217.]

Reasons for the demise of the Aztecs isn't "settled history" yet. As is usually the case, it appears to have been the coalescence of a number of factors that were ultimately responsible for the collapse of the Aztec Empire. No one factor caused the collapse.

The four factors most commonly identified with the fall of the Aztecs include the fact that they had been weakened to an extent by battles they had fought with the Indigenous Mixtec and Zapotec peoples in the surrounding area. The battles with other Mesoamerican groups angered locals and resulted in some of them becoming allies of the Spanish in fighting the Aztecs.

The scope of the Aztec's sacrifices is also thought to have been a factor in their demise. Sacrificing thousands of people each year was undoubtedly a factor in generating anti-Aztec sentiment on the part of both the Aztec population and people in the surroundings city-states from which many of the children and adults to be sacrificed came from.

Disease was also a significant factor in bringing down the Aztecs, beginning with Emperor Cuitláhuac's death from smallpox that seriously weakened Aztec leadership in the face of attacks by the Spanish conquistadors. There is evidence that about twenty-five percent of the Aztec population eventually died from smallpox, greatly weakening Aztec forces. It is also possible that the smallpox may have been brought into the region by soldiers brought in from Cuba by a Spanish Army that included Black slaves who may have had smallpox, setting off the epidemic that was a major factor in the defeat of the Aztec.

["The Fall of the Aztec Empire," www. Aztecempireproject.wordpress.com.]

Not all the deaths from epidemics may have been from smallpox, however. In 2018, biological researchers in Germany found that some of the Aztecs who died in at least three epidemics in the sixteenth century were infected with salmonella enterica bacteria, rather than smallpox. Today, salmonella is most commonly associated with food poisoning. The German researchers estimated that over a five-year-period, the disease, called "cocoliztli" locally, probably killed between seven and seventeen million people.

[Becky Little, "What Caused the Aztec Empire to Fall? Scientists Uncover New Clues," January 16, 2018, www.history.com.]

Between 1520 and 1813, there were at least five major cocoliztli epidemics in present-day Mexico, thought to have been associated with periods of drought. "The correlation between drought and the disease has been thought to be that population numbers of the vesper mouse, a carrier of viral hemorrhagic fever, increased during the rains that followed the drought, as conditions improved…Although symptomatic descriptions of cocoliztli are similar to those of Old World diseases (e.g., measles, yellow fever, typhus), many researchers believe that it should be recognized as a separate disease. [Wikipedia: Cocoliztli epidemics, and Acuna-Soto, R.; Stahle, D. W.; Cleaveland, M. K.: Therrell, M. D. (April 2002), "Megadrought and megadeath in 16th century Mexico," Emerging Infectious Diseases, 8 (4): 360-362.]

After the fall of the Aztecs, the Spanish controlled Mesoamerica and prevented any new civilization from developing. Definitions of "civilized" and "civilization" have varied over time and have generally been subjective and unclear. During the early period of European colonization, cultures were classified in stages of "savagery," "barbarianism," and "civilization." Savagery was used to define hunter-gatherer cultures, the barbarianism stage included Neolithic and Bronze Age farmers, and civilization included Bronze Age urban communities. The three stages were linked to attitudes of cultural superiority. Those that were not yet "civilized" were considered to be inferior…or those who were civilized felt that they were superior.

South American and Mesoamerican cultures tended to be more "civilized" than hunter-gatherer cultures like the Chippewa, Cherokee, Sioux, and Blackfeet…but it is important to note that the "civilizations" in South America and Mesoamerica eventually failed, whereas many of the hunter-gatherer tribes still exist today and are unquestionably "civilized." It is also important to remind ourselves that the mound builders were not some unique group, they were American Indians.

CHAPTER 21

MORE EUROPEAN IMMIGRANTS...OR INVADERS?

Although their numbers were decimated, Native Americans ultimately survived the waves of disease and depopulation, and the collateral blows of warfare, famine, enslavement, and exploitation. But they did not survive unchanged.

—David J. Meltzer
First Peoples in a New World

The French

While the Spanish focused their attention on South America and Meso-America and their gold and silver riches, Frenchman Jacques Cartier poked around the St. Lawrence River and the Iroquois village of Hochelaga in 1535 and Samuel de Champlain followed in 1605, establishing the settlement of Port Royal in Acadia, now Nova Scotia, and, in 1608, founding Quebec City on the majestic St. Lawrence River.

The French approach was considerably different than that of the Spanish. While the Spanish approach was conquest of the Native populations, some degree of enslavement, and extraction of anything of value. The French approach was to institute more of a friendly, cooperative working relationship with the Natives. They claimed lands in the northeast of North America, most of which are still Canadian ("Canada" is believed to have been a slight mispronunciation of the Huron-Iroquois word "Kanata," meaning "village" or "settlement." "Canada" appears to have materialized with Jacques Cartier in the mid-1500s, according to www.nrcan.gc.ca/earth-sciences/geography/origins-canadasgeographical-names/origin-names-canada-and-its-provinces-and-territories/9224)

Their primary interest from 1600 until they lost their lands in North America to the British in 1763 was the fur trade, primarily beaver fur, for which there was a very profitable European market. In many respects the French and the Indians of the Great Lakes regions were business partners. The Indians supplied the French traders with a variety of high-quality furs and in return they received a variety of European trade goods from the French.

If the highest priority of the French was the fur trade, the second most important priority was to spread the Catholic religion among the Indigenous populations in the region. From the very earliest days of French exploration in the Americas, Catholic priests accompanied the explorers and traders in order to spread the Gospel. The largest group of priests were from the Jesuit order, who the Indians frequently referred to as "black robes," a nod to their ecclesiastical attire.

When early explorations didn't turn up gold deposits or other precious minerals, combined with the chilly temperatures and the risks associated with life in a remote land populated largely by Indigenous peoples, most people in France seem to have lost interest in Canada. As a result, settlement was pitifully slow and almost all attention was devoted to the fur trade. It wasn't until after Louis XIV ascended to the Bourbon throne in 1663 that the French began to broaden their attention to their North American territories that stretched from the Maritime Provinces in the northeast; encompassed eastern Canada, including the region around the Great Lakes; and then ran south along the Mississippi all the way to Louisiana.

One significant limitation in those early years was the fact that the French population in America was almost exclusively male—explorers, fur traders and their minions, and Catholic priests. It was not a colony that offered much appeal to France's feminine population. The lack of women in New France also made the region unattractive for much agricultural development. It also led to many marriages, common-law marriages, and marriages of convenience with Indian women, many of which were only temporary.

The practice of Frenchmen marrying Indian women was so common that the French developed a name for the children of those unions, the "Métis," still one of three types of aboriginal peoples recognized in Canada. Interestingly, the term Métis has an ancient origin in Greek religion and mythology where Métis was a mythical Oceanid nymph and one of the daughters of the Titans Oceanus and Tethys.
[Wikipedia: Metis]

The Frenchmen weren't the only frontiersmen, mountain men, traders, or soldiers who took Native wives. One of the best accounts is an incidental aspect of the journal U.S. government trader Francis Chardon kept while running the trading post at Fort Clark on the Missouri River in the 1830s. Many of the relationships between Whites and Indian women were the result of the men actually purchasing wives from nearby tribes. Chardon purchased an Indian wife, and they had several children together. If I remember correctly, when Chardon's wife left him he simply visited a nearby tribe and purchased another "wife." It was apparently an arrangement that was acceptable to all involved. If the Indian woman wasn't treated appropriately, she was free to leave and go back to her tribe. However, many of the Indian women became life partners of the men who purchased them.

In 1600, Pierre de Chauvin, a French maritime entrepreneur, established the first French trading post at Tadoussac at the junction of the St. Lawrence and Saguenay rivers, a traditional trading site for Indigenous tribes. Commercial settlements followed at Trois-Rivieres in 1634 and Ville-Marie, later renamed Montreal, in 1642, strengthening their hold on the region.

[Truteau, Jean-Baptiste, Raymond J. DeMallie, Douglas R. Parks, and Robert Vézina, eds., A Fur Trader on the Upper Missouri: The Journal and Description of Jean-Baptiste Truteau, 1794-1796 (Lincoln, Nebraska: University of Nebraska Press, 2017), p. 3.]

The British

The British Empire extended its realm into North America in 1607 when they planted the Jamestown settlement on the James River in what became the Commonwealth of Virginia, followed in 1620 with the Plymouth settlement in Massachusetts, and 1634 with a settlement of English Catholics in Maryland. The early British explorations and settlements were almost all commercial ventures, often by people looking for cheap land and a place to practice their religions without government interference or mistreatment.

From 1754 to 1763, the British and French were involved in the Seven Years' War, as it was called in Europe, better known in North America as the French and Indian Wars. Most of the fighting actually took place in North America, pitting the British and their Iroquois allies against the French with their Indigenous allies that included the Mi'kmaq, Abenaki, Mohawk, and other Algonquin, particularly those who had accepted the Catholic religion.

New France fell to the British with the defeat of the French in 1763, leaving the French with only their lands west of the Appalachian Mountains and south along the Mississippi River to their bastion at New Orleans, and north of the St. Lawrence River. Most French Royalists, or loyalists, left, undoubtedly fearing mistreatment by the British, while the Indians stayed in their traditional lands.

Having fought the Indians, and not interested in repeating that experience anytime soon, the British treated the Indians very differently than the French had. British Commander-in-Chief General Jeffrey Amherst didn't trust them and let the Indians know that in all sorts of different ways. He made every effort to disarm them, and when he couldn't get their guns, he would made it illegal to sell them ammunition or gunpowder. The Indians were also forced to give up all of the White prisoners they had taken during the war, and the gifts that both the British and French had been freely giving to the Indians were terminated.

In those last days of the French and Indian Wars and the controversial peace that technically ended the war, there was a growing Indian movement to return the French to power and to expel the British. The movement was led by an Ottawa war chief from Michigan by the name of Pontiac. Long before Chief Pontiac would have an trendy automobile named for him, his name was attached to a rebellion that showed that the British could in fact be defeated…that maybe it would be possible not just to send the British settlers back to England, but maybe it would be possible to chase all the Whites out of the Americas.

Pontiac's Rebellion began in May of 1763 when Pontiac himself led an attack on Fort Detroit. British officials at the fort had been warned, however, and they were able to drive the Indians out of the fort. The Indians then set up a siege and held the fort captive from May 9 until the October 31, 1763. Meanwhile, a total of eight British forts were destroyed during the rebellion and hundreds of colonists were killed. On June 3, local Chippewa and visiting Sauk Indians successfully took control of Fort Michilimackinac in Michigan, located at the Straits of Mackinac where lakes Huron and Michigan meet. The strongly palisaded fort was headquarters for much of the fur trade on the northern lakes. Fifteen of the thirty-five British soldiers stationed at the fort were killed in the attack and another five died as the result of torturing that occurred afterward. The fort was only returned to British control after the local Ottawa tribe intervened and took possession of the fort and the handful of survivors.

As a result of the losses by the British, fear of the Indians extended all the way to Paris and Versailles and on October 7, 1763, King George III issued the Royal Proclamation of 1763, in an effort to console the Indians who remained in the previous French lands. The proclamation made the vast region west of the Appalachian Mountains an Indian reserve that was off-limits to Whites, especially White settlers.

The Indians must have been pleased. However, most of the White settlers were angered. Whites had already begun to settle on the virgin lands west of the Appalachians; the proclamation by the King made that illegal. Some will argue that the proclamation was a factor in generating support for the Revolutionary War that followed in a decade. The truth be told, however, the British never made much of an effort to keep Whites out of the lands west of the mountains, although the very fact of the proclamation definitely aggravated White settlers.

To adequately patrol thousands of acres of rugged mountainous lands, the British would have required a major military commitment…to protect the lands for the Indians, who they had been battling not long ago and who faced the possibility of having to battle them again. No, it was easier to look the other way and let settlers do as they would. So White settlers streamed across the crest of the Appalachians and carved out homesteads on the best farmlands they could find. That aggravated the Indians.

While the agreements that ended the French and Indian Wars held and Pontiac's Rebellion was quashed, widespread dissatisfaction among both Indians and Whites was not eliminated. It would continue to build, and that path would lead eventually to the War of 1812.

The Dutch

In 1615, the Republic of the Seven United Netherlands—the Dutch, for short—founded Fort Nassau on Castle Island in the Hudson River, near where Albany, New York is located today. In 1623, New Netherland Province was established, the following year the first Dutch colonists arrived, and in 1626 Peter Minuit purchased the Island of Manhattan from the Lenape Indians for a pittance. The Dutch must have been short on explorers because they had hired Henry Hudson, an Englishman, to search out lands they might be interested in. He named the river in New York State and the massive bay in northeastern North America after himself.

The Dutch interest in North America was a commercial one and, not surprisingly, involved an attempt by the Dutch to carve out a lucrative share of the fur trade. To do that, they aligned with the Iroquois Confederation in northern New York State, hoping that the powerful Iroquois could help them to take over some of the British fur trade. To sweeten the pot, the Dutch began providing guns and ammunition to Indians throughout the region, giving them an advantage in their conflicts with surrounding tribes. It was a situation that the French and British had tried to avoid by limiting gun sales to the Indians. While the gun sales did help the Dutch to expand their share of the fur trade, it was not enough to make them a major actor.

Eventually, the British tired of the Dutch incursion into the fur trade and their agitation of the various Indian tribes. In 1664, a strong

British military and naval force invaded Dutch lands and took control. Interestingly, Dutch civilians were allowed to remain and the change in control apparently had little effect on day-to-day activities. In repayment for their lost New York properties, a subsequent treaty between the Dutch and British gave the Dutch control of Suriname, Tobago, Saba, St. Eustatius, and Tortola, that had previously been captured by the British. The name New Amsterdam was subsequently dropped and the region was renamed New York.

The further exploration of the St. Lawrence River, the Great Lakes, and, eventually, the Mississippi River and its major tributaries were driven by three factors: the still unsatisfied desire to find a sea route to the Orient, the religious mission to convert the natives to Catholicism, and the commercial opportunities provided by rich natural resources of the region, especially the seemingly unlimited supply of valuable beaver furs and Indians who were willing to harvest them in exchange for European trade goods.

Unlike other imperial powers, France—through Champlain's efforts—fostered especially good relationships with native peoples as they expanded westward. He learned that becoming friendly with the native people was essential to successful trade. Champlain explored the Great Lakes, Hudson Bay, and eventually made it to the Mississippi River. The French made an alliance with the Hurons and Algonquians. Champlain even agreed to fight for them against their enemy, the Iroquois. [www.khanacademy.org/humanities/us-history/colonial-america]

While the French aggressively explored North America, always on the lookout for valuable territories they could annex, "the great expanse of New France remained largely unpopulated. Due to the lack of women, intermarriages between French and Indians were frequent, giving rise to the Métis people who were part French and part Indian.

The low French population in New France remained a persistent problem. At the beginning of the French and Indian War (1754-1763), for example, the British population in North America outnumbered the French 20 to 1."

[Truteau, Jean-Baptiste, Raymond J. DeMallie, Douglas R. Parks, and Robert Vézina, eds., A Fur Trader on the Upper Missouri: The Journal and Description of Jean-Baptiste Truteau, 1794-1796 (Lincoln, Nebraska: University of Nebraska Press, 2017)]

Between its founding in 1608 and 1650, New France received approximately 25,000 immigrants, but only about 15,000 settled permanently. Of those settlers, 10,000 left descendants in the colony. The overwhelming majority of the early migrants — originating mainly from Normandy, the area around Paris and central western France — were men: soldiers, indentured workers, clerics, and even someprisoners.
[www.thecanadianencyclopedia.ca/en/article/peuplement-de-la-nouvelle-france]

The predominance of men among settlers in Canada, was a problem on a couple levels. First, and these aren't in any particular order: It was hard to get male settlers to make long commitments to remaining in Canada absent prospective wives.

Jean Talon, the Intendant of New France—the colony's top administrator—proposed that the King sponsor the transportation to New France of at least 500 women. "The King agreed, and eventually nearly twice the number were recruited. They were predominately between the ages of 12 and 25, and many had to supply a letter of reference from their parish priest before they would be chosen for emigration to New France."

The women came to be known as filles du Roi, or "King's Daughters." One historical demographer has determined that a total of 770 to a high of 850 King's Daughters settled in New France between 1663 and 1673. In addition to covering their transportation costs, the French government also provided each woman with a small dowry.

"Those chosen to be among the King's Daughters and allowed to emigrate to New France were held to a scrupulous standard, which were based on their 'moral calibre' and whether they were physically fit enough to survive the hard work demanded by life as a colonist."

There has always been a rumor that many of the King's Daughters were prostitutes. The rumor has no basis in fact.

[Wikipedia: "The King's Daughters." *The author is the descendant of a fille du roi.]

In 1524, nearly a century before the arrival of the Dutch in North America, the site that later became New Amsterdam had been named New Angoulême by the Italian explorer Giovanni da Verrazzano, to commemorate his patron King Francis I of France, the former Count of Angoulême. The first recorded exploration by the Dutch of the area around what is now called New York Bay was in 1609 with the voyage of the ship Halve Maen (English: "Half Moon"), captained by Henry Hudson in the service of the Dutch Republic, as the emissary of Maurice of Nassau, Prince of Orange, Holland's "stadtholder"

[Chief Magistrate of the United Provinces of the Netherlands]. Hudson named the river the Mauritius River. He was covertly attempting to find the Northwest Passage for the Dutch East India Company. Instead, he brought back news about the possibility of exploitation of beaver by the Dutch who sent commercial, private missions to the area the following years. [Wikipedia.org/wiki/New Amsterdam]

The Dutch, whose presence in North America lasted only about 40 years, were interested primarily in trade and viewed Indians as something to be tolerated, like the cold winters and hot summers. In general, the Dutch appeared to have little interest in learning about the Indians and their culture. Like other Europeans, the Dutch never questioned the idea that Dutch culture was richer, stronger, more highly developed, and closer to God than the Indian cultures. From an Indian viewpoint, the Dutch were seen as not being hospitable for they gave few presents and charged for repairing guns. The Dutch had generally followed a policy of live and let live; they did not force assimilation or religious conversion on the Indians.

Copper, axes, knives, cloth, and the technologies that produced them were the most important aspects of Native peoples' "discovery of Europeans," and the most important reason that Native leaders persistently sought alliances with Europeans. Arrowheads fashioned from scrap copper and, later, firearms purchased from traders spawned Native American arms races that required people to ally with Europeans or succumb to those with access to superior weapons. It is little wonder then, that rumors of the marvels to be had in exchange for beaver pelts and other furs apparently preceded the axe-makers wherever they went; a constant theme in European accounts of first explorations of bays and rivers is the appearance of canoe-loads of people waving beaver pelts they desired to trade...The beaver, the deerskin, the corn, or whatever else could be traded for European goods could also increase the political power of Native leaders and their communities in a system where exotic material goods embodied the strength that came from alliances with their sources.

[Early Narratives of the Northwest, 164-1699 (New York: Charles Scribner's Sons, 1917), pp. 11-16, online facsimile edition at www.americanjourneys.org.]

CHAPTER 22

THE MYSTERIOUS DISAPPEARANCE OF THE MOUND BUILDERS

We now know that the mound-building impulse faded gradually from the country. In Ohio, mound activity ended thirteen or fourteen centuries ago. In the Southeast, it lingered on into the late seventeenth or early eighteenth century. In the far North, the effigy-mound people were building their low pictorial mounds into the late eighteenth century.

—Robert Silverberg
The Mound Builders

After five millennia, the mound building tradition in the Americas disappeared at about the same time that White Europeans showed up along the Atlantic Coast. "The end came," summed up historian Robert Silverberg, "We do not know how and why." Whether there is any correlation between the arrival of Europeans and the end of the mound-building tradition is totally speculative and lacking any explanation that will hold water.

That, by the way, is one explanation that has been presented to explain the end of the mound-building. There are those who think it was weather related, specifically changes in temperatures that led to severe flooding. That, however, doesn't work for explaining a phenomenon that took place from southern South America to areas north of the Great Lakes in Canada. Other possible explanations include conflicts between tribes, degeneration of the mound-building cultures, widespread deaths due to the spread of European diseases, opposition to human sacrifices, and that the Indians simply lost interest, mainly because of the tremendous amount of work involved in building and maintaining the mounds and associated structures.

It is possible, of course, that there may be many explanations for why the cultures gave up on building mounds. Maybe once a few cultures gave up the practice, others followed suit and ended the time-consuming practice. With the arrival of the Europeans, the Indians may simply have realized that they didn't need to build mounds or make human sacrifices in order to establish and maintain trade relations with other distant tribes, which had to have been one of the most important benefits of the cultural interactions. We may never fully understand why mound-building came to an end. Given some of the negative aspects of the practice, particularly the human sacrifices, the end of mound-building may have been a good thing.

When the First Americans came south from Beringia and Alaska, they came in tribal groups…sort of. We don't really know, but it is likely that the groups that made the difficult trek from the Bering Sea Land Bridge either knew each other or they had some commonality, such as coming from the same basic geographic areas or communities, or they were related, although not necessarily closely related. We don't know the extent to which those traveling groups remained together after they arrived at some favorable locations in the Americas. Somehow, the three known groups of Asians who immigrated must have interacted and produced offsprings, or else members of a traveling group who were not closely related reproduced. What we do know is that the populations of First Americans and Native Americans must have grown quite rapidly from the original three groups that totaled 500-1,000 individuals.

Pre-Columbian estimates of the Indigenous populations are ridiculously varied, from 8.4 million to as much as 112.5 million…take your pick! Regardless of what figure you decide to use, the increase in the Indigenous population from their first arrival in the Americas until 1492 is staggering, multiplying the starting population by at least 16,000, or as much as 112,500. That would have occurred over a period of perhaps 12,000 to 15,000 years, or maybe more.

It is unlikely that the original three groups of migrants constituted what we today refer to as a "tribe." More likely, they were family and friends, and maybe friends of friends who were willing to attempt the incredible journey. (Although there really isn't any way they could have had any accurate understanding of the distances involved. It is highly unlikely that they knew there was a Western Hemisphere.) It is possible that by the time they reached a possible homesite in the Americas they were a "tribe," or at least something close to being recognized as a "tribe."

Numbers of those who made the long trek could also have become a tribe when they settled someplace in the Americas. A group that traveled together could also have broken up into a number of "tribes," based on where they wanted to settle, how they got along, relations, how they saw their group functioning, the languages they spoke, food preferences, religious beliefs, and so on.

A tribe could also have been formed by a group of Indians who ended up in the same area. That may well have happened at places like Watson Brake when mound-building ended. There were Indians from a variety of regional tribes who had been involved with the Watson Brake community who may simply have stayed in the area, forming a de facto new tribe.

Tribes also undoubtedly began to form within a short time after the First Americans arrived in the Americas, or even before they arrived. Given that, at the time Watson Brake came to a halt, there could well have been Indians who had been involved in the project for several thousand years. If they decided to remain in the area, they may have formed a de facto tribe, or they may have decided to associate with one of the southern tribes located in the area, and there were several of those.

CHAPTER 23

THE MYSTERIES OF EUROPEAN DISEASES THAT ATTACKED THE AMERICAN INDIANS

> When smallpox broke out among tribes in the Saginaw Valley [MI] in 1837 it is reported…that whole villages and bands were decimated and during the summer many were left without a burial at the camps in the woods and were devoured by wolves.
>
> **—Ellis, in Thompson and Micketti**
> Almost an Island

"Before the American Indian communities could fully comprehend the surprising arrival of Europeans with their dramatically different lifeways and their matchless trade goods, viral diseases that the newcomers inadvertently brought with them began to sweep through Native America like a broom of death. Smallpox was the greatest of these killers, but measles, mumps, chicken pox, and influenzas in their ever-evolving forms were nearly as deadly. Bubonic plague and hemorrhagic fevers similar to Ebola might also have been part of the gruesome mix.

"As early as 1585, at Roanoke on the Outer Banks of North Carolina, English colonists reported that Native people "began to die very fast, and many in short space" after the English colonists visited their villages. "In some towns about twenty, in some forty, in some sixty, and in one six score perished. Similarly, in 1616 a French missionary said that the Native people of Acadia "often complain that, since the French mingle with and carry on trade with them, they are dying fast, and the population is thinning out."

A Dutch chronicler was likely not exaggerating when he wrote in 1650 that "the Indians…affirm, that before the arrival of the

Christians, and before the smallpox broke out amongst them, they were ten times as numerous as they now are." "Le Jeune heard the Innu story about the first arrival of the French in 1633 on the eve of the great smallpox epidemic. The image of persons who "drank blood (wine) and ate wood (hard ship's biscuits)" thus takes on a prophetic tone. For Native people, the discovery of Europe was a discovery of death on an unimaginable scale and of a struggle for cultural survival that continues to this day."

It was probably inevitable that the rapid expansion of the Bay Colony sooner or later would create some friction with the natives over boundaries, as, in fact, it did among the colonists themselves. The first such disputes did not appear until 1633, but no sooner had they arisen than, in the words of a Puritan chronicler, "God ended the controversy by sending the smallpox among the Indians." Between the fall of 1633 and the summer of 1634 several thousand New England natives succumbed to the worst epidemic since 1616-1617…Seven hundred Narragansetts perished, and travelers to the Connecticut Valley reported that the disease had interrupted all trade there. To the east, all tribes were affected as far as the Piscataqua River in Maine. Although a few Puritan colonists gloated at this sudden destruction of their heathen neighbors, the majority responded with characteristic charity."

"By the time the epidemic had run its course, many Indian villages had been exterminated and others had sustained heavy losses, while only two English families had been affected. The implication of this disparity in casualties was not lost on the Puritans. Surely this was proof positive of the Lord's intention of making New England a haven for His true church, for as Governor Winthrop put it, "If God were not pleased with our inheriting these parts, why did he drive out the natives before us?" "The recorder of the Charlestown Records observed that "without this remarkable and terrible stroke of God upon the natives, [we] would with much more difficulty have found room, and at far greater charge have obtained and purchased land." [Alden T. Vaughan, New England Frontier: Puritans and Indians, 1620-1675, 3rd ed. (Norman, OK: University of Oklahoma Press, 1995), p. 103-104; Gilder Lehrman, Document 7: First Encounters of the Ho-Chunk Nation and the French, 1634: Account of the first contact of the Ho-Chunk (Winnebago) with explorer Jean Nicolet in Green Bay in 1634, and the later marriage of a French soldier to the daughter of a Ho-Chunk chief, as related in the early twentieth century to ethnologist Paul Radin.]

The lethal epidemics of European diseases to which the American Indians had no immunity to were to have a devastating impact on the American Indians for generations. It could be argued that the residue of the epidemics is still having a negative effect on American Indians today.

It wasn't just the deaths from the epidemics that harmed the Indians. Many of the Europeans that inadvertently carried the harmful disease germs also had their eyes fixed on the millions of acres of prime lands that had heretofore been the common property of the Indians by right of discovery and the rights of occupation. In most instances the White settlers did not recognize the ownership rights of the Indians. From that point onward, it can easily be argued that relations between Indians and Whites were "all about land," or at least primarily about land.

Efforts to acquire lands from the Indians became the precise, unwavering focus of U.S. Government policies toward the First Americans. It was the focus in 1787 when the first U.S. Government took office, and it remains a focus today, although the primary mission today is simply to retain the millions of acres that have been "acquired" from the American Indians.

"Secretary of War Henry Knox reported to Congress in 1787 that the settlers and the Indians were ever prevented from being good neighbors because, "the one side [Indians] anxiously defended their lands which the other side [settlers]…claim."
[Quoted in Sheehan, Seeds of Extinction, p. 268.]

The same year a congressional committee reported that "an avaricious disposition in some of our people to acquire large tracts of land and often by unfair means, appears to be the principal source of difficulties with the Indians."

[Quoted in Prucha, Documents of United States Indian Policy, 3rd ed., (Lincoln: University of Nebraska Press, 2000), p. 10]

"President Jefferson's government wished ultimately to distribute the vast Indian-occupied acres among the members of civilized society, and consequently intended to take most of the land away from the Indians."
[Bernard W. Sheehan, Seeds of Extinction: Jeffersonian Philanthropy and the American Indian (Chapel Hill: University of North Carolina Press, 1973), p. 167, quoted in William M. Osborn, p. 75.]

According to William M. Osborn, "The Jefferson position demonstrates one of the defects of a democracy. It was difficult for any president to resist the settlers' demands that their need for land be satisfied by the government, or at least that the government stand aside while they satisfied that demand themselves."
[William M. Osborn, The Wild Frontier, (New York: Random House, 2000), p. 75.]

"The Virginia legislature in 1711 appropriated 20,000 pounds "for extirpating all Indians without distinction of Friends or Enemies." [Fergus M. Bordewich, Killing the White Man's Indian, (New York: Doubleday, 1996), p 35, quoted in Osborn, p. 77.]

Hatred, of course, led to calls for revenge. Just as Indians had sought revenge, Andrew Jackson wrote William Henry Harrison in 1811 stating, "The blood of our murdered countrymen must be revenged. The banditti ought to be swept from the face of the earth." [Sheehan, Seeds of Extinction, p. 206, quoted in Osborn, p. 77.]

"Hatred of Indians was a pervading characteristic of the settlers, as demonstrated by this assessment from The West: An Illustrated History: Continually exposed to the dangers of Indian hostility, white frontiersmen came to hate the red man with an intensity which Americans elsewhere could not understand. To the settlers there seemed only two possible solutions. Either the Army had to conquer the savages, then put them under close guard on reservations, where they could never again make trouble; or the cause of civilization demanded that they be exterminated."

[Henry Steele Commager, ed., The West: An Illustrated History, (New York: Exeter Books, 1976), p. 235, quoted in Osborn, p. 77.]

The government never proved capable of controlling westward expansion or the frontier areas. Proclamation of 1763 by the King was an effort to prevent war with the Indians by restricting expansion beyond the Appalachian watershed. "Neither colonists or Indians took it seriously."

[Gary B. Nash, Red, White and Black, (Englewood Cliffs, N.J.: Prentice Hall, 1992), p. 268]

In a letter written on September 7, 1783, that for all intents and purposes became the Indian policy of the Continental Congress, George Washington said that the government should establish "a boundary line between them [the Indians] and us beyond which we will endeavor to restrain our people from hunting or settling, and within which they shall not come." [Quoted in Prucha, Documents of the United States Indian Policy, (Lincoln: University of Nebraska Press, 2000), p. 1.] He did mention that they and their British allies had been defeated and that if the new country was "less generous," they could compel the Indians to move "beyond the [Great] Lakes." They had won legal title to the land by defeating both the British and the Indians, one or both of which previously held title to the land that became the United States.

He also said that "the country is large enough to contain us all." They should have drawn the line in chalk or some other media that could easily be erased, because it never slowed either Indians or Whites down. They did try a little. Congress warned Whites against purchasing or squatting on lands north of the Ohio River and sent troops to evict the squatters and burn their cabins. One result was increased fighting between squatters and Indians. In 1785, Congress authorized a 700-man militia charged with keeping squatters off government lands. In 1790, Congress created a regular federal army of 1,216, augmented by 500 militia to police federal lands and keep order among the settlers and Indians. Washington ordered that a line be drawn between the U.S. and the Cherokee, but admitted that "anything short of a Chinese Wall, or a line of troops, will restrain land jobbers, and the encroachment of settlers upon the Indian Territory."

["General Washington to James Duane, September 7, 1783, in Francis Paul Prucha, Documents of United States Indians Policy, 3rd ed., (Lincoln: University of Nebraska Press, 2000), pp. 1-2.]

In his letter to James Duane, a member of the Congress of the Confederation from New York, President George Washington outlined the principles for the new country's policy toward Native Americans, including those who had sided with Great Britain in the Revolutionary War. He specified that any prisoners held by the Indians needed to be "delivered up." He also wanted the Indians "to be informed that after a Contest of eight years for the Sovereignty of this Country, Great Britain has ceded all the Lands of the United States within the limits described by the article of the Provisional Treaty.

Washington also noted that in spite of much advice and admonition at the outbreak of the Revolutionary War, some tribes became allies of the British, "to share their fortune [or, in this case] their misfortune]. So, consequently, with a less generous People than Americans they would be made to share the same fate; and be compelled to retire along with them beyond the Lakes. But as we prefer Peace to a state of Warfare, as we consider them as a deluded People; as we persuade ourselves that they are convinced, from experience, of their error in taking up the Hatchet against us, and that their true Interest and safety must now depend upon our friendship. As the Country is large enough to contain us all;and as we are disposed to be kind to them and to partake of their Trade, we will from these considerations and from motives of compassion, draw a veil over what is past and establish a boundary line between them and us beyond which we will endeavor to restrain our people from hunting or settling, and within which they shall not come, but for the purposes of trading, treating, or other business unexceptionable in its nature."

"In establishing this line, in the first instance, care should be taken neither to yield nor to grasp at too much. But to endeavor to impress the Indians with an idea of the generosity of our disposition to accommodate them, and with the necessity we are under, of providing for our Warriors, our Young People who are growing up, and strangers who are coming from other countries to live among us, and if they should make a point of it, or appear dissatisfied at the line we may find it necessary to establish, compensation should be made them for their claims within it.

"The limits being sufficiently extensive (in the new country) to comply with all the engagements of government and to admit such emigrations as may be supposed to happen within a given time not only from the several States of the Union but from Foreign Countries, and moreover of such magnitude as to form a distinct and proper government; a Proclamation in my opinion, should issue, making it Felony (if there is power for the purpose and if not imposing some very heavy restraint) for any person to Survey or Settle beyond the line, and Officers commanding the Frontier Garrison should have pointed and peremptory orders to see that the Proclamation is carried into effect.

Washington went on to express concern that "Banditti" will claim property that should have been reserved for the Indians, potentially resulting in a renewal of hostilities with the Indians. He also favored restricting trade with the Indians to agents of the government, or individuals licensed by the government to trade with the Indians, to insure that the Indians were not taken advantage of. He favored purchasing land from the Indians, rather than trying to drive them off their lands by military force. "There is nothing to be obtained by an Indian War," he concluded, "but the soil they live on and this can be had by purchase at less expense, and without that bloodshed, and those distresses which helpless Women and Children are made partakers of in all kinds of disputes with them."
[Letter, "George Washington to James Duane, September 7, 1783," in Francis Paul Prucha, 3rd ed., Documents of United States Indian Policy (Lincoln: University of Nebraska Press, 2000), pp. 1-2]

In response to Washington's policy recommendations regarding Indians, the Continental Congress issued the following proclamation on September 22, 1783: "…the United States in Congress assembled have thought proper to issue their proclamation, and they do hereby prohibit and forbid all persons from making settlements on lands inhabited or claimed by Indians, without the limits or jurisdiction of any particular State, and from purchasing or receiving any gift or cession of such lands or claims without the express authority and directions of the United States in Congress assembled.

"And it is moreover declared, that every such purchase or settlement, gift or cession, not having the authority aforesaid, is null and void, and that no right or title will accrue in consequence of any such purchase, gift, cession or settlement..." "Proclamation of the Continental Congress," September 22, 1783, in Francis Paul Prucha, 3rd ed., Documents of United States Indian Policy (Lincoln: University of Nebraska Press, 2000), pp. 2-3]

The Congressional Proclamation was followed by a succession of treaties with Indian tribes, delineating their property and prohibiting Whites from settling on Indian lands: 1784 Treaty of Six Nations (Fort Stanwix), 1785 Treaty of Hopewell with Cherokee; 1785 Treaty of Fort McIntosh with Ohio lands, Fort Detroit, and Fort Michilimackinac.

While the government of the United States had begun the process of establishing treaties with the Indian tribes, they really knew little about the country west of the Mississippi River and the tribes that occupied those lands. To help correct those deficiencies, in 1804 President Thomas Jefferson organized and empowered the Corps of Discovery to explore the lands from the Mississippi River to the Pacific Ocean.

The 1804-1806 Lewis and Clark Expedition, also known as the Corps of Discovery Expedition,

came in contact with nearly fifty Native American tribes and soon learned that the various groups had different lifestyles, languages, and opinions of the White men. Some welcomed the explorers and were eager to trade and interact; others acted fearful or threatened. President Jefferson had instructed the Corps of Discovery to befriend the Indians, develop trade relations, and collect military and scientific information.

Over the course of their travels, Meriwether Lewis and William Clark developed a ritual when they encountered a new tribe. They held a conference, gave gifts, and explained that the land belonged to the United States with Thomas Jefferson as their new "great father." Lewis had worked closely with Jefferson to ensure he was well prepared with Indian presents which included pipe tomahawks, sheet iron, flannel, handkerchiefs, combs, cloth, beads, butcher knives, pocket looking glasses, ribbon, bells, needle cases, lockets, earrings, rings, and corn mills. Lewis and Clark gave more than 80 Jefferson medals to chiefs they encountered on their expedition. Sacagawea was a great asset in establishing good relations. William Clark wrote, "A woman with a party of men is a token of peace."

Generally, Native Americans helped the explorers as they traveled in the new land. The Indians offered food and valuable advice about geography. The Nez Perce, who considered killing the strangers when they first staggered out of the mountains, provided aid at a time when their help was critical to the survival of the expedition members. In September 1805, the men were nearly starving and Clark reports, "those people [the Nez Perce] gave us a small piece of buffalo meat, some dried Salmon berries and roots in different states…I find myself very unwell all evening from eating the fish and roots too freely." On their return trip, Lewis and Clark again benefited from the generosity of the Nez Perce who gave horses to be used for food. Lewis writes in May 1806, "This is a much greater act of hospitality than we have witnessed from any nation or tribe since we have passed the Rocky Mountains."

Lewis and Clark used their medical supplies and expertise to foster good relations with the Indians and to trade for desperately needed provisions. Clark treated the sore back of a chief's wife by rubbing camphor and applying warm flannel. For payment, Clark obtained two horses. The "physician-captains" frequently dispensed eye wash as "sore eyes seem to be a universal complaint among those people." Lewis and Clark agreed that Clark would be the Indian's physician as, "he was their favorite."

However, encounters with Native Americans were not always favorable. The Teton Sioux Indians' perception of the white men as competitors for the control of trade almost resulted in an armed conflict. On the west coast, the Chinooks angered the Corps by stealing, and Clark writes about the need for, "the protection of our stores from theft." A tragic interchange occurred in July, 1806, only several months before the trip's end. Lewis, in a political blunder, informed a band of Blackfeet warriors that Americans would give guns to Blackfeet enemies who agreed to a comprehensive peace plan. Under the cover of darkness, the infuriated Blackfeet warriors attempted to steal guns from the expedition. Lewis records the ensuing fight in his journal, "R. Fields as he seized his gun stabbed the Indian to the heart with his knife; the fellow ran about 15 steps and fell dead." Once the Indians realized the Americans were awake and armed, they tried to run off and steal the expedition's horses. Lewis's narrative continues: "I called to them…that I would shoot them if they did not give me my horse and raised my gun, one of them jumped behind a rock and spoke to the other who turned around then stopped at a distance of 30 steps from me and shot him through the belly, he fell to his knees and on his right elbow from which position he partly raised himself up and fired at me, and turning himself about crawled in behind a rock which was a few feet from him."

Indian health practices were worthy of the Lewis and Clark Expedition's notice as in some ways they were equal to or more advanced than those of the white settlers. Similar to the white man's medicine of the time, the Indians relied on experience and observation rather than strict scientific experiments. The Native Americans practiced bloodletting and purging, induced sweating and vomiting, and mingled their medicine with mysticism and ritual. They treated constipation with herbs and gave enemas by utilizing horns and animal bladders. Indians chewed certain roots, made decoctions, and administered drugs in teas or by inhaling fumes. They had a good understanding of sweating, emesis, menstruation, and childbirth. Plans were used to encourage abortion, speed delivery, or prevent pregnancy…Early nineteenth century Native Americans utilized splints, traction, and immobilization for fractures; employed poultices, heat, washing, and dressing for wounds; and drained abscesses. According to Maurice Gordon: "The American

Indians handled their wounds, empyemas [Empyema is the medical term for pockets of pus that have collected inside a body cavity. They can form if a bacterial infection is left untreated, or if it fails to fully respond to treatment. The term empyema is most commonly used to refer to pus-filled pockets that develop in the pleural space.], fractures, and dislocations as well, if not better, than the 18th century white physicians…The Indians definitely added 59 drugs to our modern pharmacopeia. Drugs used by the Indians and unknown in Europe include cocaine, quinine, ipecac, and witch hazel. Some plants increased palatability, but had no medicinal value, such as sassafras. Native Americans used sweat baths for a variety of reasons" and treated William Bratton who was in considerable pain and had difficulty walking. The day after undergoing sweating treatment he said he felt much better "and is walking about today and says he is nearly free from pain." [http://exhibits..hsl.virginia.edu/lewisclark/natives]

"Father Pere le June, one of the earliest missionaries, remarked "I think the savages, in point of intellect, may be placed in a high rank. Education and instruction alone are wanting. The powers of the mind operate with facility and effect. The Indians I can well compare to some of our own villagers who are left without instruction. Yet I have scarcely seen any person who has come from France to this country, who does not acknowledge that the savages have more intellect or capacity than most of our own peasantry."

"It is impossible to take the aboriginal view of the question and to judge calmly of the conduct of the discoverers of America, without making these preliminary concessions. Ignorant and degraded as the Indian was, from the Straits of Magellan to the Arctic Ocean, he had his natural conceptions of justice and elevation of character and was in a remarkable degree sensitive to kind acts and humane treatment, and whoever has found the secret of swaying his opinions and feelings, has been most observant of these traits of his mind. [Henry Rowe Schoolcraft, ed., Information Respecting the History, Condition and Prospects of the Indian Tribes of the United States, Part III, under the direction of the Bureau of Indian Affairs per act of

Congress of March 3rd, 1847, (Philadelphia: Lippincott, Grambo & Co., 1853), pp. 22-24, 54-55.]

"It is hardly surprising that many indigenous peoples were dismayed, if not disgusted, with the habits, behavior, and the aggressive interventions of the newcomers." [Paul Jentz, Seven Myths of Native American History (Indianapolis: Hackett Publishing, 2018)]

In his 1827 book, Tour of the Lakes, former Commissioner of Indian Affairs Thomas McKenney looked back on the history of the country's Indian policies and the actions of the Indians with a mix of both optimism and realism: It is high time the Indians had justice done their character. Nursed in war, they glory, we know, in the fight. From the beginning they used the kind of weapons which nature and their own art taught them to prepare, and adopted modes of defense, of attack, and of retaliation, such as they esteemed to be best. And does not man, everywhere, do the same? But they have been denounced as base and treacherous! I have yet to see the proof of either. I know our Indians have many vices, and that some are both base and treacherous; but of whom did they learn to be so? Let the English answer, and ourselves; for the question applies to both. [McKenney, Tour to the Lakes, (Barre, Massachusetts: Imprint Society, 1972), reprint of the original published in 1827, pp. 35-36, 45-47.]

"A persistent American tragedy has been the inability of European colonists and their descendants to live equitably with the aboriginal population…Our ancestors failed to solve the infinite problems of racial adjustment; perhaps modern America is not doing much better." [Alden T. Vaughan, New England Frontier: Puritans and Indians, 1620-1675, 3rd ed. (Norman, OK: University of Oklahoma Press, 1995), pp. ix-x, xiii]

"Our manifest destiny is to overspread and possess the whole of the continent which Providence has given us for the development of the great experiment of liberty…entrusted to us." [John O'Sullivan, New York Morning News, 1845, quoted in William M. Osborn, The Wild Frontier, (New York: Random House, 2000), p. 84.]

"Whites did not set out, directly at least, to destroy the Indians' life. They were simply following a script that had no Indians in it, except as exotic relics." [Elliott West, The Contested Plains, (Lawrence: University of Kansas Press, 1998), p. 335, quoted in William M. Osborn, The Wild Frontier, p. 75.]

In 1862, Chief Little Crow of the Santee Sioux said, "See—the White men are like the locusts when they fly so thick that the whole sky is a snowstorm." In 1630 there were 295,500 Indians and 4,600 Whites. In 1720 there were 244,000 Indians and 466,200 Whites. By 1780 Whites outnumbered Indians 2,780,300 to 210,000. The outcomes of Indian-White conflicts were then quite predictable. [James Wilson, The Earth Shall Weep: A History of Native Americans, (New York: Atlantic Monthly Press, 1998), p. 271.]

Looking back on the history of Indian and White relations, David Meltzer concluded, "Although their numbers were decimated, Native Americans ultimately survived the waves of disease and depopulation, and the collateral blows of warfare, famine, enslavement, and exploitation. But they did not survive unchanged. The consequences of European contact for American Indians were many and deep, often cascading in unpredictable ways through native culture."

According to Meltzer, "In the aftermath of epidemics, survivors abandoned old towns and regions; sixteenth and seventeenth-century documents hint of extensive refugee movements throughout North America. Refugees banded together with other survivors, who were often from previously unrelated communities, possibly speakers of different languages, and occasionally even traditional enemies." As a result, "Established relationships and alliances, as well as ritual and ceremonial systems, were abandoned, oftentimes because disease disproportionately killed the older members of a community, who were the repositories of those traditions and lore. The old rules no longer applied."
[David J. Meltzer, First Peoples in a New World: Colonizing Ice Age America, (Berkeley: University of California Press, 2009), pp. 333-334.]

CHAPTER 24

AMERICA'S GREATEST MYSTERIES

> White men seem to have difficulty in realizing people who live differently from themselves might be travelling the upward and progressive road of life.
>
> —**Luther Standing Bear** (Lakota)
> Land of the Spotted Eagle, 1933

The story of the populating of the Americas by the "First Immigrants," "First Americans," the "Discoverers"—is an amazing saga, one of the greatest adventure stories in the history of the world. We have only touched on a small percentage of the story, but even this abbreviated version is both fascinating and thought provoking. It is also impossible to avoid

the overpowering, gut-wrenching sadness of the story, at least it is for me and many others.

Sadly, we know so little about it, and there is so much of the story that we will probably never know. The inviolable imperative is: if history is not preserved by writing it down or somehow passing the accurate details along to subsequent generations, it will in all likelihood soon be corrupted by inaccurate reporting and eventually knowledge of that history will simply disappear, like bison, mastodons, and saber-toothed tigers that once roamed our lands. One day, they were simply gone, and it was too late to do anything about it.

Another tragic loss, but a loss that may be at least partially recoverable, are the thousands of years of human history, especially the histories of American Indians who traveled here from the frozen north, who became the First Americans, who multiplied and spread from sunrise to sunset and ocean shore to ocean shore, who developed numerous unique lifestyles, and who, without any outside assistance, generated their own Agricultural Revolution that equaled those that led to the "modernization" of Europe, Asia, and the Middle East, American Indians built pyramids and temples larger than those in Egypt, constructed elaborate irrigation systems, and built some of the largest cities in the world...with little if any contact with the outside world. Unfortunately, in many cases we don't know the "how" and the "why" of the monumental projects. In some cases, records had been kept, but they were destroyed by the Spanish Conquistadors who ravaged the cultures in South America and Meso-America.

In North America, American Indian tribes lacked written languages until 1821 when Sequoyah, a Cherokee, created a written syllabic, a system based on the sounds of various words. It was the only written system in use by a tribe in North America until after the Europeans arrived. Sequoyah's system was similar to the systems used by the Maya and Olmec cultures in South America. In addition to the Maya and Olmec, the Mesoamerican tribes of Mixtec's and Zapotec's also had written systems. The lack of any written language in North America until 1821 meant that the only ways that histories were preserved were through oral histories and graphic "reminders" on a tribe's winter count. That was tragic. Thousands of years of tribal histories could not be effectively preserved, and those years included the trips south from Beringia and the movements throughout the Americas by the First Americans. What a story that must have been! A continent with a handful of new arrivals and a lot of megafauna, including a considerable number of animals that would undoubtedly have seen the Indians as "dinner."

The development of radiocarbon dating technology, genetic analysis, language analysis, dental analysis, lidar radar, and other scientific techniques have made it possible to determine some pieces of the puzzle that would have been totally unintelligible in the past. As those techniques, and others that are still being developed, come into use we will undoubtedly be able to gradually increase our knowledge of the continent's remarkable past.

In the sidebar quote at the opening to this chapter, Chuck Cleland asked the question, "Does it really make a difference whether we get our beliefs about Indian origins from the myths and legends passed down by the Indians or the stories pieced together by archaeologists or ethnohistorians? Professor Cleland noted that, "One is left to wonder, which version is correct?"

History clearly documents that the archaeologists, ethnohistorians, and individuals from all backgrounds who have attempted to sort out the prehistoric story of the Americas have frequently gotten it wrong…frequently. "Clovis First," for example, was a major error. We "scientists" develop theories and hypothesis to try to explain what happened in the past, or why something happened, then we alter our theories and hypothesis as we develop more facts. That's "the scientific method." Taking "wrong turns" is simply part of the process of trying to eventually arrive at the truth.

But this book is just the start of the story. The immigrants from Siberia, Beringia, and what is now Alaska, who came here by way of what is now Canada, and who became the First Americans, the First North Americans, the First South Americans, and whose children became the First Native Americans and today's American Indians, First Nations, Indigenous, Aboriginals, and Métis--it has got to be an epic story—the first story of America. Hopefully, we have managed to capture some of it here.

Unfortunately, thousands of years of Indian history are missing here…a Millenium actually. With no written language, Indians depended upon their storytellers to document and save the history of the tribe. Some of that history has survived, much has been lost. Some Indian history has been reconstructed by archaeologists and others, most will never be.

Granted, some of the myths and legends seem to be totally fictional constructs, but there are undoubtedly many of the less fantastic stories that have some connection to actual historical events. Given that potential, it would be irresponsible for we historians to discard those often-cherished tales that have diligently been passed down for countless generations by the Indigenous storytellers. We just need to figure out how to separate historical facts from fictions and how to interpret the stories passed down to us.

Sadly, the answers to most of our questions are undoubtedly lost in the thick fog of time. That is so unfortunate; it must be one heck of a story. Actually, it must be dozens—or hundreds—probably thousands of fascinating stories spanning every human emotion—every joy, every pain, every fear, every disappointment, every dream. As Charles Mann, author of 1491 and 1493, summed things up, "the Western Hemisphere before 1492 was a thriving, stunningly diverse place, a tumult of languages, trade, and culture, a region where tens of millions of people loved and hated and worshipped as people do everywhere." [Mann, Charles C., 1491: New Revelations of the Americas Before Columbus, 2nd ed., (New York: Vintage Books, 2011), p. 31.]

It must have been a shock to the First Americans when they gradually spread out across the great expanses of the Americas and discovered that they were the only human inhabitants. A second shock would have come sometime later when it finally registered with them that they and their descendants were going to be the sole inhabitants for thousands of future years.

Long after that shocking discovery, they were undoubtedly amazed to find out in 1492, or sometime shortly thereafter, that they were no longer alone. The Spanish had arrived, first in the Caribbean, then at other locations around South America and North America, and the British, French, Dutch, even the Swedes and the Russians weren't far behind. The immigrants from Siberia, Beringia, and what is now Alaska, who came here by way of what is now Canada, and who became the First Americans, the First North Americans, the First South Americans, and whose children became the First Native Americans and today's American Indians, First Nations, Indigenous, Aboriginals, and Métis—theirs is an epic story, an epic mystery story—The first story of America. Hopefully, we have captured some of the magnificence of the story here.

BIBLIOGRAPHY

Abbot, John S. C., The Adventures of the Chevalier de La Salle and His Companions, in Their Explorations of the Prairies, Forests, Lakes, and Rivers, of the New World, and Their Interviews With the Savage Tribes, Two Hundred Years Ago, (Scholar Select reprint of the original 1875 book published in New York: Dodd & Mead Publishers, 1875).

Abbot, Geoffrey, "Scalping: Rite of Warfare," www.britannica.com/topic/scalping.

Adam, John, "Letter to the Editor," The Michigan Historical Review, Historical Society of Michigan, Vol. 48, No. 1 (Spring 2022), pp. 171-173.

Adams, David Wallace, Education for Extinction: American Indians and the Boarding School Experience, 1875-1928, 2nd ed. (Lawrence: University of Kansas Press, 2020).

Adovasio, J. M., and Jake Page, The First Americans: In Pursuit of Archaeology's Greatest Mystery, (New York: The Modern Library, 2003).

Adovasio, J. M., and David Pedler, Stranger in a New Land: What Archaeology Reveals About the First Americans, (Buffalo, NY: Firefly Books, 2016).

Anderson, Carol, The Unspoken Truth of Our Racial Divide (New York: Bloomsbury, 2017).

A Relation of the Invasion and Conquest of Florida by the Spanish (London, 1686) in "Perceptions of Native Americans—Document 2: Native Americans Discover Europeans, at www.gilderlehrman.org.

Armour, David A., ed. Attack at Michilimackinac 1763: Alexander Henry's Travels and Adventures in Canada and the Indian Territories between the years 1760 and 1764, originally published in 1809 by I. Riley, New York (Mackinac Island, MI: Mackinac State Historic Parks, 1971, 7th printing, 2016).

Treason At Michilimackinac: The Proceedings of a General Court Martial held at Montreal in October 1768 for the Trial of Major Robert Rogers (Mackinac Island: Mackinac Island State Park Commission, 1972 rev. ed.).

Alan Axelrod, Chronicle of the Indian Wars from Colonial Times to Wounded Knee, (New York: Prentice Hall, 1993.

Axtell, James, and William C. Sturtevant, "The Unkindest Cut, or Who Invented Scalping," The William and Mary Quarterly, Vol. 37, No. 3 (July 1980), pp. 451-472.

Bahn, Paul, ed., Witten in Bones: How Human Remains Unlock the Secrets of the Dead, (Buffalo: Firefly Books, 2012).

Bailyn, Bernard, The Barbarous Years: The Peopling of British North America: The Conflict of Civilizations, 1600-1675, (New York: Random House, 2013).

Brandão, José António, ed., Mémoires of Michilimackinac and the Pays d'en Haut: Indians and French in the Upper Great Lakes at the Turn of the Eighteenth Century, (East Lansing: Michigan State University Press, 2019).

Baraga, Frederic, Short History of the North American Indians, a translation by Graham A. MacDonald of Baraga's 1837 book (Calgary, Alberta, Canada: University of Calgary Press, 2004).

The Diary of Bishop Frederic Baraga: First Bishop of Marquette, Michigan (Detroit: Wayne State University Press, 1990) covering June 27, 1852 to July 16, 1863.

Beatty-Medina, Charles and Melissa Rinehart, eds., Contested Territories: Native Americans and Non-Natives in the Lower Great Lakes, 1700-1850 (East Lansing, MI: Michigan State University Press, 2012).

Berkhofer, Robert F., Jr., The White Man's Indian (New York: Random House-Vintage Books, 1979).

Berger, Lee, and John Hawks, Cave of Bones: A True Story of Discovery, Adventure, and Human Origins, (Washington DC: National Geographic Explorer, 2023).

"Beringian Standstill and Spread of Native American Founders," journals.plos.org'plosone/article?id=10.1371.

Blackbird, Andrew, History of the Ottawa and Chippewa Indians of Michigan, (Ypsilanti, MI: Ypsilanti Auxiliary of the Women's National Indian Association, 1887).

Boulton, William, Complete History: Alpena County Michigan (Alpena, MI: Argus Book and Job Rooms, ,1876), facsimile reprint by the Central Michigan University Press from an original in the Clarke Historical Library, Central Michigan University.

Bowes, John P., Land Too Good for Indians: Northern Indian Removal (Norman: University of Oklahoma Press, 2016).

Bridenbaugh, Carl, Early Americans New York: Oxford University Press, 1981).

Brown, Dee, Bury My Heart at Wounded Knee: An Indian History of the American West (New York: Henry Holt & Co., 1970).

Brown Eyes, Lance, Native Americans Have Always Been In America: The Reverse Migration Theory, (Middletown, DE: Privately printed, 2023).

Callaway, Colin G., The Indian World of George Washington (New York: Oxford University Press, 2018).

Our Hearts Fell to the Ground: Plains Indian Views of How the West Was Lost (Boston: Bedford/St. Martin's, 2018

One Vast Winter Count: The Native American West before Lewis and Clark, (Lincoln: University of Nebraska Press, 2003).

Casas, Bartolomé de Las, A Short Account of the Destruction of the Indies, Nigel Griffin, ed. (London: Penguin Books, 2004), first published in 1875.

Catlin, George, North American Indians (New York: Penguin Books, 2004). Began living among Indians in 1831. In Albany, NY, in 1837 preparing his gallery of 310 oil paintings of Indians, plus clothing, drums, other articles. Taken together, Catlin's works constitute the first, last, and only "complete" record of the Plains Indians ever made at the height of their splendid culture, so soon destroyed by traders' liquor and disease, rapine, and bayonets. It is the second (1832-1839) of three classic accounts of the Indians and landscapes and wild creatures of the American West written in the first half of the nineteenth century. The first was the Journal of Captain Meriwether Lewis (1803-06), the third was Francis Parkman's The California and Oregon Trail (1849).

Centers for Disease Control and Prevention, "History of Smallpox," at www.cdc.gov/smallpox/history.

Chakraborty, Tuhin, "Michigan Indian Education Before and After 1934: From Oppression to Neglect," The Michigan Historical Review, Vol. 48, No. 1 (Spring 2022), pp. 63-80.

F. A. Chardon, Chardon's Journal at Fort Clark: 1834-1839, (Lincoln: University of Nebraska Press, 1997, edited version of the 1932 original with a historical introduction and notes.)

Cleland, Charles E., Rites of Conquest: The History and Culture of Michigan's Native Americans (Ann Arbor: The University of Michigan Press, 1992).

Clifton, James A., ed. The Invented Indian: Cultural Fictions & Government Policies, (New York: Routledge, 1990).

Coates, Ken S., A Global History of Indigenous Peoples: Struggle and Survival (New York: Palgrave Macmillan, 2004).

Cook, Darius B., Six Months Among Indians, Wolves, and Wild Animals: The Historical Account of the Winter of 1839-1840, a reprint of the book originally published in 1889 at Niles, MI, by the author. (AuTrain, MI: Avery Color Studios, 1992).

Coward, John M., The Newspaper Indian: Native American Identify in the Press, 1820-90 (Urbana: University of Illinois Press, 1999).

Danziger, Edmund Jefferson, Jr., The Chippewas of Lake Superior (Norman: University of Oklahoma Press, 1979).

Deloria, Vine, Jr., Custer Died for Your Sins: An Indian Manifesto, (Norman: University of Oklahoma Press, 1988).

Red Earth, White Lies: Native Americans and the Myth of Scientific Fact, (New York: Scribner, 1995).

Denevan, William M., ed., The Native Population of the Americas in 1492, 2nd ed., (Madison: University of Wisconsin Press, 1992).

Dougherty, Martin J., The Aztec, Inca & Maya Empires (London: Amber Books, 2018).

Driver, Harold E., Indians of North America, 2nd ed., Rev., (Chicago: University of Chicago Press, 1969).

Dunbar-Ortiz, Roxanne, An Indigenous Peoples' History of the United States (Boston: Beacon Press, 2014).

Dunbar-Ortiz, Roxanne and Dina Gilio-Whitaker, "All the Real Indians Died Off:" And 20 Other Myths About Native Americans (Boston: Beacon Press, 2016).

Eccles, W. J., The French in North America, 1500-1783, Revised Edition (Markham, Ontario, Canada: Fitzhenry & Whiteside, 1998).

Egan, Timothy, Short Nights of the Shadow Catcher: The Epic Life and Immortal Photographs of Edward Curtis (Boston: Mariner Books, 2013).

Elia, Scott Armstrong, "First /Americans Lived on Bering Land Bridge for Thousands of Years,"

Scientific American, March 4, 2014.

Fagan, Brian M., The Great Journey: The Peopling of Ancient America, Updated Edition of 1987, (Gainesville: University of Florida Press, 2004).

Feldman, George Franklin, Cannibalism, Headhunting and Human Sacrifice in North America: A History Forgotten, (Chambersburg, PA: Alan C. Hood & Co., 2008)

Finger, John R., Cherokee Americans: The Eastern Band of Cherokees in the Twentieth Century (Lincoln: University of Nebraska Press, 1991).

Funk, Caroline L., "The Bow and Arrow War Days on the Yukon-Kuskokwim Delta of Alaska," Ethnohistory (October 2010) at elbdisliker.at.ua/Inuitt/The-Bow-and-Arrow-Days-on-the-Yukon.

Gibson, Jon L., Archaic Earthworks of the Lower Mississippi Valley: Interpretations from the Field, (Baton Rouge: Louisiana State University Press, 2019), pp. 11, 19, 33, 38.

Greenman, Emerson F., The Indians of Michigan (Lansing, MI: Michigan Historical Commission, 1961).

Greer, Allan, ed., The Jesuit Relations: Natives and Missionaries in Seventeenth-Century North America, The Bedford Series in History and Culture, 2nd ed. (Boston: Bedford/St. Martin's, 2019).

Greshko, Michael, "Ancient DNA reveals complex migrations of the first Americans, www.nationalgeographic.com/science/2018/11.

Halverson, Melissa Sue, "Native Americans and the Smallpox Epidemic," at www.varsitytutors.com.

Hancock, Graham, America Before: The Key to Earth's Lost Civilization, (New York: St. Martin's Griffin, 2019).

Haywood, John, "Vikings in America: The Europeans who arrived 500 years before Columbus," www.historyextra.com.

Henige, David, Numbers From Nowhere: The American Indian Contact Population Debate, (Norman: University of Oklahoma Press, 2022).

Hey, Jody, "From Few to Many: New World Founded by Surprisingly Small Population," PLOS BIOLOGY, June 3, 2005.

"On the number of New World Founders: A Population Genetic Portrait of the Peopling of America," PLOS BIOLOGY, June 3, 2005 at www.ncbi.nlm.nih.gov.

Hibbard, Claude W., "Animal Life in Michigan During the Ice Age," Michigan Alumnus Quarterly Review, Vol. LVII, No. 18 (May 26, 1951).

Hickerson, The Southwestern Chippewa: An Ethnohistorical Study, American Anthropological Association Memoir, No. 92, Vol. 64 (June, 1962), p. 67.

Hinsdale, W. B., Primitive Man in Michigan: Indians and Michigan Pre-History (AuTrain, MI: Avery Color Studios, 1992), reprint of the original book printed in 1925 by the University of Michigan's University Museum.

Hoffman, Alice M. and Howard S. Hoffman, "Reliability and Validity in Oral History: The Case for Memory,"

www.semanticscholar.org/paper/Reliability-and-validity-in-oral-history-Hoffman

Jackson, Helen Hunt, A Century of Dishonor: The Classic Exposé of the Plight of the Native Americans (Pantianos Classics), first published in 1885.

Jennings, Francis, The Invasion of America: Indians, Colonialism, and the Cant of Conquest (New York: W. W. Norton, 1975).

Jentz, Paul, Seven Myths of Native American History (Indianapolis: Hackett Publishing, 2018).

Johnson, Robert G. and Janey Westin, The Last Kings of Norse America: Runestone Keys to a Lost Empire (Edina, MN: Beaver's Pond Press, 2012).

Joseph, Frank, Advanced Civilizations of Prehistoric America: The Lost Kingdoms of the Adena, Hopewell, Mississippians, and Anasazi, (Rochester, Vermont: Bear & Company, 2010).

Josephy, Alvin M., Jr., Indian Heritage of America, (New York: Bantam Books, 1976).

500 Nations: An Illustrated History of North American Indians (New York: Alfred A. Knopf, 1994).

Keeley, Lawrence H., War Before Civilization: The Myth of the Peaceful Savage, (New York: Oxford University Press, 1996).

Kelly, Robert L., Maybe we do know when people first came to North America; and what does it mean if we do? Quarternary International, 109-110 (2003), 133-145.

Timothy Kent, Rendezvous at the Straits, (Ossineke, MI: Silver Fox Enterprises, 2004).

The Indians of the Western Great Lakes, 1615-1760 (Ann Arbor: The University of Michigan Press, 1965).

King, Thomas, The Inconvenient Indian: A Curious Account of Native People In North America (Minneapolis: University of Minnesota Press, 2012).

Klein, Christopher, "New Study Refutes Theory of How Humans Populated North America," August 10, 2016, www.history.com/news/new-study-refutes-theory-of-how-humans-populated-north-america.

Kupperman, Karen Ordahl, Settling With The Indians: The Meeting of English and Indian Cultures in America, 1580-1640, (Totowa, NJ: Rowman and Littlefield, 1980).

LeBeau, Patrick Russell, Rethinking Michigan Indian History (East Lansing, MI: Michigan State University Press, 2005).

Lepore, Jill, Encounters in the New World – A History in Documents, "Document 8: Encounters in the New World: A History of Documents," (New York: Oxford University Press, 2000), p. 91.

Lewis, Jon E., ed., The Mammoth Book of Native Americans (London: Constable & Robinson, 2004).

Lewis, Meriwether and John B. Ordway, The Journals of Captain Meriwether Lewis and Sergeant John Ordway: Kept on the Expedition of Western Exploration, 1803-1806, Milo M. Quaife, ed. (Madison: State Historical Society of Wisconsin, 1916).

Link, Mardi, "Feds appeal decision in Burt Lake Band case, Traverse City Record Eagle, May 31, 2020.

Loewen, James W., Lies My Teacher Told Me About Christopher Columbus: What Your History Books Got Wrong (New York: The New Press, 2014).

Mann, Charles C., 1491: New Revelations of the Americas Before Columbus, 2nd ed. (New York: Vintage Books, 2011).

1493: Uncovering the New World Columbus Created (New York: Vintage Books, 2012).

Mansfield, Howard, "Op-Ed: Pandemic tells the true story of the Pilgrims at Plymouth Rock," Los Angeles Times, at www.msn.com/en-us/travel/tripideas.

Manypenny, George W., Our Indian Wards, (Cincinnati: Robert Clarke & Co., 1880), a Scholar Select reprint of the original.

Maslen, Geoff, "Racism and discrimination against aboriginal staff rises," www.universityworldnews.com/post.php?story=20181010182528471, October 10, 2018.

McDonnell, Michael A., Masters of Empire: Great Lakes Indians and the Making of America (New York: Bill and Wang, 2015).

McKenney, Thomas Loraine, Indian Tribes of North America: With biographical sketches and anecdotes of the principal chiefs, Vol. 1 (Carlisle, MA: Applewood Books, reprint of 1872 original).

Sketches of a Tour To The Lakes, of the character and customs of the Chippeway Indians, and of incidents connected with the Treaty of Fond du Lac (Barre, Massachusetts: Imprint Society, 1972), reprint of the original published in 1827.

Meacham, Jon, American Lion: Andrew Jackson in the White House (New York: Random House, 2009).

David J. Meltzer, Jeremy A. Sabloff, ed., Search for the First Americans, (Washington, DC: Smithsonian Books, 1993).

First Peoples in a New World: Colonizing Ice Age America, (Berkeley: University of California Press, 2009).

Menzies, Gavin, and Ian Hudson, Who Discovered America? The Untold History of the Peopling of the Americas, (New York: William Morrow, 2013).

Milanich, Jerald T., Florida's Indians: From Ancient Times to the Present (Gainesville: University of Florida Press, 1998).

Milner, George R., The Mound Builders: Ancient Societies of Eastern North America, 2nd ed., (New York: Thames & Hudson, 2021).

Morison, Samuel Eliot, Admiral of the Ocean Sea: A Life of Christopher Columbus (Boston: Little, Brown and Company, 1942).

Mosteller, Kelli, "For Native Americans, Land is More Than Just the Ground Beneath Their Feet," www.theatlantic.com/politics/archive/2016/09/for-hative-americans-land-is-more-than-just-ground.

Mowat, Farley, People of the Deer (New York: Carroll & Graf, 2005).

The Desperate People, (Boston: Little, Brown and Company, 1959).

Nabokov, Peter, ed., Native American Testimony: A Chronicle of Indian-White Relations from Prophecy to the Present, 1492-2000, Revised Edition (New York: Penguin Books, 1999).

National Museum of the American Indian, Smithsonian Institution, Do All Indians Live in Tipis? (New York: Collins, 2007).

Newell, Margaret Ellen, Brethren by Nature: New England Indians, Colonists, and the Origins of American Slavery (Ithaca: Cornell University Press, 2015).

Nies, Judith, Native American History: A Chronology of a Culture's Vast Achievements and Their Links to World Events (New York: Ballentine Books, 1996).

"North Carolina American Indian History Timeline," www.ncmuseumofhistory.org.

Onuf, Peter S., "We Shall All Be Americans: Thomas Jefferson and the Indians," Indiana Magazine of History, Vol. 95, No. 2 (June 1999), pp. 103-141.

Osborn, William M., The Wild Frontier: Atrocities During the American-Indian War From Jamestown Colony to Wounded Knee (New York: Random House, 2000).

"Our state history is a cautionary tale in selective facts," Viewpoint: Traverse City Record Eagle, reprinted in The Alpena News, July 19, 2022, p. 4A.

Owings, Alison, Indian Voices: Listening to Native Americans (New Brunswick, NJ: Rutgers University Press, 2012).

Pauketat, Timothy R., Cahokia: Ancient America's Great City on the Mississippi (New York: Penguin Books, 2010).

Pauketat, Timothy R. and Diana DiPaolo Loren, eds., North American Archaeology, (Malden, MA: Blackwell Publishing, 2005).

Pokegon, Simon, The Red Mans' Greeting (Hartford, MI: C. H. Engle, 1893).

("The) Poverty Point, Adena, Hopewell, and Mississippian Cultures," www.encyclopedia.com › humanities › mound-builders.

Pratt, Richard H., "The Advantages of Mingling Indians with Whites," Proceedings of the National Conference of Charities and Correction, 1892, pp. 761-762.

Pratt, Stacy, "The History of Indigenous Mounds in America," www.ranker.com, September 23, 2021.

Price, Michael, "Closest-known ancestor of today's Native Americans found in Siberia," www.sciencemag.org, June 5, 2019.

Prucha, Francis Paul, ed., Documents of United States Indian Policy, 3rd ed. (Lincoln NB: University of Nebraska Press, 2000).

Raff, Jennifer, Origin: A Genetic History of the Americas, (New York: Twelve – Grand Central Publishing, 2022).

Reddy, M. D., Statistical Record of Native North Americans, 2nd ed. (Detroit: Gale Research Co., 1995).

Rees, William, www.historytoday.com/history matters/Canada's-first-nations

Restall, Matthew, Seven Myths of the Spanish Conquest (New York: Oxford University Press, 2003).

Riggenbach, Jeff, Why American History Is Not What They Say: An Introduction to Revisionism (Auburn, Alabama: Ludwig von Mises Institute, 2009).

Andrés Reséndez, The Other Slavery: The Uncovered Story of Indian Enslavement in America (Boston: Houghton Mifflin Harcourt, 2016).

A Land So Strange: The Epic Journey of Cabeza de Vaca, (New York: Basic Books, 2007).

Santoro, Nicholas J., Atlas of the Indian Tribes of North America and the Clash of Cultures (New York: iUniverse, 2009).

Saunt, Claudio, Unworthy Republic: The Dispossession of Native Americans and the Road to Indian Territory (New York: W. W. Norton, 2020).

Schaetzl, Randall, "Native Americans in the Great Lakes Region," at geo.msu.edu/extra/geomich/paleo_indians.

Schoolcraft, Henry R., ed., Information Respecting the History, Condition and Prospects of the Indian Tribes of the United States, Part III, under the direction of the Bureau of Indian Affairs per act of Congress of March 3rd, 1847, (Philadelphia: Lippincott, Grambo & Co., 1853). Illustrations by Seth Eastman.

Algic Researches and Personal Memoirs of Thirty Years With the Indian Tribes on the American Frontier: With Brief Notices of Passing Events, Facts, and Opinions, A.D. 1812 to A.D. 1842 (Philadelphia: Lippincott, Grambo and Co., 1861).

Sheehan, Bernard W., Seeds of Extinction, (Chapel Hill: University of North Carolina Press, 1973).

Shoemaker, Nancy, "How Indians Got to be Red," The American Historical Review, Vol. 102, No. 3 (June, 1997), pp. 625-644.

Sleeper-Smith, Susan, Indian Women and French Men: Rethinking Cultural Encounter in the Western Great Lakes (Amherst: University of Massachusetts Press, 2001).

Sloan, Kim, A New World—England's First View of America (Chapel Hill: University of North Carolina Press, 2007).

Smith, Alice E., The History of Wisconsin, Vol. 1, From Exploration to Statehood (Madison: State Historical Society of Wisconsin, 1973).

Steeves, Paulette F. C., The Indigenous Paleolithic of the Western Hemisphere, (Lincoln: University of Nebraska Press, 2021).

Strickland, Ashley, "Vikings in America" CNN Science – Wonder Theory, October 23, 2021.

Students on Site, A Unit of the Arts of Citizenship Program, University of Michigan, "Native Americans: Early Contact."

Tanner, Helen Hornbeck, ed., Atlas of Great Lakes Indian History (Norman: University of Oklahoma Press, 1987).

Taylor, Alan, American Colonies: The Settling of North America, (New York: Penguin Books, 2002).

Thornton, Russell, American Indian Holocaust and Survival: A Population History Since 1492 (Norman: University of Oklahoma Press, 1987).

Toups, Eric, "More Than Just a Missionary: The Jesuits, the Wyandot, and Colonial Crises in French Detroit, 1728-1751," The Michigan Historical Review, Vol. 46, No. 1, Spring 2020, pp. 1-28.

Trafzer, Clifford E., American Indians, American Presidents: A History, (Washington, D.C.: Smithsonian—National Museum of the American Indian, 2009).

Treuer, Anton, Everything You Wanted to Know About Indians But Were Afraid to Ask, (St. Paul: Borealis Books, 2012).

Treurer, David, The Heartbeat of Wounded Knee: Native America From 1890 to the Present (New York: Riverhead Books, 2019).

Trudel, Marcel, Canada's Forgotten Slaves: Two Hundred Years of Bonadage, George Tombs, translator (Montreal: Véhicule Press, 2013).

Truteau, Jean-Baptiste, Raymond J. DeMallie, Douglas R. Parks, and Robert Vézina, eds., A Fur Trader on the Upper Missouri: The Journal and Description of Jean-Baptiste Truteau, 1794-1796 (Lincoln, Nebraska: University of Nebraska Press, 2017).

Vaughan, Alden T., New England Frontier: Puritans and Indians, 1620-1675, 3rd ed. (Norman, OK: University of Oklahoma Press, 1995).

Viola, Herman J., PhD., Thomas L. McKenney, Architect of America's Early Indian Policy: 1816-1830 (Chicago: The Swallow Press, 1974).

Wahlgren, Erik, The Vikings and America. (New York: Thames and Hudson, 1986)

Waitley, Douglas, Best Backroads of Florida: Coasts, Glades, and Groves, Vol. 2, Rev. Ed. (Sarasota: Pineapple Press, 2011).

Waldman, Carl, Atlas of the North American Indian (New York: Checkmark Books, 2000).

Warren, William W., History of the Ojibway People, 2nd ed. (St. Paul: Minnesota Historical Society Press, 2009). First published in 1885 by the Minnesota Historical Society as Vol. 5 of their "Collections." 2009 edition has introduction, editing, and annotations by Theresa Schenck.

Wernick, Robert; The Seafarers: The Vikings, (Alexandria, VA: Time-Life Books, 1979).

Weston, Mary Ann, Native American in the News: Images of Indians in the Twentieth Century Press (Westport, CT: Greenwood Press, 1996).

Wikipedia, "Burt Lake burn-out."

Wikipedia, “Cultural assimilation of Native Americans,” en.wikipedia.org/wiki/Cultural_assimilation_of_Native_ Americans.

Wikipedia, “History of Native Americans in the United States,” en.wikipedia.org/wiki/History_of_Native_Americans_in_the_United _States.

Wikipedia, “Native American Diseases and Epidemics,” XXXxistence.org/wiki/Native_American_diseases_and_epidemics.

Wikipedia, “Norse Colonization of North America,”

en.wikiedia.org/wiki/Norse_Colonization_of_North_America.

Williams, Timothy, “Higher Crime, Fewer Charges on Indian Land,” New York Times, February 20, 2012.

www.encyclopedia.com, “The Poverty Point, Adena, Hopewell, and Mississippian Cultures.”

Young, Henry J., “A Note on Scalp Bounties in Pennsylvania (1957), www.journals.psu.edu.

Zinn, Howard, A People’s History of the United States (New York: Harper Perennial Modern Classics, 2015).

Zurawik, David, “500 Nations is not good history and not good TV,” The Baltimore Sun, April 20, 1995.

Made in the USA
Columbia, SC
22 March 2025

e5118234-6f17-4f9a-96f1-eaf9069da2bcR02